Communication
and Assertion Skills
for Older Persons

Communication and Assertion Skills for Older Persons

LEILANI DOTY

Gerocounselor
Counseling Resources, Inc.
Gainesville, Florida

● **HEMISPHERE PUBLISHING CORPORATION, Washington**
A subsidiary of Harper & Row, Publishers, Inc.

Cambridge   New York   Philadelphia   San Francisco   London   Mexico City   São Paulo   Singapore   Sydney

COMMUNICATION AND ASSERTION SKILLS FOR OLDER PERSONS

1 2 3 4 5 6 7 8 9 0   E B E B   8 9 8 7 6

This book was set in Times Roman by Hemisphere Publishing Corporation. The editors were Christine Flint Lowry and Elizabeth Maggiora; the designer was Sharon Martin DePass; the production supervisor was Peggy M. Rote; and the typesetter was Cynthia B. Mynhier.
Edwards Brothers, Inc. was the printer and binder.

Library of Congress Cataloging-in-Publication Data

Doty, Leilani, date.
    Communication and assertion skills for older persons.
    (Series in death education, aging, and health care)
    Bibliography: p.
    Includes index.
    1. Interpersonal communication. 2. Interpersonal
relations. 3. Assertiveness (Psychology) 4. Aged—
Psychology. I. Title. II. Series. [DNLM: 1. Aged.
2. Assertiveness—in old age. 3. Behavior Therapy—in
old age. 4. Communication—in old age. 5. Interpersonal Relations. BF 637.C45 D725c]
BF724.85.I57D67   1987   158'.2   86-19474

ISBN 0-89116-400-6
ISSN 0275-3510

Dedicated with great love and appreciation to my primary mentors

Grandmother, Takouhy Musserian Mangerian
A woman who asserted caring for others in her lifestyle

Mother, Armenoohy Mangerian Jacobson
A woman who asserts her commitment to high values by her lifestyle

Contents

II ADVANCED SKILLS

Preface

Communication and Assertion Skills for Older Persons is a two-part book that coaches the reader in four areas: (1) life in transition (aging), (2) personal and interpersonal awareness, (3) communication skills, and (4) selective assertiveness training. The text calls attention to the positive aspects of aging. The attitudes and values expressed in the book endorse continuous development throughout life. Used on an individual basis or in a supportive, life-enriching class setting, the concepts and skills explored in the text will stimulate learning and growth.

Learning plays a necessary role in one's continued growth and development. As one ages, learning becomes more comprehensive. It builds on previous learning and becomes integrated into all of one's activities.

A lifelong learning approach provides an experience that is relevant to the lives of mature readers. Lifelong learning refers to learning throughout one's lifetime and learning information that may be incorporated into one's daily life experiences.

The book introduces basic concepts in simple language. After reading an explanation of the concept, the reader has a chance to try an exercise that should help link the concept to the reader's personal experiences. Personalizing the ideas in this way cements the learning process. This, in turn, stimulates personal growth. The individual who understands the concept in a personal way will be better equipped to teach others. This may occur in a casual way, such as in a friendship, or in a more formal way, such as during an agency workshop.

The discussion exercises contribute to individual and interpersonal growth. Reflecting on personal experiences in the discussion exercises, individuals will learn more about who they are, how they function best, and in what way they may develop further.

The term *older persons* refers to people 55 years of age and older. The materials in the text, however, are meaningful to adults 20 years of age and older. This is especially true of adults who are involved personally or professionally with older persons.

In group or class settings, the book provides resources for participants to contribute to a shared learning experience that will develop interpersonal closeness and self-confidence in the midst of others. Participants in group sessions should be encouraged to share personal experiences whenever appropriate. However, it is essential to respect each other's desire to keep private information unshared. Participants should not be "pushed" to share deep secrets that they are unwilling to disclose.

When participants do not wish to share private information, their wishes are respected conscientiously. The exercises focus on understanding oneself and initiating a change in behavior. The secrets of each other's lives are not the focus of this type of learning experience. Primary interest lies in how one functions and behaves with others. People are respected for being human and are encouraged to fulfill their potential.

Maintaining confidentiality within the group is also a concern. Personal information that is shared within a group should not be discussed with others outside the group unless special permission is granted or someone's safety is at risk.

These materials were developed as a result of classes and conference programs on communication and assertion. The information and discussion exercises have been used successfully with older persons from different socioeconomic and cultural backgrounds. Professionals, paraprofessionals, service providers, educators, and researchers have explored the information in conference seminars and workshops. Older persons, 55–87 years old, in age-aggregate homes have used the materials in 10-week classes. The classes ranged in size from 5 to 15 members. People from the industrial setting find the materials helpful in developing skills for approaching problems or projects that require a team or group effort.

In the college or professional setting, the material is supplemented by reference readings. The materials may be taught in more depth for this group. In a group setting of older persons, the material is supplemented by life experiences. The materials may be adapted easily to be more general, to focus on one main idea for each concept, and to expand the time learning from personal experiences that are shared in the group.

Readers are encouraged to read the materials thoughtfully in a way that relates the information to their personal lives. Participants are encouraged to become intimately involved in the learning. They are discouraged from treating the information in a distant academic way.

The discussion exercises are designed as group discussions for personal and interpersonal exploration. Participants are requested to share on a personal level with other group members. In each discussion exercise Directions for the Learner provide guidance for the student readers. Guidance for implementation of the discussion exercises, thought-provoking comments, and questions for the instructors or group leaders using this text are provided in the Directions for the Leader. The exercises are designed to stimulate the discussion of feelings.

Participants are encouraged to make positive comments to each other during the sharing. This enhances the positive growth of group members. Encouraging each other and exchanging positive feedback, participants will feel respected, significant, and worthwhile.

Some readers may choose to work through the text alone. Used in this way, the book provides direction for personal development. Some exercises, however, concentrate on interaction. The individual reader may benefit from the focus on relationship skills by choosing a trusted friend with whom to work on certain exercises. A lighter, less emotional part of the exercise may be discussed at first. Then a deeper level of discussion may be tried. It is important to work carefully and respectfully when dealing with personal issues.

People over 60 years of age tend to take 2 to 3 times the suggested time to complete the discussion exercises. Some of their reasons are:

1. "I've never been asked to think about myself. All my life I always planned and worked for other people. I have to get used to thinking about me for a change."
2. "I have so many experiences in my life to choose from. It's hard to pick only one to think on."
3. "I could answer that, but I'm sure you'd rather hear from someone else." (The speaker is implying, "Mine is not as important as someone else's answer." This level of shyness or low self-esteem merits some attention from the leader.)

The information is designed for easy reading and quick comprehension. The communication and assertiveness strategies are designed for smooth acquisition. There are, however, two levels of skills, basic skills and advanced skills. It is important that the reader have a solid foundation of communication skills as taught in Part I: Basic Skills of this book before progressing to the higher level of skills in Part II: Advanced Skills.

The ideas, the skills, the discussion exercises, and the level of reading in Part I are very easy. The ideas, the skills, the exercises, and the level of reading in Part II are at a more advanced level. Parts I and II may be used together as a sequence or they may be used as separate units. They have been field tested and were found to be highly satisfactory under both conditions.

At the end of each chapter there are reference suggestions for readers who would like more details about the information covered in the particular chapter. Each reference follows a major topic word. If the reader would like to read more about the major topic that is identified, then the reader may look up the references that are listed. A Bibliography, containing additional reading suggestions, and Index are included at the end of the book.

As individuals develop more ease in communication, they are more able to think through and deal with personal issues. This becomes even more important in relating with other people.

Traveling through the pages of this book, the reader will act as an individual and as a member of a group. Working in both ways, the reader may become more aware of and in tune with the self, others, and changing society. The reader will also strengthen and enhance communication and assertion skills that will result in a better personal and professional lifestyle.

The author wishes to thank the many people who helped in the development of these materials: the Area Agency on Aging, Gainesville, Florida; Dr. Harold C. Riker, Professor of Counselor Education, University of Florida; and my family, Keith, Kahil Peter, Erin Gerith, and Lyana Charmise. Kahil, Erin, Lyana, and Gus Kuldau, our neighbor's son, did all the artwork.

A special thanksgiving to the older persons who participated in the development of the material on the following pages. They continue to be a rich part of my life adventures.

Leilani Doty

1

Basic Skills

Introduction

As people age, they undergo continuous, multifaceted change. Change involves personal and environmental concerns. It involves joyous celebrations, such as the birth of a newborn. It involves international devastation, such as in the tragedies of a major war. As older people meet the challenges of change each year, they become increasingly experienced and wise in ways to meet the continuous transitions of life.

With an attitude of lifelong learning, one's change may involve self-awareness, understanding, and growth. After going through the experience of getting to know oneself, a person may be more willing to reach out to others. Then personal awareness expands into another dimension, awareness and sensitivity to others, as one develops relationships with other people.

Interpersonal relationships are important to the survival of people of all ages. Without relationships many people fail to thrive. Establishing links to others becomes an important aspect of maintaining physical and mental wellness.

Healthful, solid relationships depend on strong communication skills. Knowing how to listen carefully and to respond effectively intensifies a relationship. Missing the true message may result in frustration, hurt feelings, and undesirable decisions.

Communication is strengthened with selective assertiveness. Developing appropriate assertive behaviors and attitudes provides the resources for an avenue of honest, respectful communication. With the skills of selective assertiveness, an individual is free to choose a path of purpose in life. Then aging becomes an experience of success and fulfillment.

There are ways to develop purpose and direction to achieve a sense of fulfillment. The reader will have the opportunity to learn how to set and meet goals. The reader will also explore the steps involved in making a decision.

A goal is a general aim or the end result toward which a person works. Objectives are the specific steps taken to help a person achieve the goal. Each objective may be made up of several, individual steps. It is critical that the reader establish personal goals and objectives in approaching the material in the following pages of the book. Until those personal goals are formed, the author will set out some goals and objectives. These are to establish a beginning direction for the reader's work toward self-understanding and growth.

The following are goals for personal and social development:

1. Awareness of self
2. Improved communication skills
3. An individualized assertive attitude and lifestyle

Pursuing the following objectives will help readers attain the three goals stated above, to:

1. Build self-confidence
2. Improve social interaction
3. Listen to oneself and others
4. Give and receive positive feedback
5. Express personal feelings, opinions, and experiences
6. Respect one's own (personal) rights
7. Respect the rights of others
8. Increase the practice of selective assertiveness

The chapters in the text focus on helping the reader meet the goals and objectives just listed. Topics covered are transition in life, personal awareness, relationships of family members and friends, specific communication skills, selective assertiveness, and reflection on the learning experience.

Understanding the personal self, listening, and talking are important for meaningful relationships. People who relate to others what they really want communicate effectively. It helps the speaker feel more effective and stronger as a person. It helps the listener to understand what is really happening. It provides a better opportunity for the listener to contribute meaningfully to the situation and the relationship.

As they become accustomed to effective communication, people help each other grow. Their relationships become more productive. They become willing to risk being more honest about what they really feel. They become eager to continue the relationship and share creative ideas. They are not so easily moved into wrong directions and undesirable activities. They make better choices. They activate their ideas into plans. They become energized and more self-sufficient. They meet the challenges of change in a manner that is realistic and rewarding.

2

Change

Change in life is a natural, normal, and desirable process. It establishes progress in the environment. It provides for individual development, different experiences, deep relationships, and the stimulation of constant learning. Over the centuries in the environment, a seed becomes a mighty redwood tree. In the last century one of the changes in lifestyle is observed in the modifications made in methods of transportation. The car has replaced the horse and buggy in the lives of most people in the United States.

Undergoing change, the baby grows up to become a youth and then an adult. The human being is a participant in the natural course of living things. Over a lifetime the human being develops into a full person, rich with the complex experiences of life.

Aging, then, is the process of richness of change in the ongoing transitions of life. Aging is development. It involves growing and learning new lessons in life.

For many people the adventure of change and the richness of opportunities in life have been avoided for the security of sameness. They limit taking risks in order to pursue familiar activities and behaviors. They use up a great deal of energy to prevent change. They prefer the safety of the familiar. They accept only what they have known and believed for a very long time. Thus, they limit their style of living to the same level of physical and mental comfort that they have always known.

Often, older people become victims of stereotypes. Stereotypes are negative attitudes or beliefs. Agism is one widespread stereotype that interferes with the freedom of older persons to live a fulfilled life. Agism includes negative attitudes toward any age group, but it typically is used to refer to older persons. Agism often contributes to stagnation and loneliness.

Agism distorts and is restrictive. It sets arbitrary or inappropriate age limits for behavior. Or, it distorts perceptions of what people should be like according to their age, the number of years they have lived. Examples of age distortion are the attitudes that 20 year olds must be in college or employed full time and that 70 year olds should be finished with schooling, be fully retired, that is unemployed, and should be resting.

An example of age restrictiveness is the attitude that grandmothers 55 years of age or more are too old to roller skate, even if they are in good physical condition and enjoy that activity.

In another instance of age restrictiveness, many people feel that individuals 60 years or older can no longer be productive in business or serve usefully as leaders. As they age, people typically fulfill their own negative, age stereotypes rather than realistically assess their personal resources and plan accordingly.

Few significant signposts in society alert people to the aging process. This is especially true in the United States, a youth-oriented culture. The ideal person in the mass media is portrayed as a young adult under 25 years of age. Television, especially, focuses on young, energetic, unwrinkled people who are flawless in beauty and involved in constant activity.

Intent on perpetuating their youth and, consequently, inattentive to the gradual changes of time, many individuals find themselves suddenly facing their own physical maturity. It has been a long time since they looked at themselves and saw what was really there. All at once, they notice how they differ from the popular image of the mass media, especially the television screen. They feel overwhelmed by the differences they see.

For many, turning 40 or 50 years old is the first signpost that makes them aware of their own change. They suddenly face a built up need to accommodate the demands of aging. They feel unsure of themselves and are overwhelmed by their lack of foresight and preparation for this new stage of life.

Having fun fulfilling dreams.

Older adults often feel isolated by the various changes that occur throughout their lifetime. As environments change, as society's values change, and as their bodies change, older persons feel unsure about their place and role in life.

In the increasingly mobile American society, family members and friends move more often. As their loves ones leave them through distant moves or death, older persons feel insecure. As change continues, they experience confusion and then fear. When fear hinders coping, they withdraw. They enter a personal energy crisis. They drain the energy of those around them as they cling to others for help.

Slowly older people lose the personal energy that helps them to cope and to live. Then they die, an untimely death, a wasted resource. Great, untapped reservoirs of perspective, experience, and developed skills in older people become wasted in premature death.

Men and women slowly develop the personal energy crisis that leads to the waste of premature death. From childhood to womanhood, females learn cultural attitudes and behaviors that interfere with the implementation of their full potential.

Less direct than men, women measure the same amounts of hidden or displayed hostility on psychological tests as do men. Allowing themselves to remain dependent and undeveloped, women often carry overwhelming loads of anger, despair, and depression as they age.

Throughout life males, on the other hand, have learned social values that interfere with their expressions of feelings. They become entangled in platitudes, such as being strong and silent like a "real man." Whether or not it is natural to their personality, they behave in ways that show self-control, logical thinking or intellectualizations, and aggression.

They become unable to express spontaneous, genuine feelings. This inadequacy often leads to emotional pain. Sometimes it results in confusion and turmoil in their relationships. Over the years men begin to feel increasingly distant from others and lose their sense of who they really are.

COMMUNICATION

The long-established pattern of behaving in a cautious, nondirect manner blocks open, frank communication for men and women. Older persons are unsure about sharing their real wants with others. They mull over bothersome questions and comments, such as: "How will they feel if I come out and say it?" "I couldn't stand hurting him." "She can tell what I feel; I don't have to say it in words." "She's so sensitive. I'd rather forget it."

It is difficult to overcome customary caution and uncertainty in order to think, feel, or do something that is one's own choice. Sometimes things build up until the inside storm of emotion explodes. After losing one's temper and clearing the air, a person may feel emptied of tension, but embarrassed and probably wonder, "Why didn't I say something before this happened? Next time . . ." But somehow the next time never seems to come.

Or, when a friend asks for a favor and a person wants to refuse, what happens? The individual feels tired, is busy, or wants to spend the afternoon alone in the garden. Does that person hide true feelings and preferences and respond, "Sure, I'll pick up some stamps for you at the post office right away." Or, does that person communicate the more honest, "No, I've already made plans for today. Next time, I would appreciate your calling me earlier in the week so we could plan together."

The inability to communicate adequately to others and the confusing transition of aging may be accommodated in various ways. Skills such as communication techniques and assertion training are important tools. However, before learning the "tools of the trade" (the communication trade), it is important to develop the person who will be using these tools.

Thus, in the following chapters, some time will be spent developing an awareness and understanding of oneself and the other people in one's life. The information and discussion exercises should help to enrich one's personal and social self. In this way, the communication skills will add more richly to continued growth and development as one continues in the ongoing experience of daily living.

The following discussion exercise, MEMORY EXPERIENCE, provides an opportunity to review a past experience in life. The exercise explores the factors involved in undergoing a change sometime in the past. It provides an opportunity to think about the steps involved in personal change.

Should I say it?

DISCUSSION EXERCISE

Memory Experience

DIRECTIONS FOR THE LEARNER: Think about a specific incident that occurred many years ago and that resulted in a significant, positive change in your life. What was the incident? Who was involved? How long did it take? What helped you in the experience? What interfered? What are some of your pleasant or unpleasant feelings now as you think back to that experience? Try to remember and get into the circumstances of that past situation. Make an attempt to recapture that event.

In the space provided below, write some brief responses to the questions above regarding your MEMORY EXPERIENCE.

DIRECTIONS FOR THE LEADER: This exercise may be used as an individual or group experience. The purpose of this exercise is to help the learner realize that personal change is possible. Through the examination of a past experience, the learner becomes aware of the parts and importance of personal change. Hopefully, the experience will motivate the learner to acquire new skills for dealing with daily life.

On an individual basis, each person may think of the different parts, the people and experiences, involved in the change. Questions the individual may consider are:

How different am I now as a result of that experience? What feelings did I experience then and what feelings do I experience now as I remember that incident of long ago? What strength did I show during that experience? What kind of person was I at that time? What new things do I see in that situation now that some time has passed?

As a small group activity, this exercise provides the opportunity for the sharing of each one's incident and the feelings remembered from that time. The questions suggested in the previous paragraph may be considered and discussed. As people in the group listen to each other, they should think of positive ways to respond to the one sharing personal information. What may be said to that person who is "opening up" so that they feel heard and appreciated? Refer to the section in Chapter 5 on POSITIVE FEEDBACK for some helpful information.

PERSONAL GOAL SETTING

Goal setting is a way of accomplishing positive change in one's life. A goal is a desired end result. It is the aim or point of finishing one's activities. It may be a simple job, such as doing one load of laundry. It may be a large, complicated task, such as building a new home or establishing a new business. Usually time is an important factor to consider when setting a goal. The time that it takes to do a job involves sensible planning. An individual needs to consider what reasonable amount of time is needed to complete a specific task or goal.

Goal setting helps people to plan the development of their lives in a desirable direction. Individuals may form goals for the coming year during each New Year's Day. An individual may start every morning with a new goal for that day. A grandparent may plan six months ahead to make special toys or clothing for a grandchild's summer visit. Business people may establish two-year, five-year, or longer-term goals to maintain their company's development and success.

Setting goals to improve communication helps one develop specific behavior to improve listening and speaking skills. In addition to attaining the goals are the benefits of feeling competent and, soon thereafter, confident about one's abilities.

One way to begin setting goals is to think in terms of actions or tasks that may be completed in a short period of time. For example, a person may decide to clean out a bureau drawer or organize the tool box in the next two days. Accomplishing smaller tasks will provide a feeling of success and enough self-assurance to feel competent about taking on another, more challenging goal. After success with many smaller goals, a person may feel ready to take on an even bigger challenge, such as painting the house or losing 20 pounds in three months.

Establishing a reward system encourages one to strive for goals. A reward may be a powerful motivator. A reward should match the level of the goal that is set. In the beginning rewards should be small and tangible for goals that are relatively easy to complete. Later, as the level of the goal becomes more challenging, the reward may be larger, more highly valued, or abstract.

For example, having a cup of coffee with a friend may reward a small, short-term goal. Some new clothing may reward a bigger goal, such as a large weight loss. Feeling good about one's appearance, self-discipline, and competence may be the intangible rewards that develop much later in one's goal-reward experiences.

The following discussion exercise, YOUR PERSONAL GOALS, provides practice in setting up a goal and the small steps toward meeting the goal over a time span of four days.

Where do I start?

DISCUSSION EXERCISE

Your Personal Goals

DIRECTIONS FOR THE LEARNER:

DIRECTIONS FOR DAY 1: Take a few moments to think about two personal goals that you would like to work on in the next four days. Try to think of goals related to improving your communication skills. It is important to make the exercise as meaningful to you as possible. With this in mind, it may be more helpful for you to select goals that involve another area of your life, such as relationships or physical exercise.

Now write two goals down below. Next to each goal, write down the reward you will receive for accomplishing each goal.

GOAL	REWARD
1.	
2.	

DIRECTIONS FOR DAY 2: Make the goals more detailed by developing three to five specific steps to take in order to accomplish each one. For example, cleaning out a bureau drawer may involve:

1. Setting aside 30 minutes tomorrow morning
2. Putting an empty wastebasket nearby
3. Getting out some scissors and shelf-paper for relining the drawer
4. Unplugging the telephone for 30 minutes to provide some uninterrupted time to complete the job.

GOAL ONE

STEPS:

1.

2.

3.

4.

5.

GOAL TWO

1.

2.

3.

4.

5.

DIRECTIONS FOR DAY 3:   Evaluate your progress in approaching each goal. Write down what interferes and what facilitates reaching each one.

GOALS	INTERFERES	HELPS
1.		
2.		

DIRECTIONS FOR DAY 4:   Redefine unmet goals. Write them down as new goals and set up some new rewards. Reward yourself as you planned for the goals that you have completed. You have earned your reward!

REDEFINED GOALS	NEW REWARDS
1.	
2.	

DIRECTIONS FOR THE LEADER: This is an exercise that needs some interaction. This activity should be done as a group—people may share the progress of each day in small groups of two or three persons. Or, it may be done on an individual basis—the learner may select a personal friend with whom to share. The purpose of the exercise is to provide a clear, easy way to meet goals and reward those efforts.

Questions to consider after sharing the final day of progress: What was the easiest part of this exercise? What part of it seemed to be challenging? What part of it was impossible? How does it feel to set out a plan and follow through on it? How does it feel when conditions seem to slow down or interfere with progress toward your goal?

Remember, positive feedback should be provided to those who share information about themselves. Individuals should be encouraged to give themselves credit for what has been accomplished and their willingness to open up a bit to others. This self-credit is a way of developing a personal positive feedback system. Refer to the section on POSITIVE FEEDBACK in Chapter 5 for some assistance.

GOAL SETTING FOR A NEW DIRECTION IN LIFE

Now that you have practiced setting up and meeting a simple goal on the previous pages, you may be interested in trying a bigger challenge. Think of a goal that is a little more challenging and provides new direction. It should be something you would really like to do or experience. The results of the goal should give you a sense of accomplishment. At this point it should not be the type of goal that may become a burden to accomplish. After developing skills in goal setting and understanding more about how you operate to meet goals, you will be better prepared to meet larger challenges.

After you have thought of your goal, set it up in the same way outlined in the previous discussion exercise. You may want to adjust the set-up to make it better for your personal situation. For example, the time structure may be WEEK 1, WEEK 2, etc., instead of DAY 1, DAY 2, etc. Or, you may put in a reward every step or every other step of the way in order to keep yourself motivated. Make the plan suitable for you.

DECISION MAKING

Some people have great difficulty in making a decision. Others may want a little time to ponder a bit before deciding. For some individuals, the ease in decision making depends upon circumstances. For instance, they may make personal decisions easily, but have great difficulty making choices that involve others. It may be easy for them to shop for family members, but difficult for them to decide on a gift for a friend.

Some persons, however, seem to make decisions spontaneously. Making decisions seems easy. In fact solving problems may be so automatic and natural for them that they are unable to determine the intermediary steps between a problem and its resolution. They can easily choose a book to read, a new car to purchase, the right greeting card to send, or which relative to visit for the holidays.

Decision-Making Steps

The method of making decisions may be approached with various problem-solving procedures. If one understands the process involved in making easy, daily decisions, one may apply that method to an issue where one seems confused or stuck, unable to make a choice or unable to move in any direction. The following four steps are useful to make decisions (Gelatt, 1962; Schein, 1969):

1. Define the problem
2. List sensible choices
3. Predict possible end results
4. Act on and evaluate choices

STEP 1: DEFINE THE PROBLEM

The problem may be easy to identify. Sometimes, however, the problem may be hard to see. Thinking ahead to possible end results may uncover a better understanding of the real problem. This is especially true when the problem is entangled with feelings. When a simple problem involves many emotions, it may result in a complex, confusing situation.

STEP 2: LIST SENSIBLE CHOICES

One should think about all the possible choices that may be real alternatives. It may be helpful to consider all kinds of choices at first. Then one may narrow down the possibilities to a few practical choices. A person should consider the sequence of activities needed to arrive at the final solution or to complete the final task. In completing a task, it often seems easier to follow many small steps than one big, complicated step.

STEP 3: PREDICT POSSIBLE END RESULTS

For each choice in STEP 2, one should think of the result that will probably follow. This is the appropriate time to consider possible negative outcomes that may occur as a result of a particular choice. The idea is to think ahead about possible consequences to determine the best choice of action. Foreseeing end results often helps one stay clear of major errors.

STEP 4: ACT AND EVALUATE

After selecting the best choice, one is ready to begin action. As one acts, one should begin to evaluate. The individual may think about whether the action is appropriate and how it helps progress toward a satisfactory solution. An occasional evaluation during the action allows one to determine the worth of the action. Then one may slow down or stop when it seems to be in good sense. Sometimes an evaluation brings up the need for further work at a certain stage before the next step is taken on the decision.

Evaluation may be casual, such as thinking over the pleasant points and unpleasant points of the situation. Or, an evaluation may be formal, such as asking a number of people to fill in a questionnaire. It may involve interviewing a random sample of a select group of people.

One should take time to enjoy the satisfaction of a decision that resulted in a successful solution. If the decision is not appropriate, then a person should try again by beginning at STEP 1, redefining the problem.

The following discussion exercise, THE FOUR-STEP DECISION, provides a chance to practice the steps involved in making a decision.

The Four-Step Decision

DIRECTIONS FOR THE LEARNER: Using the four steps just discussed, describe the procedure you would follow in one of these two situations, (1) to awaken in the morning after a night's rest and get ready for the day, or (2) to take a 30-minute break from working or studying. Pick situation (1) or (2) and itemize the four steps that are involved in reaching a final decision.

1. **Define the problem:**

2. **List sensible choices:**

3. **Predict possible end results:**

4. **Act and evaluate:**

DIRECTIONS FOR THE LEADER: This exercise is for individuals to do on a private basis. The purpose of the exercise is for them to apply the above four-step method to a personal problem, where they seem to be stuck. Often a careful, simple method, such as this, may help someone reach the resolution of a problem. When the resolution still seems impossible, then sometimes this method provides movement toward the next step, closer to the final solution. Moving one step is much better than staying stuck.

Questions that the individual may think about are: What new perspective is provided by this type of exploring? What kind of pressures do I feel to bring this problem to a solution? What kind of pressures do I feel to avoid bringing this problem to a solution?

The following space is provided to outline briefly the personal problem using the FOUR–STEP DECISION model described above. As the learner thinks and writes, does some direction for a solution become evident?

PERSONAL PROBLEM OUTLINE

1. **Define the problem:**

2. **List sensible choices:**

3. **Predict possible end results:**

4. **Act and evaluate:**

THE FULCRUM MODEL OF DECISION MAKING

THE FULCRUM MODEL is another useful method to evaluate a situation or personal problem in order to arrive at a decision. A fulcrum is a support that holds and balances a weight. The fulcrum is usually located toward the middle of the underside of a plane or board. The balancing of a fulcrum may be seen in a see-saw at a playground. The different weights of children on either end are balanced by the shifting fulcrum.

SIDE A   SIDE B

FULCRUM

The diagram above represents a personal application of balancing on a see-saw. In the diagram, the fulcrum operates to keep in balance the facts of a situation in one's daily life. In the situation the facts on either one side or the other, SIDE A or SIDE B of the horizontal plane, should compensate, complement, or balance each other for a person to be happy and satisfied. When SIDE A of the plane or life situation greatly outweighs SIDE B, a person may be undecided, unhappy, or overwhelmed. The guidelines below explain the use of the Fulcrum Model to help a person make decisions.

Begin the Fulcrum Model by dividing the various facts and feelings of the problem situation into two groups. Use the guidelines below. Go ahead and list everything you think is relevant to the situation. Include both FACTS and FEELINGS in each of the categories, SIDE A, POSITIVE; and SIDE B, NEGATIVE.

Fulcrum Model

STEP 1

Begin by thinking about a specific situation or relationship where you are having some difficulty finding direction. Think about the involved facts and personal feelings. Divide the facts and feelings into two groups, SIDE A, POSITIVE; and SIDE B, NEGATIVE. List everything relevant that you think of; include both facts and feelings for each category, the positive side and the negative side.

SIDE A is represented by positive facts and feelings in areas such as:

1. What I receive from the relationship, project, or situation
2. What I like about (him, her, or it)
3. Helps

SIDE B is represented by negative facts and feelings in areas, such as:

1. What I give or invest in the relationship, project, or situation
2. What I dislike about (him, her, or it)
3. Hindrances

SIDE A POSITIVE ASPECTS	SIDE B NEGATIVE ASPECTS

For example, Lyle is trying to reach a decision about changing his hobby. Lyle has been an antique car enthusiast for a number of years. Sometimes his hobby seems more like overwhelming work rather than a pleasant hobby. Every once in a while Lyle finds himself thinking about doing other kinds of activities while he is working to restore a car. It may be helpful to Lyle to use the above model to help him think through his concern. Lyle may think in the following terms:

SIDE A, POSITIVE	SIDE B, NEGATIVE
(What I like about refinishing old cars)	(What I put up with or dislike about refinishing antique cars)
1. Satisfaction	1. Lots of time
2. Lots of money from sales of restored cars	2. Costs more money these days to buy old parts
3. Easy work, I'm an expert after all these years	3. Hard work doing a good job
4. Enjoy the antique car shows	4. Frequent physical injuries
5. Meet interesting car buffs	5. Endure wife's nagging about collection of old car parts in messy garage
	6. Hard time to find old parts in junk yards
	7. Tired after 45 years at the same hobby

Is it worth it?

STEP 2

Now analyze the situation in order to separate the feelings from the facts. Mark each item of information on SIDE A and SIDE B as either a fact or a feeling.

For example, Lyle may look at his comments above and label them as:

SIDE A, POSITIVE	SIDE B, NEGATIVE
1. Feeling	1. Fact
2. Fact	2. Fact
3. Feeling & fact	3. Fact
4. Feeling	4. Fact
5. Fact	5. Feeling & fact
	6. Fact
	7. Fact
	8. Feeling

STEP 3

Next, consider the weight or value of each fact or feeling. Using a scale of 1 (unimportant) to 10 (highly important), write a number beside each fact or feeling according to how important each fact is or how strong each feeling is.

As Lyle looks over his list of facts and feelings about refinishing old cars, he may determine the following values:

SIDE A, POSITIVE		SIDE B, NEGATIVE	
1. Feeling	(9)	1. Fact	(5)
2. Fact	(10)	2. Fact	(9)
3. Feeling	(3)	3. Fact	(8)
Fact	(7)	4. Fact	(10)
4. Feeling	(9)	5. Feeling	(10)
5. Fact	(8)	Fact	(1)
		6. Fact	(4)
		7. Fact	(6)
		8. Feeling	(8)

STEP 4

Add up the score for facts and feelings on SIDE A and SIDE B. Draw a fulcrum with the total number on each side for facts and for feelings.

SIDE A, POSITIVE		SIDE B, NEGATIVE	
1. Feeling	(9)	1. Fact	(5)
2. Fact	(10)	2. Fact	(9)
3. Feeling	(3)	3. Fact	(8)
Fact	(7)	4. Fact	(10)
4. Feeling	(9)	5. Feeling	(10)
5. Fact	(8)	Fact	(1)
		6. Fact	(4)
		7. Fact	(6)
		8. Feeling	(8)

TOTALS			
Facts	25	Facts	43
Feelings	21	Feelings	18

Lyle's fulcrum will look like this:

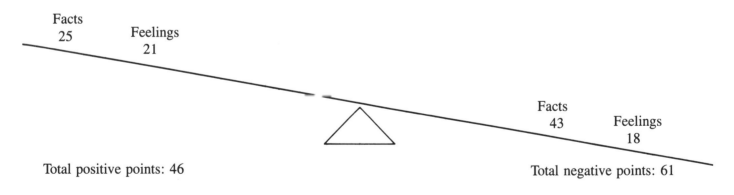

Facts
25
Feelings
21

Facts
43
Feelings
18

Total positive points: 46   Total negative points: 61

DISCUSSION OF FULCRUM MODEL RESULTS

In Lyle's situation the load of the negative factors is heavier than that of the positive ones. Based on the heavy weight of the negative factors, Lyle may decide to give up the activity altogether. This would be a reasonable decision based on the weight of the negative facts (43 points) as opposed to the positive facts (25 points).

Lyle may notice, however, that the positive feelings (21 points) slightly outweigh the negative feelings (18 points). Neglecting to evaluate his true feelings, no matter how rational and reasonable his decision was, would probably result in his being dissatisfied or unhappy. Feelings may be so important to him that he decides to ignore the facts and to continue his hobby with antique cars due to the heavier weight of the positive feelings.

Besides comparing the total scores of all feelings or all facts, other directions in decision making may be considered. Lyle may value the feelings and facts concerning other involved people, such as his wife. Some of his positive and negative scores may change after he considers her ideas and feelings and then adds those values to his own scores. She may make her own Fulcrum Model with her positive and negative facts and feelings on the topic of refinishing antique cars. Then Lyle and his wife may choose to compare and combine factors based on their different scores.

Often alternatives are available. The activity may go in a new direction. Parts of it may be changed. Minor modifications that reduce the negative facts or feelings may optimize the situation.

For instance, Lyle may decide to share the workload and profits with a partner. He may want to teach his skills to others by developing a repair manual or a continuing education course. He may exchange working on antique cars for a related hobby, such as building model cars or go-carts for children.

After carefully weighing the objective and subjective information, the involved facts and feelings, with a fulcrum analysis, an individual may face a problem situation with more alternatives from which to choose. The person's new awareness may enhance a sense of self-sufficiency. The individual may take comfort in the responsibility of carefully making the most desirable choice.

In the space provided on the next page, take a few moments to go through the four steps of the Fulcrum Model. Use a situation that is a personal concern or an unresolved problem area in your life. As you explore your concern, think in terms of learning more about yourself, what you value, and how you want your life to unfold.

Take time to get at the facts and feelings in your situation. Typically, people are so eager to arrive at a decision or conclusion that they overlook important parts of the involved facts or feelings. Overlooking such details often leads to premature decisions that may result in the same frustrations and lack of resolution encountered before.

BASIC SKILLS

WORKSHEET FOR THE FULCRUM MODEL

SIDE A, POSITIVE	SIDE B, NEGATIVE

DIRECTIONS FOR THE LEARNER AND LEADER: This worksheet provides an opportunity for the leader to work on an individual basis. After going through the exercise, it may be helpful to reflect on the following questions.

Was it easy or difficult for you to identify a concern and work out its details? What kinds of feelings did you experience as you tried to describe the different facts and feelings in the situation? Is it easier for you to see the positive or the negative parts of a situation? What new information did you learn about the situation or yourself?

SUMMARY

Transition is a natural and desirable part of life. Ongoing changes as one grows and develops occur in all areas of life. This change is the process of aging.

Society seems to focus on preserving youthfulness. It views old age with a strong negative attitude. This attitude is known as agism.

Throughout their development, maturing men and women follow the values and expectations of society. As they age, people find that the standards of culture often limit their lifestyle.

Older people have the right to make decisions and access resources that will provide them with a satisfying lifestyle. Communication skills and selective assertiveness are the tools that will help them cope effectively in order to lead rewarding, fulfilling lives.

Suggestions for Further Reading

AGISM

Atchley, R. C. (1980). *The Social Forces in Later Life.* Belmont, CA: Wadsworth.

Butler, P. (1976). Assertive training: Teaching women not to discriminate against themselves. *Psychotherapy: Theory, Research and Practice,* 13(1), 56–60.

COMPETENCE

White, R. W. (1972). *The Enterprise of Living.* New York: Holt, Rinehart & Winston.

DECISION MAKING

Gelatt, H. B. (1962). Decision-making: A conceptual frame of reference for counseling. *Journal of Counseling Psychology,* 9(3), 240–245.

Schein, E. H. (1969). *Process Consultation.* Reading, MA: Addison-Wesley.

MALE DEVELOPMENT

Brenton, M. (1970). *The American Male.* Greenwich, CT: Fawcett.

Goldberg, H. (1976). *The Hazards of Being Male.* New York: Nash.

PERSONAL EVALUATION AND LIFE PLANNING

Doty, L. (1981). Planning and preparation for the new life. *Resources in Education.* ERIC/CAPS Clearinghouse (ED 198408).

REMINISCING

Fallot, F. D. (1979–1980). The impact on mood of verbal reminiscing in later adulthood. *International Journal of Aging and Human Development,* 10(4), 385–400.

3

Communication

Communication is an important part of everyone's daily life. Whether it involves thinking alone on the front porch, holding the hand of your Grandpa as you walk in the gentle sunshine of spring, chatting with friends at work during an "orange juice" break, or sharing an important message with millions of others on a TV program, communication is important.

To work, communication must be effective. Effective communication involves skills in understanding the human being, listening well, and talking clearly. Having good skills in communication helps one person transfer information, such as ideas, experiences, and feelings, to another person.

Effective communication helps to develop and establish relationships. It helps one reach out to others and build links to others. It helps one to share oneself with others.

Relationships that exist over a long period of time depend upon good communication. Such communication involves people who can function well as a speaker and a listener.

The exchange of meaningful communication encourages further contact. Frequent, accurate communication enhances contact with others. It enlivens relationships. Limited and inaccurate communication fosters withdrawal from others. It leads to a sense of loss and lowers one's spirit. Thus, people, communication, and happiness in life are intricately interwoven.

In this chapter the study of communication will begin with the examination of two important areas, first, personal awareness, and then, relationships. Then in Chapter 4, several skills important to communication will be covered.

The format of learning follows two steps. In the first step, the basic ideas of personal awareness, relationships, and the communication skills are presented. These ideas are followed by the second step of learning, the discussion exercises. The discussion exercises provide practice opportunities for the reader to try out the ideas and skills.

SECTION I: PERSONAL AWARENESS IN COMMUNICATION

To communicate effectively, one should become aware of oneself. A person must feel free to look at personal feelings, to look inside oneself and to accept oneself. In this way a person becomes in tune with his or her own needs and wants. Then these needs and wants may be expressed as accurate messages to other people.

Sometimes a person seems to wear a shell that covers the real self or real identity. Some psychologists call this protective organization (Horney, 1945) or character armor (Reich, 1949). Many people feel that their cover protects the inner, sensitive self from hurt. Sometimes the protection covers the identity so well that it becomes hidden from others and often even from oneself.

By searching within oneself, one may begin to understand the inner human being. One way to begin this search is to learn one's perceptions and values. Attitudes and beliefs vary. The various aspects of a person's life differ in importance and significance. Understanding how one looks at people or things in life may provide clues to deeper meanings of the real person within. Then messages can carry accurate information from within oneself to others.

The following discussion exercise is PRIORITIES: NINE THINGS I LIKE ABOUT MYSELF. It is designed to provide an opportunity for the individual to consider what has value in his or her personal life. This activity may help the individual begin to develop some way to personal awareness.

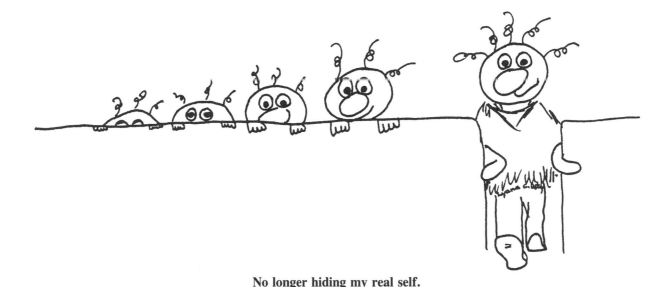

No longer hiding my real self.

Priorities: Nine Things I Like About Myself

DIRECTIONS FOR THE LEARNER:
STEP 1:   Write down nine different things . . . characteristics, feelings, people in your life, whatever you may think of, that are especially meaningful or important to you. These may be things that are part of your daily experiences now or may have been part of your life in the past.

STEP 2: Rank the nine items you just listed above from least important (9) to most important (1). Rank order three items at a time. First label 9, 8, 7, then rank order 6, 5, 4, and finally rank order 3, 2, and 1.

DIRECTIONS FOR THE LEADER: This discussion exercise may be done as a group or individual activity. The purpose of the exercise is to help the learner become more aware of what is of the most value in his/her life.
The group may find it helpful to discuss the following questions. If done on an individual basis, the learner should take a few moments to reflect on the questions.
What are the most important, top two choices? What do you hold dear in your life? How would you categorize what you hold dear . . . animals, family heirlooms, things, people, ideas, etc.? What does this information tell you about yourself? What does this information tell you about how you act in certain situations?
NOTE: The total exercise should take about 20 to 30 minutes. People who are 70 years old or more usually take a minimum of 60 minutes to complete this exercise. They have such a wide range of people and things from which to select, that it takes a while for them to select only nine items. They also prefer to take more time when they share information about their nine items with others in the group.

IDENTITY

Some theorists think of identity in terms of the onion skin theory, layers upon layers of "personality skins." The core of the onion is supposed to represent the very essence of an individual. The outer shell, the thin outer brown layer of onion skin, represents the socially presented self. A person behaves in different ways and exposes different levels of the self (or layers of onion skin) according to the situation. One's needs also influence how one shares different aspects of oneself.

In order to look within or in order to find the core of the onion, one carefully peels through the layers. Hopefully, the core is strong and healthy. An onion with a weak core quickly disintegrates into nothing. Sometimes, no amount of peeling through the protective layers of human personality skins seems sufficient to find the deeply hidden core of real self.

Erich Fromm (1955) believed that each human being differed from all others. Each person's identity is unique and tells who he or she is. When one perceives and receives into the self all sensory and visceral experiences, a person becomes more developed, more enriched, and more of an individual. That person becomes more appreciative of the self as a separate individual.

The stronger the sense of self, the stronger is one's identity. As the identity becomes stronger, the person becomes more understanding and accepting of the self and others. Paradoxically, as one becomes more individualized, one senses the common features of all humans and senses a unity, a brotherhood or sisterhood with everyone. For example, one senses the need to be loved and the need to belong that all people share. Thus, joining, sharing, and caring for one another are strengthened as one becomes more fully oneself.

The following explorations of ideas and discussion exercises concern "I" statements, roles, and self-concept. The information may help people learn more about the self. The discussion exercises provide practice in recognizing parts of the self and sharing some of that with others.

"I" STATEMENTS

"I" statements show a willingness to own up to and assume responsibility for what is said. The subject of the statement is the personal "I", not general words, such as you, they, everyone, etc. Saying "I" indicates the willingness of the speaker to be open and to share a personal feeling or opinion. "I" statements put the speaker in charge of what is being said or done. The listener has more concrete information to which to respond.

Hippocrates, 400 B.C., provided a good example of a general statement when he pointed out that what is not used, is lost. Or, the same general statement put a little more strongly by Henry Ford in 1931, "Money is like an arm or a leg . . . use it or lose it" (Davidoff, 1942, p. 231).

Though the message is spoken in different ways during different centuries, both Hippocrates and Ford establish a respectful distance with their words. The statements seem to relate to the same general idea or principle. A personal report of beliefs, experiences, or feelings of the speaker, however, is not given in the words that are stated.

The listener of these remarks would probably reply with a similarly general remark. This keeps the conversation away from intimate sharing. It remains safe. The people remain somewhat uninvolved, reserved, and distant from each other. At an important business meeting, the social distance of general remarks may be appropriate. In family communication, such distance may be undesirable.

An example of an "I" statement that reveals personal feelings and specific information about the speaker is the following excerpt from "I Cannot Sing the Old Songs" by Charlotte A. Barnard (1830–1869).

> I cannot sing the old songs
> I sang long years ago
> For heart and voice would fail me
> And foolish tears would flow.
> (Davidoff, 1942, p. 356)

Listening to Barnard's self-disclosing nostalgia, a person would likely respond with sensitivity. Further, the individual would probably share his or her own emotional experiences in singing old songs. The intimate communication involves specific content and feelings.

After their time together, the participants would experience a togetherness. They would share a sense of emotional bonding. They would experience a transformation of uplifted spirits. They have started a significant relationship by their willingness to share personal information.

Note the following differences when an "I" statement is used:

1. "Everyone needs a better salary to keep up with inflation" versus "I want to ask for a pay raise to keep up with my family expenses."
2. "Nobody cares about public transportation" versus "I like to use the bus, but I can't afford the increased fare" or "I'm upset that the weekend service is being cut."

The "I" statements provide specific information about the speaker. As a result, the listener is inclined to feel more involved in the conversation and closer to the speaker. The conversation will probably be an exchange that is meaningful to everyone involved.

The following discussion exercise, PERSONALIZING "I" STATEMENTS, provides practice in using the personal "I" to communicate in a way that is more open and shares personal information.

DISCUSSION EXERCISE

Personalizing "I" Statements

DIRECTIONS FOR THE LEARNER: How would you make the following statements more personal? Using the pronoun "I", write a personal form of each statement below in the spaces provided.

1. You get embarrassed when people talk about your thick glasses.

2. Children are so rude these days.

3. Politicians are not doing the job they should.

4. You know that your parents and grandparents love you and want the best.

    DIRECTIONS FOR THE LEADER: This activity may be done in a large or small group or as an individual homework assignment. The purpose of the activity is to help people become aware of the differences between more distant versus a closer way of talking. The responses should include "I" as well as some specific thoughts and/or feelings about the subject.
    It may be helpful for the learners to role play a conversation starting with one of the general statements above and continuing with how they would respond to such a statement. Then they could role play a conversation starting with one of the personal statements they wrote. How do the responses of the different role playing situations compare? What different kinds of information are exchanged in the more general and more personalized conversations?
    The learners should be encouraged to be alert to how people generally avoid using personal statements. They may hear actors on television using general and personal statements. How do those different kinds of statements affect relationships? It is important to try to use "I" more often, when it is appropriate of course.
    It takes about 15 minutes for the exercise and discussion.

DISCUSSION EXERCISE

Self-Concept

DIRECTIONS FOR THE LEARNER: *Write down some words that describe how the individual in the picture below is feeling. What is this individual's self-concept?*

DIRECTIONS FOR THE LEADER: *This exercise is a good brainstorming activity for a group; people stimulate each other's thinking. The purpose of the exercise is to learn about feelings that can be portrayed through an image and through body behaviors.*

Here, there are some lines on paper, only an image, and yet some feelings are transferred from the lines on the paper to the learner. The image is showing a certain kind of body behavior and that behavior sends information about feelings to the reader.

The group should think about and discuss the feelings of the above image or "individual." What clues can be seen or felt from the contents of the picture above to acquire information about the individual's current experience of self?

The exercise takes about 10 to 15 minutes.

VIEW OF SELF

Views of oneself often develop through positive or negative interactions with other people. One's view of the personal self may be obvious. It may be consistent with one's daily behavior. On the other hand, one's view of oneself may be hidden, emerging as different behaviors in various situations. One's view of oneself may even result in behavior that confuses others as well as oneself.

For example, Mable may view herself as caring and sociable. Although she may see herself as sociable and outgoing, her behaviors in two contrasting party situations indicate some differences.

In the home of her close friend with a small group of people she knows well, Mable is outgoing and a bit of a clown. In a large, formal social gathering, the welcoming reception for the new Commissioner of Education, she acts distant and cool. Perhaps Mable's sociable behavior in the small group was the result of her feeling accepted and respected by friends. The distant, unsociable behavior at the large reception may have been the result of her feeling shy, socially inadequate, less capable and incompetent when comparing herself with the others.

Briefly exploring different terms that relate to self-concept may help people understand themselves better. It may help them to see how the view of self evolves from or is comprised of different factors. The following terms point out some of the different components of self-concept.

Self-concept

Self-concept is what I think of and sense about myself. It usually undergoes frequent modifications as a result of continuous experiences. This component of self-concept is known as the cognitive element. It refers to the involvement of the cognition, intellectual thinking, the objective and subjective images and ideas I have about the person I am.

For example, I think of myself as . . .
1. I am clumsy.
2. I am quick-witted.
3. I am an athlete.
4. I am intelligent.
5. I am shy.
6. I am a repair man (woman).

Ideal Self

The ideal self is the most or the best I want to be. It is the highest level I want or think I can achieve for myself. Parents, teachers, significant historical persons, etc., may be role models or mentors that contribute values to the ideal that I desire to achieve.

For example,
1. I will dance as gracefully as Maria Tallchief.
2. After I become president of the club, I will introduce programs to support volunteerism, because helping others is so important.
3. I want to be as good a Grandpa to you as my Grandpa was to me.

Self-esteem

Self-esteem is how high or low I value myself. It is the worth I feel about myself. This emotional element refers to how much I like or dislike who (I feel) I am.

For example,
1. I hate being the one who always asks questions. I feel so stupid all the time.
2. I am proud to be an American.
3. I cannot volunteer to help. I never do well when I have to do a big job by myself.

Self-acceptance

Understanding my personal condition of worth, I respect and accept myself as I am now. I also like the person I am becoming as I grow older. I value myself. Self-acceptance leads to the acceptance of others.

For example,

1. Since I started playing the piano, I have developed a greater respect for pianists.
2. I have never done that job before, but I'll be careful and do my best.
3. Accepting my own difficulties with self-motivation helps me to be more patient with my youngest son and his struggle to do his schoolwork.

Locus of Control

The locus of control indicates where I put responsibility for the control of decisions, behavior, etc., in my life. Operating with an internal locus of control, I place the control of decisions and actions with myself. I take full responsibility for my own decisions and behavior. Operating with an external locus of control, I allow personal decisions to be made by others or by whatever others are doing. I follow the decision of the group. I believe that they know the best direction for me and that I don't.

In this sense, the introvert is a person who evaluates available choices, makes an independent decision, and accepts full responsibility for the consequences of the decision.

The extravert, on the other hand, is a person who follows the flow of the group. This is the person who goes along with the opinion of the majority, accepts little or no responsibility for the decision and, therefore, feels no responsibility for the consequences of the decision.

For example, INTERNAL LOCUS OF CONTROL:

1. Before I buy new drills, I'm going to shop around and get a set that meets my needs.
2. Even though my friends are playing tennis this spring, I'm going to try something new and sign up for golf lessons.

For example, EXTERNAL LOCUS OF CONTROL:

1. Everyone is wearing Whammo shoes. I'd better get myself a pair so I won't look out of place.
2. Working with books would be fun. I would like to volunteer for the library sale, but my family won't let me have any free time for that kind of activity.

Influences on the Self

Many factors affect the development of the self, another word for personality, or character. The self may remain the same or undergo change as a result of time and experiences. Some influential factors on the formation of the self include family, culture, stereotypes, profession, success and failure, physical and psychosocial elements, experience, values, beliefs, and trends.

Some influences are obvious, such as the influence of classroom learning. Some influences are subtle, such as the family stress of childhood and its relationship to one's adult behavior. A person may be open to new experiences. The individual may like the excitement of stimulating new influences, such as traveling in a different country or studying a new course at the community college.

Sometimes a new experience may result in hurt feelings. For example, training for a new career may not result in a job. A new relationship may lead to conflicts in values and interests instead of the anticipated deep companionship. After several emotionally painful experiences over the years, some people may become closed to further influences on the self.

For example,

1. Even though I had to quit school in the third grade, I have always loved learning. I remember how pleased my teacher was with the way I read out loud to the class. I still enjoy reading out loud. I read to my grandchildren all the time.

COMMENT: The positive influences on the self that are being expressed by the person in this example are pleasant memories, reading out loud, and spending time with grandchildren.

2. I hate to argue with another adult. I'd rather just forget it. I don't know why. My mother and father used to have some nasty spats when I was young, but I'd just go outside and play. I wouldn't worry about it. I just don't like to bother. It's not worth it.

COMMENT: Unpleasant memories, unresolved issues, anxiety about arguments and disagreements, and a tendency to withdraw from conflict, provide negative influences on the self.

In looking at what makes up the self, an individual should consider self-concept, the ideal self, self-esteem, self-acceptance, locus of control, and influences on the self. Looking at these different factors, first separately and then collectively, the individual may develop some self-understanding.

The following discussion exercise, THE PERCEPTION RECTANGLE, will help the reader explore various aspects of the self. Hopefully, some new information will be uncovered and some known information will be confirmed as one works through the exercise.

DISCUSSION EXERCISE

The Perception Rectangle

DIRECTIONS FOR THE LEARNER: Write down in the three columns below expressions that describe you in each of the following different ways, OTHERS WOULD DESCRIBE ME AS, I WOULD DESCRIBE MYSELF AS, and I WISH OTHERS WOULD DESCRIBE ME AS.

The three expressions may be composed of single words or phrases. They may be nouns or adjectives. The expressions indicate how you think you are perceived according to the title of each column, OTHERS WOULD . . . , I WOULD . . . , and I WISH OTHERS WOULD. . . .

For example, think about how OTHERS WOULD DESCRIBE (you): gray hair, shy, reluctant to join in, helpful on committees, etc.

OTHERS WOULD DESCRIBE ME AS . . .	I WOULD DESCRIBE MYSELF AS . . .	I WISH OTHERS WOULD DESCRIBE ME AS . . .
1.	1.	1.
2.	2.	2.
3.	3.	3.

DIRECTIONS FOR THE LEADER: This exercise works better in small groups. The purpose of the exercise is to help the learner expand a perception of the self to include information about how others perceive him/her. The feedback from other group members about how they perceive the individual confirms or contests the accuracy of each persons's report from their OTHERS WOULD DESCRIBE ME AS columns.

If working on the exercise as an individual, the person should try to find a trusted friend with whom s/he may confide the information recorded on the PERCEPTION RECTANGLE. Then the listening friend may be asked for some response or feedback regarding the contents of the column, OTHERS WOULD DESCRIBE ME AS.

In the class situation, the participants should break up into groups of 4 to 5 members. In each group, participants should take turns sharing the different words from their three columns that suggest:

1. *How you think others see you*
2. *How you see yourself, in other words, your self-concept*
3. *How you would like to be seen, in other words, your self-ideal.*

Sometimes it is easier for people to identify their self-concept after they have thought about how others think of or perceive them. The participants should be reminded to provide positive feedback to group members who share information about themselves. People may refer to the section in Chapter 5 on POSITIVE FEEDBACK for some assistance.

Some questions to consider in the small group discussions:

1. *Would other people in your group use the same words to describe you as the words you wrote in column one, OTHERS WOULD . . . , and column two, I WOULD . . . ? How are the words or expressions of group members different or the same as your own? What does this exercise indicate about your self-awareness?*
2. *How close or how far are your self-ideal and your self-concept? What does this indicate about you and how you operate in the activities of your life?*

It takes about 30 minutes to complete the exercise and the discussion.

SECTION II: COMMUNICATION IN RELATIONSHIPS

After learning about one's personal self, the next obvious step in effective communication is to understand about other people. Knowing about the relationships in one's life plays a large role in good communication.

Satisfying interpersonal relationships are an important part of a healthful lifestyle. Mutual expectations and gratification allow social interaction to be pleasant and fulfilling. Each one counts on the other to respond appropriately. Caring for each other is a way for people to be open to each other. Relationships of caring help individuals feel significant. This significance contributes to their experiencing meaningfulness and happiness in their individual lives.

Researchers find that for older persons, participation in at least one close, personal relationship is critical for healthful living. Having many friends is not the critical factor. Having at least one close friend does seem to make a decided difference in the health of older persons. In other words, the quality of the relationship seems to be very important.

In a 1980 study of almost 6,000 older people, one researcher, V. C. Little, found that 1,300 people had transportation needs, 4,300 needed help with home maintenance, but the greatest need was in the area of interpersonal relationships. Other researchers agree that companionship and a sense of belonging to someone else are priority needs of older persons.

FAMILY AND FRIENDS

Membership in a group broadens one's horizons. In a person's lifetime, the first group in which one participates is the family of origin, one's parents and siblings. It is considered to be the nuclear family, composed of a father, mother, and children living together. Informal groups of friends and formal groups, such as classmates or peers at work, increase the scope of social contacts.

As an adult, one may marry and form a new nuclear family, known as the family of creation. The created family usually has at least one spouse and one or more children. This family unit is also known as the conjugal family.

As the number of people increases in the family unit, the number of relationships increases. Interactions occur on many different levels and become extremely complex. In such settings good communications skills are essential to maintain positive, supportive relationships.

As one becomes older, former relationships may be replaced by newer ones. As an older person, one may have few relationships with one's nuclear family. Older adults may become involved in daily activities that include cohorts because they are located nearby and share similar interests. Cohorts are people who are about the same chronological age.

Over the years people may develop long-term friendships that seem closer than family ties. The friends may become a surrogate family. For the very old who often have difficulty replacing relationships, a surrogate family may fill the void left by the loss of intimate, long-standing relationships, such as a spouse of 60 years or a sibling of 80 years.

A surrogate family of cohorts may provide years of special caring and sharing that enrich the later years of life. Cohorts are especially appropriate as surrogate family members, because they share the same experiences of history and culture. Intergenerational relationships, however, are also rewarding.

The following discussion exercise, CONFIDE IN U, invites people to think about how they function with others. They will explore the special conditions they have in some of their relationships.

DISCUSSION EXERCISE

Confide in U

DIRECTIONS FOR THE LEARNER: In the first block of space or column below, named SYMBOL, write a word or draw a secret symbol that represents something you have done or felt, but that you have never shared with anyone. After thinking for several minutes, you may feel that, during the course of your life, you have shared everything there is to know about yourself. Then consider something about which you have been really careful, cautious, or reluctant to share.

Note that the SYMBOL information will not be discussed. It shall remain private. It is not the focus of this discussion exercise.

Next, in the right-hand block of space or column, labeled CONDITIONS, list the circumstances or provisions you would require before you would be willing to share that special, secret information about yourself.

SYMBOL	**CONDITIONS**

DIRECTIONS FOR THE LEADER: This discussion exercise may be done on an individual basis or with a group. The purpose of the exercise is subtle, not obvious at first. The exercise explores the ability of an individual to take risks in a relationship.

As a large group, the participants should share/discuss the following questions and perhaps keep a record of the conditions on a blackboard or flip chart in front of the class.

What general conditions do you require before you are willing to take a chance on sharing casual or superficial information about your family? What conditions do you require before you self-disclose personal information? What demands do you make before you are willing to share very personal information or deep secrets? Try to have a discussion about these conditions.

Now try to think of other people. How do you provide for them the same kind of conditions that you require? What attitudes or behaviors do you provide for others to let them feel safe in sharing with you? In other words, how do you provide conditions of trust for others?

Focus the discussion on the conditions of the exercise. For the purposes of this particular lesson, the SYMBOL information is not relevant. Participants should remember that everyone has a right to privacy and that the conditions of trust, not the secret, are the essential focus of this exercise.

It takes about 40 minutes to complete the exercise.

ROLES

The specific behaviors of people according to a position, social standard, or expectation, may be called a role. The roles of people change in different circumstances. Sometimes the behavior mirrors the standards set by the community. Sometimes the behavior is in response to a set of expectations that relate to one's age, job, or position. For example, a sixth grader's behavior is expected to be different from that of a college student. A grocery store clerk's behavior is expected to be different from that of a store manager.

Throughout life in different situations, people behave in various ways. The specific actions of people in their different roles may change as the circumstances change. Sometimes a change within a person may result in different behavior though the role is essentially the same. For example, a carpenter may realize artistic talents in cabinetry by applying creative designs on the face of the wood. The role of carpenter is the same, but a change in the person has resulted in a change in the end product.

A role or function may be new, may become more complex or even disappear in one's lifetime. For instance, in a natural role change, the baby grows into a youth, who soon becomes an adult. The simple roles of childhood evolve into the more complex roles of adulthood. Being a son may develop into the more complex role of father, or grandfather after a few more years.

Some roles are naturally given and may be stable, such as one's sex, male or female. Some roles are achieved, such as being a physician or an accountant. Some people have multiple roles; some have very few. One woman may act in the multiple roles of wife, mother, teacher, musician, volunteer, artist, carpenter, plumber, and chauffeur. Another woman may have the few roles of wife, homemaker, and gardener. For some individuals their stage in life dictates their amount of involvement in roles.

After studying the behavior of many people, in 1961 two sociologists, Cumming and Henry, published results indicating that older persons seem to have fewer roles than young people or middle-aged adults. They described their conclusions as the Disengagement Theory. The Disengagement Theory suggests that not only does society pull away from involving older persons in several responsible roles, but that older people also withdraw from many activities and roles.

The Activity Theory contends, however, that many older persons are just as involved in activities in later life as during their younger years. Some people substitute new roles and activities for ones that are no longer appealing. Others redistribute their roles and activities to accommodate their time and energy.

As they increase in age, many older persons become more active because of changing interests and because they may have more free time. Some older persons, on the other hand, seem to increase activities to prove that they are not aging. They want to seem vital, young, and perhaps to hear the comment, "No one would ever guess you were 80 years old with all the running around you do!" This type of comment presupposes two erroneous facts, (1) that 80-year-old people are not usually busy people, and (2) that younger people have stores of energy and are always very busy "running around."

Several theories of aging exist, but the common view of gerontologists focuses on the individuality of older people. Older persons should be sensitive to whatever is meaningful and worthwhile in their lives. They should choose the direction of their involvement with others. It is important for an adult to follow what feels right for an individual situation.

Knowing how one currently develops relationships and roles may provide some useful information about how one will behave in the future. Current interest, adaptability, and flexibility in meeting others and acquiring new roles will probably lead to similar behavior as a post-retiree.

Difficulty developing new roles and adjusting to new relationships will probably result in difficulty adjusting to change in later life. If one insists on the same activities, patterns of behavior, and relationships for 40 to 50 years, it may be difficult to change established ways. As the years pass, such reluctance to change may result in the loss of fulfilling roles and relationships.

For example, the 45-year-old mother may become depressed over the "empty nest" as the children move away from home to become independent adults. Or, she may return to school, the job market, or community programs for personal development and fulfillment. Progressing through the stages of life, a person may choose sameness and eventual despair or take up the challenge to develop new invigorating life roles.

The next discussion exercise, ROLES THROUGH LIFE, helps the individual gain an overview of his or her personal style of developing roles through the years. It provides an opportunity to project into the future in either an idealistic way or a realistic way. The exercise helps the reader understand role stability, transition, and potential for an optimal lifestyle during the later years.

DISCUSSION EXERCISE

Roles Through Life

DIRECTIONS FOR THE LEARNER: Describe yourself briefly below. What different functions, behaviors, and roles do you identify for yourself at the times specified in each column below? Use words or phrases to describe yourself, who you are and what you do, at each stage, BEFORE, NOW, and LATER.

You may have to work hard to imagine how you will look or function in 20 to 40 years. Think about the kinds of activities in which you will be involved at that future time.

BEFORE (10–20 YEARS AGO)	NOW (RIGHT NOW)	LATER (IN 20–40 YEARS)

DIRECTIONS FOR THE LEADER: This exercise is a good activity for the whole group. For the benefit of the whole group, the leader may write on a blackboard the words from the three columns, BEFORE, NOW, and LATER, of participants who are willing to share. Note any words which seem to develop roles, change function, or disappear as the time changes from column to column. Which words seem to stabilize from column to column?

For example,

BEFORE	NOW	LATER
1. High energy	1. Energetic	1. Enthusiastic
2. Daughter	2. Daughter & mother	2. Daughter & mother
3. Engaged	3. Married	3. Single

Notice the tendencies for individuals to maintain and drop roles. As time passes, especially in the final years of life, how may people work to effect a satisfying, enriching mixture of roles in their lives?

It takes about 45 minutes to complete the exercise.

SUMMARY

Better communication begins with the development of the personal self and the social self. Exploring different aspects of oneself helps to develop personal awareness. When one knows the characteristics of one's own nature, relationships with family members and friends become easier.

Personal Awareness in Communication

Knowing the total self involves an awareness of self-concept, ideal self, self-esteem, self-acceptance, and locus of control. Many factors inside oneself and outside in the world have an influence on the developing self. Looking at the self from different perspectives helps provide a better picture of the total self. Having a better picture of oneself improves one's ability to send accurate messages from within oneself to others.

Communication in Relationships

Learning to understand relationships is important also to effective communication. Relationships are important to healthful living, perhaps even essential to healthful living. Relationships may include family members and friends. Often long-term friendships seem to take on the closeness associated with family membership.

People take on different roles in their relationships. Sometimes an activity or one's position in the community may define some new roles. As people undergo transition, it becomes important for them to have relationships and roles that continue to enrich their lives.

Getting to know oneself is a lifelong process. Getting to know others better is another lifelong process. Understanding oneself and others is the key to good solid communication.

After studying about how one is connected to others through relationships, one is more ready to study specific communication skills, the techniques that strengthen such connections. The specific communication skills to be covered in the following pages include trilevel communication; feelings; reflection of feelings; empathy and sympathy; positive feedback; attending, hearing, and listening; beginning with excuses; sexism, racism, and agism; saying "No!"; and intensity.

Suggestions for Further Reading

COHORTS

Atchley, R. C. (1980). *The Social Forces in Later Life.* Belmont, CA: Wadsworth.

CHARACTER ARMOR

Reich, W. (1949). *Character Analysis.* (T. P. Wolfe, trans.). New York: Orgone Institute Press.

DISENGAGEMENT THEORY

Atchley, R. C. (1980). *The Social Forces in Later Life.* Belmont, CA: Wadsworth.

Cumming, E., & Henry, W. E.(1961). *Growing Old: The Process of Disengagement.* New York: Basic Books.

Neugarten, B. L. (1973). Developmental perspectives. In V. M. Brantl & S. M. R. Brown (Eds.), *Readings in Gerontology.* St. Louis, MO: The C. V. Mosby Co., pp. 31–36.

FAMILIES

Okun, B. F., & Rappaport, L. J. (1980). *Working with Families.* North Scituate, MA: Duxbury Press.

IDENTITY

Fromm, E. (1955). *The Sane Society.* New York: Rinehart & Co.

INTROVERT–EXTRAVERT

Rychlak, J. F. (1973). *Introduction to Personality and Psychotherapy.* Boston: Houghton Mifflin.

Schultz, D. (1977). *Growth Psychology.* New York: Van Nostrand Reinhold.

NEEDS OF ELDERLY

Belbin, R. M. (1972). Retirement strategy in an evolving society. In F. M. Carp (Ed.), *Retirement.* New York: Behavioral Pub., Inc., pp. 172–196.

Little, V. C. (1980). Assessing the needs of the elderly: State of the art. *International Journal of Aging and Human Development,* 11(1), 65–76.

Loneliness shortens longevity. (1982, July-August). *Dynamic Years,* 17(4), 60.

Lowenthal, M. P., & Haven, C. (1968). Interaction and adaptation: Intimacy as a critical variable. *American Sociologist Review,* 33(1), 20–30.

PROTECTIVE ORGANIZATION

Horney, K. (1945). *Our Inner Conflicts: A Constructive Theory of Neurosis.* New York: W. W. Norton & Co.

QUOTATIONS

Davidoff, H. (Ed.). (1942). *Quotations.* New York: Pocket Books.

ROLES

Atchley, R. C. (1980). *The Social Forces in Later Life.* Belmont, CA: Wadsworth.

Donelson, E. (1973). *Personality.* Pacific Palisades, CA: Goodyear Publ. Co.

SELF–CONCEPT

Donelson, E. (1973). *Personality.* Pacific Palisades, CA: Goodyear Publ. Co.

4

Basic Communication Skills

What kind of communication is going on in the following scene?

The setting is a large cafeteria located in the middle of a huge mall in downtown Yorcity. Weary shoppers and salesclerks are taking a lunch break during the end-of-summer clearance sales. They are lined up for lunch. They are eager to relax a while and to rest their cramped toes.

In front of the counter, a shopper, Meg, with a questioning look of concentration at the steaming pan of food before her, mumbles to her husband Teg, "Go ahead of me. I'll catch up in a minute."

Teg thinking, "I have had it with all this shopping. She's been pushing everyone all morning . . ." ignores her instruction as he studies the selection of salads.

Behind the counter, half-listening to her co-worker's fascinating story about a son in college, Wanda asks Meg, "Pardon me, Ma'am, did you say 'some ketchup with some spinach?' "

With a smile on her face, Meg responds tartly, "Now why did you give me spinach when I asked for chicken!" Meg tosses a quick glower at her husband then resumes a serious smile for Wanda.

Perry, the customer behind Meg and Teg thinks, "I heard her ask for spinach. At least she's in a good mood."

Meanwhile, Terry, way back in line, mutters to no one in particular, "Why did she demand that they speak Spanish? She could just point to what she wants. We are all held up because of her." And a soft rumble begins to grow in the line.

Tired and hungry, the customers in the cafeteria are probably focused in on their own survival needs, to get the best bargain, to eat, and to rest. The food servers are distracted by their own entertaining conversations. Like most Americans today, all of them are also trying to hurry, "to beat the clock."

Teg is not responding; he may be ignoring Meg on purpose. The messages in Meg's harsh voice tones conflict with her facial expression, the smile. Back further in line, Perry and Terry are responding to a misinterpretation of Meg's actual message.

In general the people of this scene are responding quickly to distorted messages. They are responding to what they thought they heard. They are not in tune with what was actually communicated. How does such a distortion occur? How may such modifications of actual messages be avoided?

People with good communication skills pay attention fully to all the information being sent to them. They are careful to send clear, appropriate responses. Thus they receive and send accurate messages that are on target.

It is hard to pay full attention to messages from other people, because a great deal of information is transmitted at the same time. Amazingly enough, communication occurs on many different levels. Before discussing the different levels of communication, some time will be taken on the next page to brainstorm or think about this topic.

The following discussion exercise, THE INTERACTION, challenges the reader to figure out the different kinds or levels of information that are exchanged during an activity involving two individuals. The reader should try to think about the more obvious and more hidden parts of an interaction.

The Interaction

DIRECTIONS FOR THE LEARNER: Write down briefly what is occurring in this scene. What behaviors do you see? What messages are being communicated? What specific behaviors tell you about the interaction between the two individuals?

DIRECTIONS FOR THE LEADER: This exercise is a good brainstorming tool for a group discussion. The purpose of the exercise is to think about all the factors that make up an interaction. In other words, what are the different parts of, or the activities that make up, an interaction between two individuals?

As a total group, participants should be encouraged to share their responses to the questions above in the directions. What does the picture describe to you? What kinds of words are being exchanged by the individuals? Is the interaction pleasant or unpleasant? And how can you tell? What sort of message is transferred to you even though you do not read nor hear words spoken in this picture?

The exercise takes about 10 minutes.

TRILEVEL LANGUAGE: ORAL, KINESIC, AND UNDERCURRENT

When communicating a message, a speaker provides three levels of information, oral, kinesic, and undercurrent. The oral message refers to the words of a speaker. Kinesics is another way of saying body language. Body language involves the message given by how one's body is moving. Undercurrent information is very subtle, usually hidden from the listener.

The verbal message includes the oral or spoken message as well as the written message. For the purposes of this text, the written message will not be explored. Only the oral aspect of the verbal message is discussed here.

Paying attention to all levels of trilevel language will enhance communication. Tuning into one's own style of trilevel language and that of others will improve comprehension, genuineness, and accuracy in communication.

Ignoring one or more aspects of trilevel communication may result in perceiving a distorted, incomplete, and puzzling message. This will probably result in confused, erroneous communication.

People who focus on trilevel communication hear more accurately. They use other cues to add information to what they actually hear. This improves their communication. An additional benefit is their feeling a part of the interpersonal dynamics because (1) they really understand the communication and then (2) they participate effectively.

Oral Language

Oral language is the spoken word. The oral message is verbal. Oral language includes content as well as feelings. Content involves the information or the subject under discussion. Content is WHAT is being said. Feelings involve one's attitude or emotions about the subject under discussion.

The oral message, what is being said, is important, but often carries less weight than most speakers realize. Saying something to fill space or to hide one's own or someone else's feelings is not genuine communication. Without judging or accusing, one should convey feelings as well as information about the subject in order to communicate fully and effectively. Stating one's feelings expresses an emotional attitude about the incident or the subject under discussion. This provides more information to the listener.

Saying at least a part of what is felt at the time the incident occurs is a progressive step toward appropriate communication. A person should try to be honest and open as well as respectful of others. It is also important for the individual to be in tune with his or her personal style of speaking. Expanding or developing one's natural way of talking will feel more comfortable than trying to talk in a totally different manner. Then others will perceive the new behavior as an earnest attempt to improve oneself rather than distrust the new behavior as pretentious or hypocritical.

The following examples involve both the content and feelings of the speaker. Notice the differences between the two styles of talking.

Example 1:
I'm upset about waiting 30 extra minutes for you to dress.

The speaker communicates about specific content and feelings in an "I" statement. The resulting dialogue from the listener and speaker will probably clarify, explain, and express understanding of the issue and the involved feelings. *NOTE:* Refer to the chapter, PERSONAL AWARENESS IN COMMUNICATION, for more information about personalizing statements in the section, "I" STATEMENTS.

Example 2:
You're inconsiderate. You are always so late and don't care a bit about how frustrating it is!

The speaker is judgmental and accusing. The statement generalizes . . . "You are ALWAYS so late," and "how frustrating IT is." The ensuing dialogue will probably result in hurt, misunderstood feelings, and defensive excuses.

Nonverbal Communication

In addition to using oral language, people use nonverbal means to communicate. Nonverbal communication involves kinesics and undercurrent language. By watching the movements or actions of other people, one can learn a great deal. Information can be seen easily in what is communicated through kinesics or body language.

Body language can be observed readily in the theater. Since acting is often an exaggeration of real life, communication through body language is often more obvious than that of the typical person. Actors on the stage, films, or television screen are good demonstrators of body language. An actor may express anger through glaring eye contact, a loud, harsh voice tone, a tightened facial expression, and wild throwing gestures with his arms.

One may also begin to sense some undercurrent language or a hidden message. This is an additional message. It goes beyond the message that is heard and the behavior that is observed readily.

In the angry actor just discussed, perhaps one can pick up another message. The expression of anger might be on top of another message, frustrated love for his country. Or, perhaps the actor's behavior of anger is an attempt to cover his fear for the political security of his country.

Unpleasant message.

Pleasant message.

Quite often the oral message is enriched by kinesics and undercurrent meanings. Sometimes, however, the extra information contradicts the oral message. For instance, a kind, understanding oral statement may be negated by a stiff body posture, clenched fists, and a sense of tension or anger in the person. Awareness of nonverbal behavior enhances one's perception of what is actually being communicated.

Kinesics or Body Language

Kinesics is the body movement that accompanies the spoken message. The action of the body provides cues that communicate information to other people. The communication of these body cues is called body language.

Body language is used in many ways. Some individuals may use it to establish recognition for themselves, such as strutting or swaggering when telling how well they did during the last chess tournament. Some people use kinesics to control a situation, such as the authoritative stance of a police officer on duty.

At other times people use body language in relationships, such as establishing control over others. Dominance and territoriality may be seen in strong postures. Body language components are also used to establish approval or caring.

I am so proud of my family!

The culture of a person has an influence on the development of one's personal style of kinesics. For instance, flamboyant gestures are an intimate part of the communication style of people from the Mediterranean countries. On the other hand, a calm voice and controlled body movement are the behaviors of the Indo-Chinese in proper and respectful conversation.

Watching how people express themselves indicates how different body actions enhance the oral message. One may notice a feeling that is communicated in the speaker's eyes, jaw tension, or general posture that adds to or subtracts from the spoken message.

The seven parts of body language that are explored in this text are (1) eye contact, (2) look on one's face, (3) voice, (4) body posture, (5) gestures, (6) personal space, and (7) timing.

1. EYE CONTACT: The eyes of a person may take on different activities. They may look at or away from someone. They may look down, or shift back and forth nervously. They may gaze, stare, glare, or look blank. They may give a relaxed, direct look.

2. LOOK ON FACE: The expression on a person's face may be animated or dull. It may be happy, relaxed, pleasant, tight, or angry. The jaw may be tense. The person may have a stoney look. The look on a person's face may match or contradict the spoken message.

3. VOICE: The voice may sound pleasant or unpleasant. The speaker may talk with a high, deep, loud, mellow, sharp, soft, raspy, whiny, monotonal, harsh, well modulated, or even sound. The speaker may clip words, cutting them off sharply so that they seem to attack the listener.

4. POSTURE: The posture of a person's body may be tense and rigid. It may be towering, relaxed, slumped, leaning back, or hovering over the listener. The speaker may angle away from or lean forward toward the listener.

5. GESTURES (NOTE THE DIFFERENCES AMONG CULTURES): The arms of a person may be folded in front. Arm movement may be stiff, flailing, nervous, or relaxed. Gestures may be easy and spontaneous. The legs may be crossed and pointing away from the listener. The fists may be clenched. There may be wild over-gesturing or, the opposite, no movement at all.

6. PERSONAL SPACE (NOTE THE DIFFERENCES AMONG CULTURES): The speaker may move too close, too far away, or appear to be hovering over the listener.

7. TIMING: Responses from the listener may be too soon, too late, spontaneous, or wavering. The words may seem too interruptive or too delayed for the current topic under discussion.

It is important to be aware of one's own style of communication as well as the style of other people. The following discussion exercise, THE HELPER, provides training in body language awareness. It encourages individuals to become aware of their own kinesics as well as that of other persons.

The Helper

SPECIAL NOTE TO THE LEARNER AND THE LEADER: Since this discussion exercise is rather complex, first a general explanation will be given. Next will follow SPECIFIC DIRECTIONS FOR THE LEARNER in three parts covering SHARING, FEEDBACK, and GROUP SHARING. Finally, the SPECIFIC DIRECTIONS FOR THE LEADER will be provided.

GENERAL INSTRUCTIONS FOR THE LEARNER AND THE LEADER: On an individual basis, each person should think of something they have done in the past 10–20 years (or 40–60 years for older people). This activity or helper event should be something that had a pleasant or positive effect on someone else's life. Think in terms of something you would be willing to talk about with others in a small group.

After the positive event is remembered, take a few minutes for participants to pair up. Each member of the pair will observe the other while he or she is sharing. Thus, in the pair, sometimes referred to as the dyad, one person will be the SHARER and the other person will be the OBSERVER. Then each will switch roles or jobs in the discussion exercise.

The SHARER will describe the personal experience while the OBSERVER tries to be aware of the different elements of body language that the SHARER uses spontaneously while talking. As various body movements and expressions are demonstrated during the sharing, the OBSERVER may write some of them down in the specific spaces provided in the BODY LANGUAGE OBSERVATION CHECKLIST which follows the instructions to this discussion exercise. It may be helpful to group members to review briefly the various elements of body language on the checklist before the exercise begins.

Use the specific instructions below to help you through the exercise. Remember, after the first SHARER–OBSER-VER interaction, the roles are switched. Then the first SHARER becomes an OBSERVER while the OBSERVER, the first time around, becomes the SHARER.

SPECIFIC DIRECTIONS FOR THE LEARNER, PART I: SHARING

1. *Each individual thinks of an event or activity of special significance that occurred about 20 or 40 years ago. The memory or helper event should concern a pleasant or positive effect that the participant had upon the life of someone else.*

2. *Choose a partner with whom to work. Then some partners should team up to form groups of 4–6 members. Taking turns, each dyad works in the group. First, in Part I, there is a series of sharing memories. Then in the next step, Part II, there is a series of feedback activities.*

3. *In turn, the SHARER of a dyad describes the positive memory or "helper event" in about 2–3 minutes while the OBSERVER of the same dyad notes privately the partner's body language. Then roles are switched so that the new SHARERS report their helper events while their partners take a turn as OBSERVER. After everyone in the group has had a turn sharing, the group is ready for the next step, the reports on the behavior of the SHARERS.*

NOTE TO THE SHARERS: Try to answer the following questions as you share. What are some of the feelings you experienced in the past as the event occurred? What do you feel now as you recall the experience?

NOTE TO THE OBSERVERS: Remember to make notes of your partner's body language for a more accurate exchange of information a little later on.

SPECIFIC DIRECTIONS FOR THE LEARNER, PART II: FEEDBACK

1. *In the privacy of each dyad, each one reports what body language was observed. Each twosome should take a few minutes to share notes on each other.*

2. *As usual, remember to stay positive with each other. Note the section in CHAPTER FOUR on POSITIVE FEEDBACK for assistance.*

3. *What does your partner's observations tell you about yourself? Does the feedback give you some new information about how you talk?*

SPECIFIC DIRECTIONS FOR THE LEARNER, PART III: GROUP SHARING

1. *Each pair should return to their group of 4–6 members and summarize their interactions.*

2. *Members of the group should be observant of the body language as others share.*

3. *Group members should encourage each other by using positive feedback techniques.*

SPECIFIC DIRECTIONS FOR THE LEADER: This exercise is designed for group participation. The exercise has a twofold purpose, (1) to help speakers become aware of their body language, and (2) to help listeners become more aware of the body movements that accompany the oral statements of others. The emphasis is on helping each other in a positive environment. Participants should be reminded to encourage one another.

Often this exercise must be repeated to help participants acting in the role of observer to learn how to watch body behavior. Initially the OBSERVER will be swept into the story of the oral message and will have to struggle to stay aware of body behavior. The leader may provide reminders on a blackboard or flipchart about the need for observers ''to observe.''

It is helpful to provide a demonstration for the total class or group before they begin on their own. Sometimes, however, it is helpful for them to struggle on their own. They quickly learn how easily they can be swept into the story. They have a chance to see how much work is involved in paying attention to the signals of body language.

It takes about 30 minutes to complete this discussion exercise.

CHECKLIST

Body Language Observation

DIRECTIONS FOR THE LEARNER: *Write down in the spaces below what you noticed as OBSERVER during the discussion exercise, THE HELPER.*

---

1. Eye Contact

---

2. Look on Face

---

3. Voice

---

4. Posture

---

5. Gestures

6. Personal Space

7. Timing

Undercurrent Language

Undercurrent language concerns the information underneath what the speaker expresses orally or through body movement. It is a subtle, often hidden message. The undercurrent message may involve feelings and/or content. The spoken and kinesic messages may or may not provide clues about the hidden message.

Through experience, one may develop a "sixth sense" about a hidden agenda, what the speaker is trying to convey or hide. Some people refer to the undercurrent language as "energy," vibes, or attitude. It is experienced in a different way from what is heard or seen directly. In a way, it is felt. The undercurrent message is an important part of the communication process.

The following situation depicts what may happen when undercurrent feelings are unnoticed or ignored.

Early on a Monday morning, Mrs. Nell decides to visit her neighbor, Mrs. Snoe. She wants to chat with a friend, but a phone call is not enough. She rings Mrs. Snoe's doorbell. Although Mrs. Snoe is in the middle of heavy cleaning and is embarrassed about her house being a mess after the busy weekend, she invites Mrs. Nell in with a warm welcome.

As Mrs. Nell eagerly enters the house, however, she senses tension and discomfort in the air. Even though she hears and sees language that communicates a warm welcome, Mrs. Nell feels uncomfortable. She feels estranged, but she tries to ignore the feeling.

After a brief visit, she leaves. She feels confused, frustrated, and, perhaps, even hurt. But she can't figure out the problem. She cannot remember any specific thing that happened that would result in her feeling so confused about the short, neighborly visit.

Mrs. Snoe was unwilling to communicate openly. She decided to hide her anger at Mrs. Nell's untimely visit. She wanted to say that she was too busy to visit right then, but kept silent and did not suggest a later visit. Mrs. Nell, on the other hand, considered her own needs for companionship and ignored the message of Mrs. Snoe's undercurrent language.

The lack of candid, appropriate, trilevel communication generated an experience of frustration and discomfort for both women. Open, genuine, trilevel communication would have shown respect for mutual needs. In addition, it would have strengthened their mutual trust and their interpersonal relationship.

The following discussion exercise is TRILEVEL COMMUNICATION. It provides a brief, visual introduction to the elements of trilevel communication in an interaction between two individuals.

DISCUSSION EXERCISE

Trilevel Communication

DIRECTIONS FOR THE LEARNER: Write down briefly the trilevel communication that you observe. Remember that trilevel communication involves oral, kinesic, and undercurrent messages. Use the BODY LANGUAGE CHECKLIST below as a guide. What is going on between these two individuals pictured below?

BODY LANGUAGE CHECKLIST

1. *EYE CONTACT:*

2. *LOOK ON FACE:*

3. *VOICE:*

4. *POSTURE:*

5. *GESTURES:*

6. *PERSONAL SPACE:*

7. *TIMING:*

DIRECTIONS FOR THE LEADER: This exercise is a good tool for a group brainstorming session. The purpose of the exercise is to explore the specific aspects of trilevel communication.

As each group member contributes, others should observe the obvious and subtle communication that group member portrays. Also, positive feedback should be provided to contributors.

The exercise and discussion take about 20 minutes.

FEELINGS: REFLECTION OF FEELINGS

Feelings are an important part of communication. They may enrich the spoken message. Feelings communicate the depth of interest and commitment to the message. Some people share feelings openly. As people get older, there seems to be a tendency to hide personal feelings.

In an effort to keep one's feelings private, a person may become less aware of feelings involved in different situations. The feelings may become so well concealed that self-awareness and self-understanding are hindered. Or, a rush of feelings are experienced. Sometimes the mixture of feelings may lead to confusion and difficulty in coping. Taking a few deep breaths, trying to relax, and closing one's eyes for a few seconds may help one get more in touch with one's emotions. Then one may clearly see the difference between what is actually occurring, the objective facts or the content of the situation, and one's emotions, how one feels about the experience.

For Example:

The facts or the contents of the scene may be that a person's purse was just "snatched" by a stranger who ran off with it. The victim may feel overwhelmed with confusion, turmoil, or surprise. Relaxing briefly, the victim may become sensitive to feelings of anger, fright, or mirth. (Perhaps it was an old, empty, "fake" purse.)

Taking a moment to assess what happened, the person may discover the real, personal feelings about the occurrence. In this situation the person may choose to chuckle at the purse snatcher who wasted time and effort over a worthless, empty handbag. Knowing one's true feelings about the event improves coping behavior.

Reflection of Feelings

Sensitivity to one's personal feelings and the feelings of others is very important. Aware of feelings, an individual may address those feelings and heighten the accuracy of the communication. Reflecting the feelings of others provides communication on a deeper, more personal level.

By replying with words that respond to the obvious and more subtle feelings being communicated, one shows that she or he really heard what was said. The listener shows caring and understanding. Reflecting feelings shows that the listener is really "with" the speaker. It encourages continuation of the intimate communication. Furthermore, it enhances the intensity of the conversation and the relationship.

On the other hand, not attending to the speaker's feelings encourages more superficial communication. It leads to emotional distance between the speaker and the listener. Not reflecting feelings allows the speaker to have a safe, superficial dialogue. This may be appropriate behavior for people who have just been introduced at a cocktail party or public meeting. However, for long-term relationships, reflecting feelings allows more meaningful, heart to heart communication. This is especially important to family relationships.

For Example:

Bertha, a close friend, has just joined you for lunch. She's upset as she discusses some unpleasant remarks her co-worker made to her a short while ago. Listening to Bertha, which of the responses below would you use to reply:

1. "You are insulted by what Sally said."

The statement reflects feelings and invites the continuation of intimate communication. Bertha will probably feel heard, appreciated, and supported as a result of the conversation.

2. "Why didn't you leave the room when she said that to you!"

The listener seems to ignore the hurt feelings of Bertha in an effort to recommend a personal solution. Typically, giving advice leads to defensive responses, "I couldn't think." or "That would have been stupid." Advising-defending dialogue usually results in superficial communication. Bertha will probably feel misunderstood, disrespected, and incompetent as a result of the conversation.

EMPATHY AND SYMPATHY

Empathy is often confused with sympathy. Empathy is seeing and understanding another's point of view without total emotional involvement in that experience. It differs from sympathy. Sympathy is feeling immersed in the same emotional experiences of the other person. Empathy is caring, supportive, and respectful of the other person. It provides assistance that helps another understand better a personal experience and the self.

For Example:

1. EMPATHY: "You're heartbroken about your father's death."

The statement shows understanding and concern for the other's welfare. It offers support and caring.

You are heartbroken over your Dad!

2. SYMPATHY: "I feel so badly about your father's death; I can hardly stand it."

The statement is self-centered. This overwhelmed speaker will probably be unable to assist anyone else in distress.

I can hardly stand it. What can we do?

If one is familiar with words that communicate feelings, one has a more accurate perception of the wide range of personal feelings. Then one is more likely to understand oneself better. Also, one is more likely to understand which feeling is being expressed by another person. Then one can respond more effectively to the varied feelings of others.

An individual may respond to another person's feelings by using a word that accurately captures those feelings and reflects them back to the speaker. This may be a way of showing empathy. The listener can show the speaker that she or he is being correctly heard.

This level of sensitive listening encourages further personal sharing. Knowing a vocabulary of feeling words facilitates deep communication.

The purpose of the following FEELINGS WORDS EXERCISE is to build up the reader's vocabulary of words that describe the feelings of an individual.

EXERCISE

Feelings Words

DIRECTIONS FOR THE LEARNER AND LEADER: *As you look over the following words, write down others that come to mind. Keep the list as a reference of FEELINGS WORDS to help identify specific emotions.*

abused, accepted, afraid, alienated, angry, anxious, awful

berated, better, bitter, boastful, bold, bored

calm, confident, confused

defeated, depressed, desolate

eager, elated, erratic, excited

fearful, flat, fragmented

good, great, guilty

happy, heartened, hopeless, hurt

ideal, irate, irrational

jaded, jealous, joyous

keen, keyed up, kicked around, kind

liberated, lonely, loved, loving

mad, miserable, misunderstood

naughty, nervous, nice, nothing

obedient, open, ordinary

passionate, plain, pressured

quaint, quarrelsome, quick, quiet

rash, reckless, regretful, rejected

sassy, shocked, silly, surprised, sweet

tearful, threatened, thrilled

used, useful, useless, usurped

vicious, vigorous, vitriolic

wanted, warmhearted, worthy

xerotic (dry)

yearning, yellow, yielding

zealous, zesty

POSITIVE FEEDBACK

One of the most important communication skills needed by people of all ages is POSITIVE FEEDBACK. Although it has many subtle qualities, it is a simple skill to put into practice. It requires very little effort and its rewards are tremendous. Positive feedback concerns responding back to someone else with a positive statement. It returns some positive information to that person about his or her effect on you. It helps that person to feel better about what she or he said or did.

Positive feedback is a nice way to reach out to other people. It provides the opportunity for a pleasant interaction between the speaker and the listener. It develops confidence in both persons and strengthens the relationship. It encourages both persons to seek another opportunity for an interaction, because it is a positive, rewarding experience.

Example 1:
Consider the following comments between Diane and Irene.
DIANE: "Your red dress looks lovely on you."
This is a positive response to something Irene has done.
IRENE: "Thank you, I appreciate your compliment."
This is positive feedback to Diane. Irene did not respond as most people usually do in this situation, "Oh, this old thing. It's just a rag that's hung in my closet for years." This type of response would have resulted in both people feeling awkward and uncomfortable.

Example 2:
Now consider the following comments between Harold and Frank.
HAROLD: "I liked your enthusiastic motion at the meeting. I agree that we should have a costume party this Halloween."
This is a positive response to the specific behavior of Frank at the meeting that the men just attended.
FRANK: "I'm glad you said that. I feel better knowing that you back up my idea."
The positive feedback to Harold enhances their relationship. Frank did not say, "I probably should not have said anything about it," or "I don't know why I made such a crazy suggestion." Even though it would have been directed toward himself, either derogatory remark may have resulted in both men feeling embarrassed. They may have even regretted talking to one another. Perhaps, they would become more cautious about talking to each other in the future.

Positive feedback is a genuine response. It is not meant to be dishonest. The speaker focuses on positive feelings or attitudes in the situation and does not worry about dislikes or disagreements.

For Example:
When the host offers, "Would you like coffee or tea?" a positive response may be, "Thank you, I would enjoy some tea." Saying, "I hate coffee" or "I can't stand coffee, I'd rather have tea," may be honest, but is negative and hurtful to a host. Focusing on what one prefers or likes keeps the course of the relationship and communication positive and open to further development.

Positive feedback has the following qualities:

1. It says something in a complimentary or beneficial manner.
   For Example:
   DO SAY: "I enjoy your garden. The camelias are such a lovely pink."
   DON'T SAY: "How nice. All your camelias are in blossom. It's a wonder the frost doesn't get them."

2. Positive feedback is sensitive to its effect on others.
   For Example:
   DO SAY: "Thank you, iced tea will be so refreshing. I'll take it without sugar, please."
   DON'T SAY: "How can you drink your iced tea so sweet? Don't you worry about what the sugar does to your body?"

3. Positive feedback is sensitive to individual development and the ability of people to undergo change.
   For Example:
   DO SAY: "I like your new choices of colors. The green and yellow together are beautiful in this afghan."
   DON'T SAY: "I'm not sure about combining this green and yellow in the same afghan. You always put the strangest colors together. I can just imagine what the next afghan will look like."

4. Positive feedback considers the needs of the giver and the receiver. It weighs the mutual needs of the involved persons.
   For Example:
   DO SAY: "I'm glad you asked me to slow down the tennis game. I felt I could focus better on the game and enjoy it more."
   DON'T SAY: If you are that winded at tennis, maybe you should get a different partner. It might help both of us to improve our game."

5. Positive feedback describes the speaker's personal reaction or addresses a specific detail. It doesn't judge the whole person.
   For Example:
   DO SAY: "I like your wording in this petition. I can clearly understand the importance of stop signs at Main Street."
   DON'T SAY: "You're bold to write up a petition for the meeting."

6. Positive feedback is well timed. It is given as soon as possible after the occurrence of the behavior.
   For Example:
   DO SAY: "Thank you for taking the initiative to introduce yourself first. This is my first time at the club and I'm so glad to meet you."
   DON'T SAY: "Do you remember six months ago when I attended my first club meeting . . ."
   However, when saying "Thanks," the rule is: Better late than never.

7. Positive feedback is rephrased for accuracy to insure clear communication.
   For Example:
   DO SAY: "I enjoyed your story about hunting for blackberries. I enjoyed the sense of adventure and mystery in your voice when you told about hunting blackberries as a young boy."
   DON'T SAY: "I liked that story about when you were young. You know the one I mean. It's hard to forget it."

Readers may practice some of the preceding seven qualities of positive feedback in the next discussion exercise, THANK YOU.

DISCUSSION EXERCISE

Thank You

DIRECTIONS FOR THE LEARNER: *Participants may work in one large group or may divide into several small groups. Each group member takes a turn making a positive statement to another group member, who receives the remark with positive feedback. This is done round robin fashion. In other words, everyone has a turn.*

As an alternative, one person may agree to be the focus of many positive remarks. As the center of attention, the person is bombarded with positive statements, such as,

"I like your relaxed way of talking."

"I have enjoyed your sense of humor."

The person who is the focus of the remarks should respond after each remark with positive feedback, such as, "Thanks, I like hearing that." Positive bombardment seems especially helpful to self-conscious older persons who frequently think of and refer to themselves in negative terms.

DIRECTIONS FOR THE LEADER: *This exercise requires group interaction. The purpose of the exercise is to provide an opportunity for people to give and receive positive feedback.*

Sometimes people feel very awkward with this exercise. They might need some help in keeping their comments positive. Usually the hardest part of this exercise is for people to accept completely and unconditionally the positive comments that others say to them. It seems to be difficult for people to hear so many pleasant or nice comments about themselves.

The feelings of group members should be shared at the end of the exercise. Consideration of the following questions may help people as they discuss their experiences during the exercise.

1. *Do you feel pleasant or unpleasant when you make a positive remark to someone else? When you said something positive, what special feelings did you experience?*

2. *Did you feel pleasant or unpleasant when you heard someone say something nice to you? When you heard those nice remarks, what special feelings did you experience and how did you act?*

3. *After completing this exercise, how do you feel as a group?*

It takes about 30 minutes to complete the exercise and discussion.

ATTENDING: HEARING AND LISTENING

Paying full attention to a speaker involves being completely attuned to what is said and how it is said. The listener pays attention to verbal and nonverbal messages. The listener shows by his or her own body posture that full focus is on the speaker. The listener shows caring and interest in the speaker and the communicated message.

Some ways in which a person may communicate intense listening are by looking directly at the speaker, showing an attentive facial expression, and sitting or standing in a comfortable, alert position. An individual may indicate that she or he is attending to what the speaker says by an occasional nodding of the head.

An attitude of half-hearing shows disinterest and a lack of respect for the speaker. Partial listening may result in misunderstood, distorted verbal information. A person who is barely listening may show this through body language. This behavior may include restless fidgeting, a posture turned or angled away from the speaker, arms folded across one's chest, a dull facial expression, eyes that stare into space, and attention paid to everything but the speaker. Such behavior may indicate partial listening or complete disregard for what is being said. Real listening involves work, but results in the reward of solid communication.

In the following discussion exercise, LISTENING, the reader has an opportunity to experience the difference between being ignored and being heard in the process of communication.

DISCUSSION EXERCISE

Listening

DIRECTIONS FOR THE LEARNER: Break up into tryads, that is, groups of three members each. You will practice talking and listening. There are three steps to this exercise. Each small group should finish STEP 1 and proceed to STEP 2 at the same time. Then each group should move to STEP 3 at the same time. At the end of STEP 3, the whole class should discuss the differences experienced between each of the three steps in two areas (1) one's own manner of active listening and (2) the experience of feeling heard by others.

STEP 1:

As a group, discuss recent national or international events. Each person taking a turn to add to the discussion should not refer to what was just said. Do not link the new comments directly to the previous comments.

For example, SPEAKER A says, "Europe is concerned about problems with inflation." Then SPEAKER B may add, "I saw a television documentary about an old religious temple in Japan."

Take about five minutes for the discussion. Briefly write down in the space below and then discuss in your tryad how you felt about participating in this conversation.

STEP 2:

This time the topic of conversation should concern the importance of having or being a good friend. Taking a turn to add to the conversation, each member should reflect about (1) the feeling and (2) the content of the previous speaker.

For example, SPEAKER A says, "I have a special friend that is like a brother to me." Then SPEAKER B may say, *"You really care (the reflected feeling) for your close friend (the reflected content)." Then SPEAKER B may add, "I have a friend whom I have known for 50 years."*

Take about five minutes for the discussion. Briefly, write down in the space below and then discuss in your small group some of your feelings about the conversation as you participated.

STEP 3:

This section is the final step of the discussion exercise. It is usually an intense experience. It has a special identity; it is known as the PETE AND REPEAT TRYAD.

Assign roles of (1) SPEAKER, (2) LISTENER, or (3) OBSERVER to each member in the tryad. Each person follows their assigned role as indicated in the set of instructions that follows immediately.

1. *SPEAKER: Describe briefly for about three minutes an event that happened to you when you were in your early 20s. The event should concern something that made you happy. As an alternative, the speaker may choose to discuss a recent experience of feeling happy.*

2. *LISTENER: After you hear the speaker's story, try to summarize the feelings and content of what was just said. Remember to keep your comments positive.*

3. *SPEAKER: After the listener summarizes the content and feelings of your story, provide feedback to the listener. Correct any distortions that the listener reports back to you. Have the listener summarize again until you feel the information is correct.*

4. *OBSERVER: Observe carefully the interactions between the speaker and the observer. Watch their trilevel communication. Remember, this includes the oral, the kinesic, and the undercurrent messages. When they have completed their interaction, report to them the trilevel communication that you observed. Provide positive comments when possible.*

Rotate the roles of SPEAKER, LISTENER, and OBSERVER until everyone has a chance to practice the three different parts.

DIRECTIONS FOR THE LEADER: This exercise requires interaction. The purpose of the exercise is to refine the skills of listening.

After STEPS 1, 2, and 3 are completed in the tryads, the class as a total unit should discuss the experiences of the groups. The discussion should involve comparing the three levels of listening.

What new personal information did group members learn about themselves? What speaking and listening skills were enhanced through the conversations in the tryads? In daily circumstances outside of the group activities here, in which of the three types of conversations does each person usually participate?

A SPECIAL NOTE: The discussion exercise, LISTENING, catalyzes group cohesiveness. For this reason, it is better to use this activity after group members have met together a few times, such as during the middle or toward the end of the term. Often the tryads refuse to stop the sharing in STEP 3 until they feel finished. The flexible leader may feel comfortable in allowing the small groups to become more independent. The leader may be willing to change the established structure of the learning environment by letting the groups take more than the allotted time for the exercise or by creating a different way of ending the exercise. The author has witnessed powerful experiences of positive growth and the unleashing of creative energies among group members who are given the freedom to develop the PETE AND REPEAT TRYAD in a way that meets their personal needs.

STEPS 1, 2, and 3 of the discussion exercise take about 20 minutes. It takes about 45–60 minutes to complete all the steps of the exercise and to allow enough time to share the deep feelings that result from the intense listening and sharing of group members.

OPINION VERSUS FACT

Opinion differs from fact. Everyone has the right to feel and express an opinion. Although most people think they are in dispute over actual facts, usually they are disagreeing about differences in personal opinions. Older persons have a tendency to integrate information from their many experiences over a long period of time. As a result older persons often have difficulty separating the objective facts from their feelings or opinions about the situation under discussion. Note the following differences between opinion and fact.

Opinion

An opinion is *subjective*. It involves personal feelings, beliefs, or assumptions about a situation. The opinion may be a notion, an attitude, or a personal evaluation. Everyone has the freedom to hold a personal opinion. Freedom to express a personal opinion in a nonhurtful way is guaranteed by the Constitution of the United States.

For Example:
Bob says, "It's going to rain today."

Bob thinks this is true. He sees clouds in the sky and he remembers that it rained yesterday about this time of the morning. Bob may be right or he may be wrong. He believes that he is correct.

Fact

A fact is *objective*. It is information that can be verified or documented. It is what has actually occurred. Sometimes it takes a great deal of research to identify the real facts. In the history of civilization the facts of earlier centuries are disproven sometimes by the objective findings of later centuries. Therefore, one should be careful when identifying information as facts.

For Example:
Barbara says, "The temperature is high today. It's 102 degrees Fahrenheit."

Barbara read the thermometer and is reporting factual, objective information. The information is relatively accurate. Barbara is correct.

However, if Barbara had said, "It is so hot today. What miserable weather!" many would agree that she was correct in what she said. They would agree with her opinion. On the other hand, some may disagree. They may feel relaxed and comfortable in the Arizona desert sunshine at 102 degrees Fahrenheit.

The next discussion exercise, OPINION OR FACT, provides some practice in thinking about the differences between opinion and fact.

DISCUSSION EXERCISE

Opinion or Fact

DIRECTIONS FOR THE LEARNER: Determine which of the following statements are opinions and which ones are facts. Put an "O" before OPINIONS and an "F" before FACTS. Discuss the results as a large group or class.

_____ 1.   Paying taxes is the obligation of every American citizen.

_____ 2.   Eating a balanced diet helps a person to feel good.

_____ 3.   Watching television helps a person to relax.

_____ 4.   A person has to have at least one friend to feel worthwhile.

_____ 5.   When you drive over the speed limit, you are breaking the law.

_____ 6.   People should be kind to each other.

_____ 7.   When a person has no job to do, that person is not worth much at all.

_____ 8.   Older people must get involved in the Silver Haired Legislature if they want to see policy changes in the government.

DIRECTIONS FOR THE LEADER: This exercise works well as a homework assignment that is discussed with group members at a later time. The purpose of the exercise is to provide some practice in differentiating between opinions and facts.

Some statements may seem easy to identify. Other statements may need to be discussed or explored in further depth before being labeled as opinion or fact.

Group members should be encouraged to discuss their different responses. Using some of the previously discussed communication skills, such as "I" STATEMENTS and POSITIVE FEEDBACK, may help the flow of communication. It is important for group members to try to communicate effectively the different ways of thinking that led to their different responses.

Many group members agree that the correct responses are (1) F; (2) F; (3) O; (4) F; (5) F; (6) O; (7) O; and (8) O.

The discussion exercise takes about 20 minutes to complete.

BEGINNING WITH EXCUSES

Many people develop the habit of beginning their sentences or responses with extensive apologies. They make excuses about what they are going to say and how they will say it. Then they explain their general inability to do anything well.

They make so many excuses and apologize to such an extent that the listener begins to doubt the strength of what is about to be said. The listener feels unsure about the speaker's ability to contribute any worthwhile information to the discussion. For some people, the larger the group of listeners, the more excuses they make before they begin their contributing comments.

As they age, older persons often lose their confidence to speak in front of others. Sometimes this is a result of physical changes in hearing or speech. Very often, however, it results from the belief in stereotypes of aging, that the elderly have less capacity to do things well. They ignore the wealth of patience, sensitivity, and perspective that they have accumulated through years of experience.

Thinking in terms of loss instead of development, they show their lack of confidence through excuses. After a while, they believe their excuses and feel they have no skills. Introducing themselves with apologies, they convince others of their lack of skills. In this way, they encourage disrespect, dislike, and distance to develop in their relationships.

Sometimes a polite apology is appropriate. The apology, however, should be genuine, brief, and to the point. For instance, the late Arthur Fiedler, past conductor of the Boston Pops Orchestra, would occasionally stop his musicians after the first few chords of the concert. He would turn to the large, awaiting audience and quietly say, "Excuse us, we will start again." Then they would proceed to play a program of magnificent music. Fiedler's apology was direct, brief, and suitable.

The following examples show the differences between the appropriate and inappropriate use of excuses.

Appropriate Excuses:
1. "I'm sorry I'm late. My car had engine trouble. Let's start the meeting."
2. "Excuse me, I read that incorrectly. It actually reads like this . . ."

Notice that in both examples the speakers are sorry, but eager to correct the error and to proceed with the scheduled activity. The speakers show self-respect and respect for others in the two responses located above. They apologize willingly. They admit their faults, but proceed to handle the situations in a competent, fitting way. The activities in both situations will probably flow along smoothly.

Good choices.

Inappropriate Excuses:

1. "Oh, I couldn't possibly tell you about my new litter of kittens. I know it wouldn't come out right. I always say things backwards. Let someone else say something."

I couldn't . . .

2. "I don't know if this report is going to sound right. The committee did meet, but I'm not sure this is what we decided. I'm not good at this. You probably can't understand my voice. Do you want me to read it? I didn't write it up too well. Should I summarize the previous meeting?"

Notice that the last two, inappropriate examples are drawing attention to all kinds of personal inadequacies in each speaker. The nervousness about speaking correctly is a result of a lack of self-confidence, but it is expressed as inability. Most of the introductory remarks of the speakers do not relate to the subject under discussion. The speakers seem to be saying, "You don't want to listen to me; I'm not worth your attention."

Most listeners respond to multiple excuses with (1) impatience, (2) disgust, or (3) rescuing behavior. Eager to reach the point of discussion, the impatient listener feels restless about so much time idling away with meaningless messages. Sad, frustrated, and then angry about self-effacing excuses that seem endless, the disgusted listener begins to suspect that whatever is said will be worthless information.

As a rescuer, however, a listener may try to help the floundering speaker. The rescuing listener may use soothing words of worth and ability to help the speaker feel better. If the interaction continues, the rescuer and speaker will probably become sidetracked to a "yes, you can" . . . "no, I can't" debate.

Inappropriate excuses distract from the content of the discussion or report. By the time a committee report is read, the audience of listeners may be uninterested. Further, the members may suspect the value of the information presented in such a faltering manner. After listening to a wealth of apologies, the audience may forget the original point of the issue. At a meeting, the hour may grow too late for the presentation of the actual report.

Inappropriate excuses hinder useful communication. The social situations in the preceding examples will probably become boring, confusing, and discouraging to awaiting participants.

Appropriate excuses, on the other hand, would have taken care of the initial discomfort or error. Then the individuals may have proceeded with fitting behavior. Soon goals would be met. In addition, other people at the meeting would feel a sense of accomplishment regarding the progress of events. Thus, effective communication can lead to a satisfying evening.

Many good examples of inappropriate excuses may be identified in daily life. The reader may begin to be aware of incidents of excessive excuse behavior within the class or at home. Typically, spontaneous interaction is fraught with excuses.

For example, in a group the first person to ask a question for clarification or further information may apologize profusely before getting to the point of the question. Before presenting information to a group, a member may apologize for being inadequately prepared. Before starting a meeting, the convener may apologize for nervousness, self-consciousness, and uncertainty. Alert to these daily occurrences, the reader may begin to determine how to apologize appropriately and how to groom a sense of confidence in the presence of others.

The next discussion exercise, A SYMBOL OF ME, provides an opportunity for the individual to discuss a familiar topic in front of other people. It will help the individual to practice developing confidence when presenting meaningful information to a group of people.

DISCUSSION EXERCISE

A Symbol of Me

DIRECTIONS FOR THE LEARNER: Think about something that you are wearing that tells something about you. Identify a specific article, such as eyeglasses, shirt, piece of jewelry, etc., that you are wearing or have with you. Think about how this item tells a story about you.

Think in terms of something you are willing to talk about with others in the group. Then tell a story to the whole group about the item you have chosen.

Stay in the large group. Individuals may take about 3–4 minutes each to share their symbol and story in front of the others.

DIRECTIONS FOR THE LEADER: This exercise works better in large groups of 15 to 25 people but can be effective with a group of 5 to 10. The purpose of the exercise is to strengthen the speaking skills and confidence of people in the sharing of personal information.

The leader of the session plays an active role with group members in this discussion exercise. When individuals make spontaneous excuses as they begin to speak, the leader should interrupt them in a respectful way. Encourage them to reflect on the comments they just shared. Help them evaluate their remarks in terms of appropriate and inappropriate excuses. Next, invite the speaker to restate the information in more positive, confident terms.

The leader is encouraged to invite group members to participate in the leader's job of excuse intervention. This helps the group to become more aware of that kind of behavior. It simultaneously encourages self-reliance and interdependency. The group members become more willing to encourage and support each other. They develop facility in working with each other toward mutual growth.

It will be helpful for group members to include different aspects of positive feedback in their words of encouragement to each other.

The discussion exercise takes about 45 minutes to complete.

DISCUSSION EXERCISE

Male or Female

This discussion exercise allows the reader to assess personal feelings and opinions that result from individual life experiences before the ideas are discussed on the following pages.

DIRECTIONS FOR THE LEARNER: In each of the following statements, which sex is the speaker? Put an "M" before a statement you believe to be spoken by a male and an "F" before one you think to be spoken by a female.

_____ 1. I was hurt and needed to learn to make my own decisions.

_____ 2. I'd like to be friendly with my coworkers instead of being so competitive all the time.

_____ 3. I enjoy rocking my two-year old grandchild to sleep even though it takes a while to settle Cutie Pie down.

_____ 4. I would feel much better if my feelings about the divorce would settle into place.

_____ 5. I like to go into a store, look around, and compare prices before I buy something.

_____ 6. Before every date I would get so nervous, I would pace up and down the hall of my flat.

_____ 7. I never have any luck with other people. They must sense it, somehow.

_____ 8. In most new situations, I usually rush in, but then I back off because I get scared.

_____ 9. I hate to ask questions, because I feel so stupid.

_____ 10. I wish I could talk to men about my real feelings.

DIRECTIONS FOR THE LEADER: The exercise works well as an individual or homework assignment, the results of which are discussed later in the total group. The purpose of the activity is to stimulate thinking about one's attitudes, beliefs, and ideas and how they become intimately entwined in communication to others.

As a total group, people should discuss their responses to the ten statements above and some of the following questions. Which statements do most group members agree seem to be more masculine or feminine? What "isms" or stereotypes become so well integrated in our lifestyles that they are nearly impossible to recognize? What do people learn as social or cultural rules or habits that interfere with open attitudes and acceptance of others? What preformed expectations do people carry about male or female behavior? Which of the above statements are said by both men and women?

It take about 20 minutes to complete this discussion exercise. Note that the answers to the above statements are either "male" or "female" or both for each of the ten items.

SEXISM, RACISM, AND AGISM

Although not its typical meaning, "ism" is used to indicate a stereotype in this section on sexism, racism, and agism. In this sense, an "ism" is a distorted belief or a limited perception of a topic. It is a negative view or attitude. Some isms are so well learned that they are nearly impossible to recognize. Isms may block personal awareness and growth.

For example, unwilling to take time to listen and learn about the special qualities of each individual, the ism-bound may see slowness as laziness in a particular group of people. However, further exploration may show that the behavior is actually thoughtfulness. In another group, close-minded people may see carefulness as weakness rather than as sensitive consideration.

People should be open to the uniqueness of each individual. Openness allows one to see the richness of contributions that result from differences in people. Variety enhances complex life experiences.

Racism, agism, and sexism are common isms. Sometimes it is difficult to recognize the negative, demeaning attributes of these attitudes.

For Example:
1. SEXISM: Men are strong. Women are weak.
2. RACISM: Non-Blacks are self-serving. Occidentals are disrespectful. Non-Native Americans are untrustworthy.
3. AGISM: Old people are forgetful. Young people are irresponsible.

Preformed attitudes limit one's personal ability to develop new dimensions. An open attitude is reflected through open communication. It shows willingness to listen carefully and to speak considerately.

At this point the reader may want to review the previous discussion exercise, MALE OR FEMALE. In the light of what is being learned and discussed, would some of the responses be different now?

SAYING "NO!"

People who are non-assertive often say "yes" to requests for the wrong reasons. They are unable or unwilling to communicate their true feelings and wishes. They agree to do something to avoid an unpleasant interaction. Sometimes they agree in order to preserve the sameness of the relationship. Many people who want to say "no" often say "yes" because of the following reasons:

1. To avoid hurting someone else's feelings.
    For example, thinking, "I've got to go bowling with the group tonight. I can't let them down."

2. To feel included, valued, respected, useful, accepted, or loved.
    For example, thinking, "I'll contribute to the office party fund one more time, so they will think of me as one of the group."

3. To meet social expectations, such as in protecting the family name, personal reputation, or professional image.
    For example, thinking, "The Smiths have always made a substantial donation to the annual country fair, so we'd better donate again this year."

4. To make others feel grateful or indebted.
    For example, thinking, "If I agree to give you the car, then I expect you to drive me to the grocery store when I need it."

Not taking the responsibility to make decisions that satisfy one's own needs and wishes has consequences. Some unpleasant effects may be minor distress, a lack of self-respect, and no time for oneself.

Being unable to say "no" may result in emotional distress and physical illness. As one continues to serve others and work at great personal cost, resentment and anger may develop. Often the individual awaits his or her due with much bitterness.

Sometimes the build-up of stress results in psychosomatic problems, such as headaches, skin rashes, a low-grade fever, or upset digestion. A consultation with the family physician may clarify symptoms that merit medical treatment versus symptoms that need self-awareness, motivation, and active change for relief.

Say NO! to:
1. Something that would make you feel unpleasant or uncomfortable.
2. Inconsiderate requests or demands.
3. Taking care of whatever someone else should be doing.
4. Behavior that violates personal values or beliefs.

How to say NO!:
1. Start the response with "no."
   For example, "No, I don't want any more magazines. I have enough subscriptions."

2. Keep the answer short and clear.
   For example, "No, I don't want any dessert."

NO! I do not want any dessert. Thank you!

3. Speak in a clear, strong voice that genuinely communicates the message. Sound as if you really mean it. Don't hesitate or falter.
   For example, "No thank you, I do not want to attend."

4. Think of upcoming events. Plan ahead.
   For example, "I want you to know ahead of time that I will be out of town for the rally. I will not be participating this year" *or,* "I have developed different interests and commitments this year. Please remove my name from the Rally Committee list."

5. Practice saying "no" in easier situations before you try it in more difficult ones. For some people, it is easier to start participating among strangers, such as in a department store. For others, it is easier to practice first among family members and friends, then with strangers.

Above all, say "YES!" when you want to participate. Make a decision about what you want to do and say what you mean, YES or NO.

INTENSITY

Intensity involves the degree of feeling or the amount of energy that one uses in communication. For the purposes of this text, intensity is considered as a continuum of feeling or general energy from a person's body. Intensity is various levels in strength of emotion or energy that is expressed by an individual. The continuum of intensity ranges from a very low level to a medium, moderate level up to a very high level. The continuous levels may be thought of as a range of numbers from 1 to 10 in the following descriptive diagram.

INTENSITY SCALE

1	2	3	4	5	6	7	8	9	10

Very low energy (shallow, laid back)	Medium energy (attentive, alert, active interest)	Very high energy (powerful, high excitement)

This INTENSITY SCALE shows that many energy levels are available to express a wide range of feelings and responses.

For example:
You may be at a 1 to 2 level of intensity as you doze lazily in the Florida sunshine. When a friend invites you to have a cup of cold iced tea, you may perk up to a 4 to 5 level of intensity and appreciate the refreshing drink.

When a dragonfly flitters by and lights on your toe, you may reach a 6 to 7 intensity level of alertness as you appreciate the dragonfly's colorful, iridescent wings. When some nearby children, tossing a frisbee, abruptly knock your iced tea all over your chest, you may reach a fuming 9 to 10 level of intensity.

Different levels of intensity are appropriate for different situations. Some people have a range of two or three numbers for all of their behaviors. Others may use a range of six to seven numbers that are never too low or too high a level of intensity for the situation. Some individuals typically operate at the lower end of the scale at levels 1 and 2. Others operate at the higher energy levels, represented by 9 and 10 on the scale.

Having a repertoire of behaviors, actions at different levels of intensity for different situations, provides interesting variety in one's lifestyle. On the other hand, staying within a range of two or three numbers on the continuum probably indicates that the individual is somewhat limited in choices of behavior. In other words, no matter how varied the circumstances, the person responds nearly the same way each time. With such a well-established pattern of behavior, the individual probably feels limited, bored, and stuck. Few choices seem available.

Or, the individual may not understand how the behaviors fall into a typical pattern. They may feel as if they express themselves with great variety and use all levels of intensity. They may not see themselves as others do. Others may see them as predictable, usually excited or usually expressionless. The others do not respect the impact of some of their messages, because the oral message is generally contradicted by the level of intensity.

For example, a person who is typically overemotional may operate at an intensity level of 8 to 9 nearly all the time. It may be hard for the person to convince others that he or she is no longer upset about a situation. The oral message may reflect forgiveness and calmness, but the level of emotion remains strong and, perhaps, intimidating. The conclusion of the listener will probably be that the speaker is insincere and has little self-control. The listener may decide to be more careful during their future interactions.

In another example, the manager of an office may function generally at an intensity level of 2 to 3. The manager feels that level of intensity is appropriate for a professional. It may be hard for the manager to convince the other employees that serious changes are needed on the job.

The manager may speak clearly and use descriptive diagrams, but remain unconvincing because of the relaxed, low-key intensity level used in communication. The workers may agree with the manager's ideas. They won't be convinced about the serious need for change, because, somehow, it did not seem serious. The intensity of the communication contradicted the oral message. The weak, relaxed style of communication had too little strength or vigor to impress them.

Becoming aware of one's own style of behavior, a person may expand the level of intensity by practicing and implementing trilevel language strategies. For example, one may use arm gestures to intensify the expression of anger. One may try to smile with one's eyes and mouth to communicate pleasure. Opening one's mouth more to form words, using fuller (not necessarily louder) voice tones, and changing sound levels in one's sentences add variety to a person's customary level of intensity. These actions may help to make a person's experiences in life more interesting and fulfilling.

The following discussion exercise, INTENSITY, provides an opportunity for the reader to think about the strength and energy that they express in personal feelings and behavior in different situations.

DISCUSSION EXERCISE

Intensity

DIRECTIONS FOR THE LEARNER: On the blanks available below, write an intensity range of two numbers, such as 4–5 or 7–8, to indicate the appropriate level of intensity you would experience in each situation.

_____ 1. You announce the changed date of your committee, potluck luncheon meeting.

_____ 2. You tell everyone in your single level apartment complex that the supermarket across the street is on fire.

_____ 3. You are thanking your host for a delicious dinner.

_____ 4. Your five-year-old granddaughter got into your sewing basket or tool box and you tell her to stop.

_____ 5. You are asking the cashier at the drug store for a package of cotton applicators.

_____ 6. You still can't hear what the representative at the city hearing is saying.

_____ 7. You read your nine-year-old foster child's thank-you letter for your camping trip together last weekend.

_____ 8. You finished a snack of cheese, homemade bread, and hot tea. Now the house is quiet and you are relaxing in your armchair on the sun porch.

DIRECTIONS FOR THE LEADER: The purpose of this exercise is to become familiar with the range and appropriateness of different intensities. This exercise works well as an activity for the individual or a group. The individual may think about and the group may discuss the exercise in terms of the following ideas and questions.

The activity above should be evaluated in terms of the variety of answers given. The eight different examples should cover many levels of intensity in emotion and energy. If the total pool of answers shows a wide range or a narrow range of intensity levels, that may be an indication of the reader's range of intensity behavior in daily life.

How does your intensity vary in each statement? What body language changes occur as people and circumstances changed in each situation? How does the level of intensity in your responses compare with the responses of other people? What does this information tell you about yourself?

It takes about 30 minutes to complete the exercise and discussion.

SUMMARY

Many skills may be used to facilitate communication. Paying close attention to a speaker helps the listener hear more accurately. Understanding the spoken message, the body language message, and the hidden message, a careful observer may obtain, not only the obvious, but also the subtle information being communicated.

Specific skills, such as positive feedback, saying "NO," and appropriate intensity, help one respond genuinely to others. Being aware of sexism, racism, and agism help a person become more open to the special qualities that different kinds of people contribute to life. Confining debates to the facts and sharing opinions respectfully enhance relationships. Apologies are appropriate to relationships, but long, belabored excuses may interfere with the flow of information between people. Although specific techniques are important, good communication attends to the feelings of people as well as the contents of their messages.

Suggestions for Further Reading

EMPATHY AND SYMPATHY

Egan, E. (1975). *The Skilled Helper.* Monterey, CA: Brooks/Cole.

FEELINGS

Alpaugh, P., & Haney, M. (1979). *Counseling the Older Adult.* Los Angeles, CA: The Ethel Percy Andrus Gerontology Center.

POSITIVE FEEDBACK

Golembiewski, R. T., & Blumberg, A. (1970). *Sensitivity Training and the Laboratory Approach.* Itasca, IL: Peacock.

Hansen, J. C. Warner, R. W., & Smith, E. M. (1976). *Group Counseling: Theory and Process.* Chicago, IL: Rand McNally College Pub. Co.

Phelps, S., & Austin, N. (1975). *The Assertive Woman.* San Luis Obispo, CA: Impact.

Standards for the Use of the Laboratory Method. (1969). Washington, DC: NTL Institute for Applied Behavioral Science.

SAYING NO!

Alberti, R. E., & Emmons, M. L. (1975). *Stand Up, Speak Out, Talk Back!* San Luis Obispo, CA: Impact

Fensterheim, H. (1971). *Help Without Psychoanalysis.* New York: Stein & Day.

TRILEVEL LANGUAGE

Alberti, R. E., & Emmons, M. L. (1974). *Your Perfect Right.* San Luis Obispo, CA: Impact

Donelson, E. (1973). *Personality.* Pacific Palisades, CA: Goodyear Pub. Co.

Phelps, S., & Austin, N. (1975). *The Assertive Woman.* San Luis Obispo, CA: Impact.

UNDERCURRENT MESSAGES

Egan, E. (1975). *The Skilled Helper.* Monterey, CA: Brooks/Cole.

Gazda, G. M., et al. (1977). *Human Relations Development* (2nd ed.). Boston, MA: Allyn & Bacon.

5

Selective Assertiveness

Selective assertiveness implies the most desirable behavior for a given situation. Hopefully, most of the time a person will choose to be assertive, that is, open and honest. In evaluating a dilemma and its possible solutions, one may decide upon a non-assertive course of action. One may choose to be passive, that is, silent and helpless. Or, a person may select aggressiveness, which is explosive, over-reactive behavior.

Usually assertive action is the best choice. Sometimes, however, after carefully evaluating the situation, a person may choose passive or aggressive behavior as the most appropriate resolution of the specific situation. Choosing to be non-assertive differs from automatic non-assertive behavior. In this book selecting the most desirable and most sensible alternative is acting with selective assertiveness.

For example, in a discussion at a social gathering, Carol and Debra are disagreeing heatedly about a political question. They disagree on whether the government should spend federal tax dollars on defense programs or cancer research. Carol begins to feel "pushed" in the discussion and decides to stop trying to clarify her point of view. She perceives that Debra is being over-emotional. She knows that Debra is stressed right now from the recent death of an older brother and from baby-sitting her four grandchildren for the past two weeks.

Carol says, "Debra, this is an important issue for me. I want to talk more about it with you. Why don't you come to my place for lunch next week? Meanwhile, let's get refills on the punch and see how many new voters Mary registered at the library last week."

Carol has chosen to bypass the current emotional confrontation and behave in a passive way. Because she actively selected passive behavior from different available alternatives which she thought over carefully, her action is considered to be selective assertiveness. Carol did plan another time for further discussion, however. At that time she may choose to argue the facts and present her viewpoint assertively.

In situations such as in the preceding example, the decision to behave passively or aggressively is called selective assertiveness. Even though passiveness and aggressiveness are not assertive actions, the process of considering and choosing sensible action is assertive.

A person should evaluate carefully the needs and possibilities of an occasion. When a person has made a careful choice, accepted the responsibility for the chosen behavior, and is prepared to deal with the consequences, one may feel confident that the selected assertive, passive, or aggressive actions were probably the most suitable for the situation.

The objectives of selective assertiveness are twofold. The first objective is to enlarge and enrich a person's repertoire of behaviors, in other words the number of and types of behaviors. The second objective is to help a person to be assertive as often as possible.

NONASSERTIVENESS

Nonassertiveness is behavior that avoids dealing directly with the situation to provide an appropriate solution. Typically, nonassertiveness is inadequate coping behavior. People who are nonassertive usually act too soon or too late. Their immediate response is often inappropriate and does not deal directly with the dilemma at hand.

The nonassertive person may behave as an over-emotional bully or as a powerless, helpless victim. After their inappropriate responses, these people usually feel embarrassed or frustrated. They think of the right action or answer in a few minutes, or much later, when they have left the scene or the people. Their greatest frustration, however, is that they continue to be dissatisfied with their unassertive handling of situations.

Nonassertiveness or nonassertion fits into two categories, (1) situational nonassertiveness or (2) general nonassertiveness. Situational nonassertiveness occurs on specific occasions. General nonassertiveness is a general or almost total lifestyle and attitude of nonassertive behavior. Whether they behave nonassertively in specific situations or as a general lifestyle, nonassertive people seem to be caught in a pattern of inadequate coping and wish they had acted differently.

Situational Nonassertiveness

Most people have an issue in their lives that falls into the category of situational nonassertiveness. Usually the person that has this concern is emotionally healthy. The person copes adequately and feels satisfied and fulfilled in life in most situations. In certain incidents or with certain people, however, the person becomes overwhelmed by tension, built up emotions, a sense of failure, etc. The person relies on an inadequate passive or aggressive response to cope. The individual wants to develop new methods of dealing with problems that always seem to end up in the same discomfort or embarrassment.

For example, a type of situation that requires asking someone in authority for money may seem overwhelming to someone. Whenever in that type of situation, the person may feel embarrassed, unworthy, and incompetent. The person may be able to ask favors of most people, but may feel incapable of asking the boss at work for a raise. The individual would like to learn assertive behavior in dealing with this specific type of situation.

Another example is the following interaction between Mr. and Mrs. Lepa. They have been married for 45 years. Every time he complains of a headache, she becomes stoney and silent. His low grumbling quickly grows to yelling as he slams out the kitchen door.

She thinks to herself, "I know he's under tension at work. All those young kids and that new machinery plus his retirement next year. He's worried about the grandchildren again; it's been so long since they have written. I'm worried, too. I know all about it. He's so emotional. He brings those headaches on himself. I can't help him. He has his own stubborn ways."

At the same time he is thinking to himself, "Why can't that woman talk! I know she's worried about my retirement and having enough money to pay all the bills. The garden was so dry, she couldn't do much canning this year. This house is getting too big. The cost of repairs is sky high. I like to putter around the house, but that heavy winter snow gets worse every year. She's always busy, picking up this, picking up that. She caused this headache and won't do anything about it. She's not suffering! That banging in the kitchen is just enough to drive me out of the house for keeps. Well, she won. I hope she's happy with what she's done."

After working in his tool shed for two hours, he'll come into the house quietly. She'll serve dinner efficiently. They'll go on with their daily lives, including headaches, pans banging in the kitchen, and the resumption of regular roles after the frustration simmers down.

Here is a look at a different confrontation. It involves a couple. It ends in a way that is similar to the behavior of Mr. and Mrs. Lepa.

Every time Pat asks for help in balancing the checkbook, Lee has a temper tantrum, yells abusive words, bangs a few doors, and goes out shopping. Pat gets the message, but Lee always feels embarrassed and miserable about the behavior afterward.

Lee is typically a caring, understanding, considerate person except when it comes to math. Pat, on the other hand, is usually direct, but hates to interact with someone "who's all upset." Therefore, Pat distances personal feelings in emotional confrontations and withdraws from the situation.

A few minutes later when the noise dies down, Pat figures out some remarks that would have helped solve the problem, but it's too late. Perhaps Pat will remember these soothing, helpful remarks the next time. The next time, however, never seems to come. And the years go by.

By being assertive, open, honest and respectful with each other, Pat and Lee as well as Mr. and Mrs. Lepa would have a richer relationship. They would develop and grow with each other instead of being stuck in the same old frustrating patterns of interaction.

General Nonassertiveness

General nonassertiveness is behavior that is nonassertive in nearly all circumstances. Anxious in nearly every situation, nonassertive individuals know only one way of handling their tensions, passively or aggressively. Their typical behavior and attitude toward most people is nonassertive. Passive people dislike doing or saying anything that may upset someone else. Aggressive people don't want anyone to get away with anything, important or insignificant. The passive person suffers martyrdom in silence. The aggressor has a chip on his or her shoulder and bursts out offensively at the slightest provocation.

For example, a generally passive person may think, "No matter what happens, nothing I say or do will change anything, so I just won't bother." OR:

"If the electrician (or any other person) says it should be done that way, who am I to question it? I just have to accept what they tell me. There is nothing I can do about it."

On the other hand, a person who is aggressive generally may think, "Who are they to tell me what to do? CRASH! POW!" OR:

"You don't know what you're doing. How can you be so stupid? Take lessons next time before you make a mess out of other people's lives!"

Nonassertiveness allows a person's rights to be violated by deliberate or inadvertent action. Someone may purposely infringe on another person's rights through neglectful or hurtful behavior. A person may violate someone else's rights or feelings by holding inside themselves their personal emotions, needs, or wishes.

The end results of nonassertive, inhibited reactions are usually hurt, anxiety, or sometimes, anger. Nonassertion limits emotional intimacy and interferes with close, healthy interpersonal relationships.

PASSIVENESS

Passive people act shy, helpless, and victimized. They seem unsure and powerless. It appears as if they do not have the strength or the skill to act or speak up. In an interaction the right response comes to them at a later time. Sometimes the right response comes much later, such as the next day.

They may think, "I wish I had said, 'No, I don't want any tickets to the raffle!' Why did I buy something that I don't want and can't afford?"

Passive people may think they are being very polite and kind. This kind of behavior is indicated in the popular saying "Speak only when spoken to." They may feel they are helping and protecting others from unpleasant interactions.

This attitude is reflected in the saying, "See no evil, hear no evil, speak no evil." The saying has been interpreted by many to mean: ignore what you see, discount what you hear, and never say what you feel. This interpretation encourages passive people to stay uninvolved.

It is more acceptable in the culture of the United States for women to be passive than it is for men. This provides a great deal of difficulty for men who prefer passive behavior. They are seen by society as unmanly. In fact, men are encouraged to be reckless and aggressive. Women, on the other hand, are rewarded for passive behavior. Society expects them to be helpless, waiting, dependent, and rather inept.

Men and women, accustomed to passive behavior, may be interested in acting in a more open manner. They may want to learn skills that give them choices in ways to act with others. Having a range of assertive behaviors from which to choose, these people will have more freedom to act in ways that will bring them a sense of satisfaction in their lives.

The following discussion exercise, PASSIVE, AGGRESSIVE, OR ASSERTIVE: EXERCISE ONE, provides an opportunity for the reader to explore actions that indicate a posture of passiveness.

DISCUSSION EXERCISE

Passive, Aggressive, or Assertive: Exercise One

DIRECTIONS FOR THE LEARNER: Circle the word in the above title, PASSIVE, AGGRESSIVE, OR ASSERTIVE, that describes best the following picture. Briefly write down in the space below the picture the behavioral clues you see that help you decide. Does the big figure below seem male or female to you?

DIRECTIONS FOR THE LEADER: This exercise may be done on an individual basis or in the total group. The purpose of the exercise is to identify actions and feelings that might be labeled as a specific type of behavior, namely passiveness. This exercise has been used with success as an introduction to the topic of passiveness and/or as a quiz after the topic has been discussed thoroughly.

How do people relate to the behavior the picture portrays? How do people relate to the feelings the large individual seems to be experiencing?

It takes about 10 minutes for a group to complete the exercise and discussion.

AGGRESSIVENESS

Aggressive persons stand up for their rights in a way that violates the rights of others. Aggressors make a strong, usually negative impression. Rather than express honest anger about a behavior, they overreact. Often their pent-up feelings seem to explode and attack the other person. They humiliate and insult. Aggressors respond too vigorously in a physical and/or emotional manner.

After the aggressiveness, they usually experience guilt, embarrassment, and self-doubt. Sometimes the post-incident emotional and material costs are very great. The costs may involve the repair of broken doors or windows. Sometimes hospitalization is required for the aggressor or for the victim of the aggression.

As an example, the aggressor may think during the morning after the outburst, "I didn't think I was that angry. I can't believe I hurt someone bad enough to put him in the hospital. I don't know what came over me. I was just being a man. Sometimes I scare myself."

It is more acceptable in American culture for men to be aggressive than it is for women. Often men feel pressure to act in an aggressive way. Their aggressive movements are praised. Women are usually scolded or ridiculed when they display aggression.

Aggression may be taught as appropriate behavior in certain jobs, such as the military service or police work. Often politicians stress aggressive action when they lobby for new legislation or international programs. Corporate executives emphasize aggression in their management and sales tactics.

Usually these people mean assertive attitudes and behavior. They intend to act with strength. They want to be forthright and open. Instead, they use a word that indicates harmful, inconsiderate, overemotional, and disrespectful behavior. A clear understanding of the difference between aggression and assertion would help people behave in a way that communicates their genuine intentions.

The following discussion exercise, PASSIVE, AGGRESSIVE, OR ASSERTIVE: EXERCISE TWO, provides an opportunity for the reader to explore body actions that portray aggressiveness.

DISCUSSION EXERCISE

Passive, Aggressive, or Assertive: Exercise Two

DIRECTIONS FOR THE LEARNER: Circle the word in the above title, PASSIVE, AGGRESSIVE, OR ASSERTIVE, that describes best the picture below. Briefly write down in the space around the figure the behavioral clues you see to help you decide. Does the figure below seem male or female to you?

DIRECTIONS FOR THE LEADER: This exercise may be done on an individual basis or in the total group. The purpose of the exercise is to identify actions and feelings that might be labeled as a specific type of behavior, namely aggressiveness. This exercise has been used with success as an introduction to the topic of aggressiveness and/or as a quiz after the topic has been discussed thoroughly.

How do people relate to the behavior the picture portrays? How do people relate to the feelings the individual seems to be experiencing?

It takes about 10 minutes for a group of people to complete the exercise and discussion.

ASSERTIVENESS

Assertiveness is as important and basic a need as are food, shelter, and love. When these survival needs are not being met, a person's mental and physical health enter jeopardy. Then the person may lose the ability to cope effectively with the multiple, daily changes of life.

By being assertive, a person acts on the privilege of human rights and freedom. Assertiveness helps a person learn self-respect and to respect others. Also, the person learns to become an equal participant in the opportunities and responsibilities available to all human beings.

Becoming an equal does not mean becoming the same as another. Equality refers to having the same opportunity available to experience a rich and fulfilling life. Part of the experience of equality is learning to accept more rights, such as the right to choose for oneself and the right to spend time in a personally fulfilling manner. Accepting one's rights and acting on them include acceptance of the involved responsibilities. While choosing plans that provide a self-fulfilling direction in life, the assertive person acts conscientiously. The individual is careful not to indulge in the self at the expense of hurting others.

The assertive person is open and caring. She or he makes compromises that respect both of the parties involved. The assertive individual feels capable and confident, but not cocky. Eager to develop the skills of expression, the assertive person does not harm others.

Assertiveness is the open expression of feelings and attitudes. It helps one to be more involved in the experience of being alive. It focuses on what Carl Rogers called the fully functioning person, what Abraham Maslow called self-actualization, what Erich Fromm called productive love, what Eric Erikson called wisdom and integrity, and what Gordon Allport called the mature personality.

Assertiveness enhances self-esteem and the esteem of others. Direct and appropriate, assertiveness encourages interpersonal relationships. The candid expression of one's feelings, beliefs, and opinions allows a person to stand up for personal rights without infringing on the rights of others.

The assertive person tries to deal with the issue immediately, gets involved, and makes choices. Much later, after an incident, the assertor says, "I feel I did the right thing," or "I tried my best. It didn't work . . . no regrets for trying."

The following three examples depict assertiveness:

1. A young couple cuts in front of you and your family in the ticket line at the theater. You say, "The line ends back there (or behind me). We came early to get good seats."

2. When Mr. Taylor counted his change after paying his utility bill, he was 23 cents short. He says, "I've counted 45 cents here and I should receive 68 cents in change. I gave you $55.00."

3. Mrs. Smith is having difficulty hearing the teacher in an adult evening class of 20 members. She asked him twice to speak louder. She closed the side windows to shut out background noises. She still cannot hear what is going on. She requests, "May I move to the front row to hear better?" With some confusion and moving of class members, she settles down and listens. At last she can focus on the instructor's ideas. Though she was embarrassed about interrupting so often, she is satisfied that she can finally hear and learn. Now she feels as if she is part of the class.

Assertiveness training involves building a personal value system of beliefs and behaviors. The system of beliefs includes such convictions as (1) accepting the right of individual freedom, (2) accepting oneself, and (3) knowing that nonassertion is frustrating and harmful to oneself and others in the long run. The system of behaviors includes such actions as (1) talking openly in an appropriate manner about one's feelings and concerns, (2) using body language that is in tune with the oral message, (3) developing deeper and/or new relationships with others, and (4) making appealing activities and interests part of one's life.

The following discussion exercises, (1) PASSIVE, AGGRESSIVE, OR ASSERTIVE: EXERCISE THREE, (2) ASSERTIVENESS, and (3) TRYING ASSERTION AND NONASSERTION, provide opportunities for the reader to explore ideas and actions of the body that portray assertiveness.

DISCUSSION EXERCISE

Passive, Aggressive, or Assertive: Exercise Three

DIRECTIONS FOR THE LEARNER: Circle the word in the above title, PASSIVE, AGGRESSIVE, OR ASSERTIVE, that describes best the picture below. In the space below the picture write down briefly the behavioral clues you see in the interaction to help you decide.

DIRECTIONS FOR THE LEADER: This exercise may be done on an individual basis or in the total group. The purpose of the exercise is to identify actions and feelings that might be labeled as a specific type of behavior, namely assertiveness. This exercise has been used with success as an introduction to the topic of assertiveness and/or as a quiz after the topic has been discussed thoroughly.

How do people relate to the behavior the picture portrays? How do people relate to the feelings the individual seems to be experiencing?

It takes about 10 minutes for a group of people to complete the exercise and discussion.

DISCUSSION EXERCISE

Assertiveness

DIRECTIONS FOR THE LEARNER: *Categorize the following statement as A to indicate ASSERTIVE, P to indicate PASSIVE, or AG to indicate AGGRESSIVE. Think in terms of the description of the people in the statements.*

_____ 1. Children are to be seen and not heard.

_____ 2. To the victor belong the spoils.

_____ 3. It is only natural for older people to be quiet; they have a lot more to be quiet about.

_____ 4. Girls are made of sugar and spice.

_____ 5. Boys are made of frogs and snails.

_____ 6. Show me a good loser and I'll show you a loser. (Woody Hayes, former football coach, Ohio State University)

_____ 7. Use it or lose it.

_____ 8. Children are a great comfort in your old age, and they help you reach it faster, too.

_____ 9. An appeaser is one who feeds a crocodile . . . hoping it will eat her last. (Sir Winston Churchill)

_____ 10. A fool always loses his or her temper, but the wise hold theirs back.

DIRECTIONS FOR THE LEADER: *The exercise above may be done on an individual basis or with a group of people. The purpose of the exercise is to clarify the differences between assertiveness, passiveness, and aggressiveness.*

Take some time to point out the differences between assertive, aggressive, and passive behaviors that are indicated in the situations of the statements above. When the reader thinks in terms of the setting of the situations or the attitudes of the speakers or the creators of the statements, does the category of each statement change?

It takes about 15 minutes for a group to complete this exercise and discussion. Most people agree that the answers to the statements above are (1) P, (2) AG, (3) P, (4) P, (5) AG, (6) AG, (7), A, (8) P, (9) P, and (10) A. Considering the behavior of the speaker, however, may provide different answers.

DISCUSSION EXERCISE

Trying Assertion and Nonassertion

DIRECTIONS FOR THE LEARNER: How would you respond to the following situations? Give a passive, aggressive, and assertive response to each situation described below. Write down your answers in the appropriate places indicated below each situation.

Then form small groups of 4–6 members each to share your responses. Role play the different responses. Exaggerate the behaviors that would indicate definite passive, aggressive, and assertive responses for each situation.

1. *You and your spouse or close friend are at the police chief's house for dinner. Your loved one remarks, "This is such a lovely home. I wanted to buy a house in this neighborhood two years ago, but my partner here refused to go along with the idea."*

PASSIVE:

AGGRESSIVE:

ASSERTIVE:

2. *An in-store special was just announced. In the next five minutes you have the opportunity to buy two tickets for the price of one to the present production at the local playhouse. Your friends have told you that the play is spectacular. You have enough money, but are unsure about which friend to invite. The offer seems so good.*

PASSIVE:

AGGRESSIVE:

ASSERTIVE:

3. *The full service guarantee on your $100.00 watch lasts two more days. The watch seems to be gaining five to ten minutes a day, but you're unsure. You really have become attached to the watch, but you don't seem to have the time to visit the jewelry store. Besides, the salespeople in the store seemed so unpleasant during your stop there last week.*

PASSIVE:

AGGRESSIVE:

ASSERTIVE:

DIRECTIONS FOR THE LEADER: This exercise works better as a group activity because it involves a great deal of interaction. The purpose of the exercise is to provide some practice in assertiveness and nonassertiveness.

The participants should be encouraged to overplay or overdramatize the role playing. This overacting will give them a better emotional feeling for the differences between assertive, passive, and aggressive behaviors.

What specific trilevel communication do you see as each response is demonstrated? In other words, what oral statements, body language, and undercurrent messages are observed? Participants are encouraged to provide positive feedback to each other.

It takes about 30 to 45 minutes to complete the exercise and discussion.

TRILEVEL LANGUAGE SUMMARY CHART

Passive, Aggressive, Assertive

DIRECTIONS FOR THE LEARNER: Using the information on the previous pages, list below on the three charts the different kinds of attitudes and behaviors associated with the three styles of behavior, (1) passive, (2) aggressive, (3) assertive. This information summarizes the chapter on selective assertiveness for the reader.

ORAL LANGUAGE	PASSIVE	AGGRESSIVE	ASSERTIVE

BODY LANGUAGE	PASSIVE	AGGRESSIVE	ASSERTIVE
1. Eye Contact			
2. Look on Face			
3. Voice			
4. Posture			
5. Gestures			
6. Personal Space			
7. Timing			

HIDDEN LANGUAGE	PASSIVE	AGGRESSIVE	ASSERTIVE

DIRECTIONS FOR THE LEADER: This exercise may be done individually, as a homework exercise, or in a group. The purpose of the exercise is to develop a summary sheet or reference sheet of assertiveness, passiveness, and aggressiveness. This summary has helped many individuals realize that different specific body behaviors communicate information and attitudes. It take about 15 minutes to complete the exercise.

Suggestions for Further Reading

AGGRESSIVENESS

Brenton, M. (1970). *The American Male.* Greenwich, CT: Fawcett.

Fromm, E. (1955). *The Sane Society.* New York: Rinehart.

Goldberg, H. (1976). *The Hazards of Being Male.* New York: Nash.

Phelps, S., & Austin, N. (1975). *The Assertive Woman.* San Luis Obispo, CA: Impact.

ASSERTIVENESS

Alberti, R. E., & Emmons, M. L. (1974). *Your Perfect Right.* San Luis Obispo, CA: Impact.

Butler, P. (1976). Assertive training: Teaching women not to discriminate against themselves. *Psychotherapy: Theory, Research and Practice,* 13(1), 56–60.

Corby, N. (1975). Assertion training with aged populations. *The Counseling Psychologist,* 5(4), 60–74.

Phelps, S., & Austin, N. (1975). *The Assertive Woman.* San Luis Obispo, CA: Impact.

MATURE PERSONALITY

Erikson, E. H. (1964). *Insight and Responsibility.* New York: W. W. Norton and Co.

Fromm, E. (1956). *The Art of Loving.* New York: Harper.

Schultz, D. (1977). Growth Psychology. New York: Van Nostrand Reinhold.

PASSIVENESS

Alberti, R. E., & Emmons, M. L. (1974). *Your Perfect Right.* San Luis Obispo, CA: Impact.

Phelps, S., & Austin, N. (1975). *The Assertive Woman.* San Luis Obispo, CA: Impact.

6

Reflection

Reflection provides an opportunity to look at oneself in view of the events surrounding one's life. For the purposes of this text, reflection involves looking over the experiences of the reader that have resulted from exposure to the materials on the preceding pages.

Ending one kind of experience is the first step in the beginning of the next experience or challenge in "lifelong learning." That next challenge to learn will be found in different places for each person. Each person should assume the responsibility of being on the alert for that next challenge. Such a state of readiness will help one to move spontaneously to enjoy the experience when the next opportunity or challenge surfaces.

The purpose of this text is to try to provide clarity, awareness, understanding, and skill in specific techniques. As a result of their learning, readers should be able to observe more clearly the communicative language of others. They should become more aware of the natural traits and new components of behavior within themselves. They should have some understanding of how feelings and behaviors influence each other.

In addition, they should see how the use of good communication skills and selective assertiveness techniques enhance life and improve relationships. When people can feel that they are beginning to move in these directions, then they know they have started the exciting adventure of blossoming into a more capable person.

The next part of the adventure of development for the reader may involve learning advanced skills in human interaction on the following pages, PART II: ADVANCED SKILLS. On the other hand, the reader may want to take some time to focus on adapting the basic skills from the previous pages into his or her lifestyle. No matter which step is pursued, the reader should take some time to reflect over the recent learning. The reader should try to practice the skills and integrate the meaning of the information on personal and interpersonal awareness into personal living.

The last pages of PART I: BASIC SKILLS contain three discussion exercises that are designed to help readers move from the activities in the previous pages of this text to the next developments in their lives. They provide assistance in helping participants begin to move away from the emotional closeness of the group toward other relationships in their lives.

Participants are given an opportunity to summarize experiences and express appreciation for meaningful exchanges. The exercises help group members finish activities with each other and develop a sense of completion with the experiences. The sense of completion with past experiences helps ready them for a new set of experiences.

The next discussion exercise, the GOOD–BYE HANDSHAKE, provides an opportunity to develop self-perception and the awareness of others through a common means of communication, the handshake. EXPANDING THE SELF, the second discussion exercise, helps the reader reflect over the personal and interpersonal experiences that have occurred as a result of going through the previous materials. The TIME CAPSULE, the final discussion exercise, helps people examine their own histories and identify meaningful, important characteristics that they would be willing to share with others.

Pleasant reflections.

DISCUSSION EXERCISE

Good-Bye Handshake

DIRECTIONS FOR THE LEARNER: Everyone shakes hands with as many other people as possible. Shake hands as if you were greeting each other for the first time. Do it the same way you typically shake hands in a new setting. Try to feel a sense of what each person is like when you shake each hand. Try to give a caring, but gentle handshake to people who may have arthritis in their hands.

Take some time and discuss each person's style of shaking hands. How did all the group members perceive each individual person? Remember to keep comments positive.

Now each class member may choose a partner who is among those that they know least well. The partners stand up facing each other, shake hands, and close their eyes. With hands still clasped and eyes closed, they try to communicate a message through hand contact. No words are allowed.

Next, they open their eyes and tell each other in words what they felt from one another. Feedback is provided about the accuracy of the message. Then with eyes closed, hands clasped, the message is again transmitted. Partners provide oral reports and feedback to each other once more.

To see how you feel to others, see if you can shake hands with yourself. See if you can feel in your own left-hand-to-right-hand contact what others may have experienced from their contact with you. Then try to hug yourself. What do you feel like to yourself? How does it feel to put your arms around your own body?

DIRECTIONS FOR THE LEADER: This exercise depends on group interaction. The purpose of the exercise is to experience more fully the contact made with another person through a handshake.

Participants should take some time as a total group to talk about the experiences. Consider the following questions in the discussion. How close did you come to communicating accurately what you felt the first time around? How did you feel initially when your eyes were closed? During any of the handshake experiences did you send or receive information that is hard to put into words?

How does your body feel to you? What kind of sensations did you experience when you hugged yourself? How do you communicate to yourself? How do you communicate to others? How are these two methods the same and how are they different?

The exercise and discussion take about 20 to 45 minutes depending upon the size of the group and the depth of the experiences people have with this activity. Older people will take much longer, because they will want to talk about "touching," its role in their lives, and the rules about touching in society down through the years.

DISCUSSION EXERCISE

Expanding the Self

DIRECTIONS FOR THE LEARNER: On an individual basis, take some time to respond to the questions below. Reflect over the learning that you have experienced as you have worked through the materials in this text. Remember to keep private any information you do not want to share. Be willing, however, to be open and honest with yourself.

1. *This week (or the past few weeks) I was surprised to learn about myself that . . .*

2. *Something about myself that I recently affirmed or learned is . . .*

3. *I helped someone else to . . .*

4. *One of the members of the group helped me to . . .*

5. *I had the most fun when . . .*

Now form small groups of 4–6 members and share your responses. Be sure to provide positive feedback to each other regarding effective communication demonstrated during the process of sharing. Try to thank in a direct way the people who were helpful and supportive to you. Now open up the small groups to become one larger group and share your responses all together.

DIRECTIONS FOR THE LEADER: This exercise is a group activity. The purpose of the exercise is to help people learn the value of reminiscing on a short-term level.

Sometimes it is helpful to review past events and evaluate the changes that may have occurred. The experience may reveal some appreciation of one's own ability or change. It may reveal the positive influence of someone else.

This kind of reflection provides perspective to one's recent experiences in life. It is a variation on the Life Review (Butler, 1963b), which is a review of all the events in a person's lifetime.

It takes about 20–30 minutes to complete this exercise.

DISCUSSION EXERCISE

Time Capsule

DIRECTIONS FOR THE LEARNER: A time capsule is a well-sealed container that holds information for other people to explore at a future time. On an individual basis, think about some things you would collect together to put in a time capsule. You have been selected to be a representative of the special people who developed during this century. What will you place in the time capsule to symbolize your life?

The capsule will be planted in Washington, D.C. The President of the United States 100 years from now will open up the capsule and share your information with the world.

Use the space below to write down briefly the items your time capsule would contain.

DIRECTIONS FOR THE LEADER: This exercise relies on the group process. The purpose of the activity is to help the participant reflect on values, some of which may now differ as a result of the materials in the past few chapters.

The group members should gather in a circle and share their responses. After the items of the time capsule are shared, the discussion may consider the following questions. What came to mind first as you began to think about the directions of this exercise? How do you feel about the story that is told by your time capsule? Are you surprised by the items you gathered together? How do you feel as you think of someone opening up your time capsule so far ahead in the future?

As people share, they may need to be reminded to provide positive feedback to each other regarding effective communication.

It takes about 20–30 minutes to complete this exercise.

Advanced Skills

7

The Need for Communication Today

Each generation of people has different historical and social settings that contribute to individual development. The settings contribute to the sense of who the people are, how they link with others, and who they will become. The Pilgrims who traveled to the New Land in the 1600s had a different setting from the astronauts who traveled through space in the late 1900s. Although there were few Pilgrims, well-established, close relationships and effective communication helped them to survive.

The survival of the astronauts also depends upon a well-established, support system. The relationships, however, involve contacts with a large number of people located around the world. Many of the people in the support system have close relationships with the astronauts, but there are many others, such as television viewers, builders of rocket parts, trained observers, or newspaper journalists, whom the astronauts will never meet.

As a result of such different kinds of relationships, effective communication is very important to the survival of the astronauts. The strength of their support system depends on their ability to communicate. Clear, effective communication with different kinds of people separated by thousands of miles is essential to keep their lifelines working.

The United States has evolved from an agricultural society to a microtechnological society in the last three centuries. As a result of the changes in the lifestyles of its citizens, effective communication has become essential for older people to survive within the complex support system of the United States.

As they age, the personal definition of the identity of people becomes richer and more complex. With time, the lives of people become increasingly varied. As the years pass, they develop deeper, different relationships as they live first with family members, then become involved with neighborhood friends, and later with associates at school and work.

They expand their interests and activities. Activities that were available in the local, small neighborhood may change when the child goes to school. They may change again later when the person is a young adult, graduates from a training program, finds a job in a new community, and then sets up a home.

The setting in which a person lives may extend to one county or the whole country. Some people have a business at home; others travel great distances to work. The grocer whose family business has been located in the same store for 100 years has a strong sense of identity with the small town. The sense of identity may be just as strong, but different from that of the senator who commutes cross-country every week to Washington, D. C. to represent the home state. The boundaries of the senator's work setting may extend to horizons that are thousands of miles apart.

To a certain degree, the high level of technology in society today is responsible for the expansion of experiences in people. People may enjoy adventures in remote countries without moving from the comfort of their homes. Today,

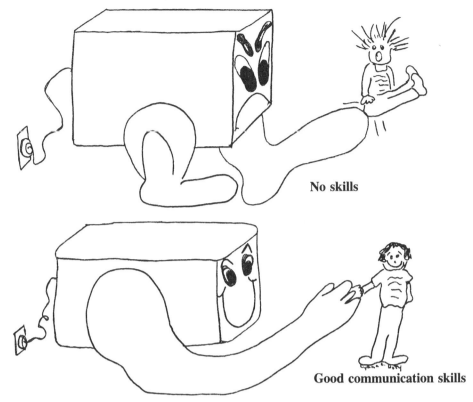

No skills

Good communication skills

Keeping up with technology.

technology provides television, radio, newspapers, and magazines that quickly deliver information about celebrations and conflicts occurring at distant places. International distances seem to have shrunk with the advances of technology. Today, people in all countries can become aware and feel intimately involved with the daily activities of other countries throughout the world.

Although aware of daily life on the international level, an individual may feel no sense of participation in the development, planning, and unfolding of these events. A complex set of political policies, economic changes, military mandates, territorial conflicts, research explorations, and ecological concerns from throughout the world spread out before the individual each day.

In the morning newspaper at breakfast, from the radio at work, or on the evening television news after dinner, a person may feel burdened with the details of life in countries that are far away. Advanced camera technology portrays striking pictures of events. The stories of strangers are vivid and real.

Stories about strangers.

Exposed to pain and confusion in the lives of many different individuals, a person may feel concerned. But, at the same time, the person may feel emotionally removed from the aching of the strangers in the situations. A sense of hopelessness may begin to creep in. The individual may realize that the ability to receive the information that stirs up feelings is accompanied by an inability to influence the turmoil and unhappiness that is occurring in such distant places.

This becomes especially frustrating to people who witness the ravages of war, earthquakes, blight, hunger, and disease. Though witnessed closely through television, world events seem beyond the influence of any single person. Doubt is stirred. Questions arise from within. How can one person be of any help? How may one individual make a difference in what happens throughout the world? Should one try to become involved? As the frustration mounts from such questions, a sense of helplessness begins.

As the sense of helplessness increases, a feeling of futility grows. As the years pass, the futility that started with frustrations about crises in foreign lands begins to overlap with issues that are closer to home. The futility begins to involve community issues, neighborhood issues, and, finally, immediate relationships. People begin to wonder how one person may influence anyone else's life?

For some, the sense of helplessness may spread further. It may spread to their personal lives. They may begin to feel powerless to plan or control the direction of their own lives. Not only do they feel helpless about issues in Asia, the local state, and the neighboring city hall, but also they feel that nothing can be done to improve their own situations in life. Life seems to be a matter of good or bad luck.

It is too much . . . I am overwhelmed, unimportant, helpless.

How may an individual develop a sense of significance when feeling so helpless? How may such a person accomplish anything? Does one life have any meaning or worth in the midst of all the events that surround these powerless individuals?

These questions become critical, personal issues for the aged. Often they begin to feel worn out by a lifetime of questions and continuing circumstances that seem beyond their control.

BEING OLD

People think of their identity or who they are in terms of what happens to them and around them. The events in their personal lives, relationships, and communities help them to understand themselves. These events help them draw up a personal definition of their lives. All the information collects into a more detailed description of their identity.

With the passing of time, they have aged. Now they are caught up in the negative feelings that society has about being elderly. Having grown up with the norms, the typical standards and beliefs of their culture, they believe as society believes. They endorse agism, the negative ideas and statements about getting old. They see and think of themselves as diseased, deteriorating, disabled, disengaged, dependent, and distant from others. Is it any wonder that many of the aged feel frightened and hopeless?

The 3 to 5 percent of the total elderly population, who are actually frail, disabled, and helpless, struggle to survive. They need skilled nursing care around the clock. They are inclined to withdraw from the challenging, invigorating events of life to hold onto bare survival. They conserve the small amount of their remaining strength to exist at a minimal level of survival. Few alternatives seem to exist for them if they want to stay alive.

About 7 percent of older people need some assistance with the routine of normal, daily life. They are able to live in the community with a team of helpers, such as a housekeeper, a home health aide, and a close relative. Approximately 85 percent of older people are independent, however, and require no assistance in their normal, daily routine.

IMPORTANCE OF COMMUNICATION AND ASSERTION SKILLS

To develop a sense of strength and significance in life, people must begin with the self. As people begin personal development, they reach a level of awareness, involvement with activities, and wellness that motivates them to reach out to others.

Developing solid relationships strengthens all parties involved. Strengthened by their relationships, people may extend their involvement into the concerns of the community and then the larger society. As a participating member of a group, the individual has a more powerful voice. United with others, he may advocate for change. United with others, she may help develop legislation that provides new direction for the country. Evidence of such united efforts may be seen in the work of silver-haired legislatures throughout the country.

As the sense of making a difference grows, a person feels more in charge of personal behavior. The person gains a sense of self-direction. Then the person feels like a significant contributor to the behavioral change in the immediate and extended network of friends.

The nexus of influence has started. One feels in charge of life. As a result of this, the person feels intimately involved in the process of living. This involvement stimulates, energizes, and transforms older persons. It brings to them a sense of happiness and satisfaction with life.

INTERPERSONAL SKILLS

Communication skills play an intimate role in helping a person make contact with other people. An individual develops relationships by being able to communicate effectively with others. Being able to talk clearly provides accurate information and the genuine sharing of oneself with others.

People make contact with one another by sharing their ideas, feelings, and concerns with each other. They influence each other's lives. They care for one another.

Being important in the lives of others makes them feel significant. Interpersonal skills are the tools that help them to make the experience of life rich with involvements, commitments, and challenges. They strengthen their sense of individual worth. Also, they strengthen their sense of "we-ness," being a part of the lives of other people.

Selective assertion, often called selective assertiveness in this text, is an important tool to use in establishing and developing relationships. Selective assertiveness is a process that helps a person make choices that are meaningful and fulfilling. The choices are respectful to the person who has made them. In addition, the choices respect the rights of the older people involved in the situation.

By choosing to say or do what one thinks is most sensible and appropriate, a person may move in a desirable direction or achieve a desired goal. This action enables the person to be in tune with the self as well as with others. It helps the person work toward fulfillment and satisfaction in life.

In the following chapters are some advanced techniques of communication and selective assertion. The techniques are explained in ways that contribute to the experience of lifelong learning, the comprehensive learning that occurs throughout life. Specific techniques to improve communication and assertiveness are described. Examples are provided in order to help clarify the ideas that are presented.

Then discussion exercises are provided to allow the reader a way to practice a specific technique or a combination of techniques. The exercises are set up to encourage group participation. The interaction of the group provides opportunities to adapt the techniques being practiced to a participant's personal style of behavior. When practiced in a small group, there is an opportunity during the exercises for participants to give and to receive feedback that is constructive, affirming, and respectful.

LEARNING

Learning refers to the incorporation of new information, meaning, and experiences into the self. It involves personal awareness, an interest in changing, and enough motivation to begin the change.

In 1982, a magazine for educators published an article about learning by U. M. L. Reck. Reck felt that students are not taught. An instructor presents the choice of a new experience to the students. Then each student evaluates, chooses, and learns. Resources are made available by the instructor, but the student decides to become involved and to learn. Following Reck's idea, the reader is encouraged to take the personal responsibility to become a real learner. In this way learning is a matter of continuous self-choosing, interaction with the new experience, and then becoming involved with the change process.

Learning: "To dive or not to dive; that is the question."

For the purposes of this text, lifelong learning is defined as (1) continuous learning throughout a person's life and (2) comprehensive, meaningful, responsible learning that integrates new information into daily life experiences. The process of acquiring new information and understanding continues throughout life. It does not stop at any age.

Lifelong learning involves all the areas of a person's life. The learning becomes a part of a person's attitude, perceptions, and behavior. It relates to how a person sees the self and others and how a person acts in the presence of others.

THE TEXT

The materials on the following pages are resources of ideas, strategies, and discussion exercises for practice. The material is written in a way that tries to show sensitivity to the life circumstances of older persons. If readers will reflect on the ideas and relate them to their personal lives, they will begin to become better acquainted with themselves. When they practice the communication and assertiveness strategies with other people, they will stimulate the beginning of some changes in their own behavior.

The author hopes that this book will help readers to operate at a higher level in the areas of:

1. Adapting to the new technology or machinery that aid communication and bring comfort to one's lifestyle,
2. Communication,
3. Dealing with feelings,
4. Selective assertion,
5. Personal awareness,
6. Interpersonal relationships, and
7. Impacting the community.

Operating at a higher level in these five areas will provide many benefits for readers. Readers will develop a greater sense of their own uniqueness. They will become more at ease with themselves. They will respect themselves and others more readily. They will understand better the meanings behind interactions with other people. They will become more effective communicators.

The implications of advanced technology, such as telecommunication systems, will be considered in a brief discussion in the following chapter. After exploring upcoming changes in machines that aid communication in Chapter 8, communication skills will be studied in Chapter 9. Next, in Chapter 10, will be a look at the role of feelings in communication. Chapter 11 will cover a more advanced level of selective assertiveness. Transition and agism will be discussed in Chapter 12. Then, roles and relationships will be examined in Chapter 13.

The final few words are in Chapter 14. This chapter will consider how to end an experience, in other words, how to say good-bye.

SUMMARY

Today, Americans are more aware of recent world events than the generations before them. Closeness to the news, however, is often associated with the lack of ability to make a difference in the direction of life events. Sometimes the sense of helplessness about world events begins to include issues that are closer to home and, then, to personal issues.

The sense of helplessness and insignificance may be helped by developing the sense of self, strengthening relationships, and participating in community concerns. Communication and assertion skills provide ways to develop personal awareness and relationships. In the modern world, now more than ever, strong communication skills and the ability to adapt in an assertive way may mean the difference between mere survival and comfortable living.

Older people who are trained in communication and assertion skills may enhance their lives personally and professionally. Using these life-coping skills will help them function better in their activities and relationships. They will be able to look more clearly at the objective world. Making good choices will help them feel self-directed and self-sufficient. It will make a difference in their own growth, the progress of their interactions, and the continued development of their community and country.

Suggestions for Further Reading

IDENTITY
Guardo, C. J. (1982). Student generations and value change. *The Personnel and Guidance Journal, 60*(8), 500–503.

LEARNING
Reck, U. M. L. (1982). Self-concept development in educational settings: An existential approach. *Educational Horizons, 60*(3), 128–131.

8

The Communication Era

The United States has passed through many stages in its development as a democratic society. In each successive stage, society has tried to improve the quality of the standard of living for its citizens. It has been an agricultural economy. It experienced the Industrial Revolution. It has entered the Space Age.

Yesterday.

Many scientists feel that the U.S.A. is in the next stage of development. The stage has been called the Age of Artificial Intelligence by some. Others call it the Intelligence Era.

Society has already begun to move beyond the Intelligence Era into the next stage of development, the Communication Era. During this new stage, assertive communication is essential. Today, messages between people, between people and machines, and between countries depend on highly developed individual skills in communication. The messages must be clear. The world depends upon it.

During the Industrial Revolution, machines took over many of the manual functions of people. The sewing machine still helps speed up the stitching of clothing and the combine, the harvesting of wheat. During the Space Age, machines facilitated travel to distant places, even the moon. During the Intelligence Era, machines took over many of the routine thinking jobs of people. Calculators can do complicated arithmetic in seconds. Computers quickly combine facts to make a diagnosis of health or illness.

The tele-machines of the Communication Era can send all kinds of messages to other machines and to people all over the world and in space. Tele-machines are the machines that carry information and other kinds of messages over great distances. Now, more than ever, people are responsible for the accuracy and appropriateness of these messages.

These new machines are better and faster than before. They improve with each new milestone in research. However, just as before, the machines have no responsibility for the final results. The responsibility lies with the people, the makers and the users of the machines. How will these incredible machines be made to serve the best interests of people?

Men and women must be able to function at a satisfactory level as "Masters of the Machines" in the Communication Era of the twenty-first century. They will need strong communication skills to assist them in the activities of normal, daily living. Their homes, places of recreation, and worship, their relationships with others, and their business transactions will require the use of machines that demand a high level of listening and speaking skills. Effective, assertive communication skills will be essential to maintain a high level of quality in their lifestyles.

CHANGES IN ROLES

As society becomes more modern in its move from an agricultural to a communications period, the variety of roles in the lives of people increases. There is an increase in the distance between the places where a person performs in the roles. A person may be a parent in one state, a grandparent in another state, and a worker in a third state. A person in the business of making sales may spend as much time with other people throughout the country as is spent with immediate family members.

As a result of urbanization and the mobility of families, the roles of an individual may determine with whom and how time is used. The roles of people may determine the direction of their lives. Often only a part of the personality is seen by others. People do not have a chance to be whole human beings with one another. Neighbors may see each other only when they travel together in the elevators up to their apartments. The salesperson who waits on a customer may never see that customer in any other role. Indeed, the salesperson may never see that particular customer again.

The styles of living and making friends seem to change more as each year passes by. People need to keep up with the continuous transformations of society. They should pace their own development to incorporate change. Maintaining good communication and assertion skills will help.

OLDER PEOPLE OF TOMORROW

As the years go by, older people will represent an increasingly larger ratio of the national population. Right now, more than 26 million Americans are 65 years of age or older. Many experts predict that in the year 2000, the social and economic health of the nation will depend significantly upon the ability of older people to attain a decent standard of living.

A decent standard of living includes the physical as well as the mental well-being of individuals. Inflation, social security, housing, health care, employment, transportation, and nutrition are some of the many issues that affect the physical well-being of a person. Self-concept, relationships, feelings of significance, and self-sufficiency are important aspects of the emotional well-being of a person.

There is a great concern about the economic limitations of society. As costs increase, the needs of older people increase, and resources in the country decrease. In many states, programs that provide services for older people are reeling from Federal cuts. Medicaid and medicare benefits, shared living arrangements, neighborhood legal services, resources for the handicapped, and long-term care facilities are being reduced. In some circumstances, the programs are being eliminated.

On the other hand, some states are responding to the economic crunch with creativity. They are seeking new ways to enhance the well-being of the elderly. For example, Oregon and Idaho are just two of the states that have tax breaks to assist families that provide care for frail older persons in need.

Volunteers help a great deal in SPICE (School Programs Involving Our City's Elderly). Located at an elementary school in Seattle, Washington, the program offers inexpensive meals and social activities to older people. The senior citizens feel a sense of being connected to one another, to citizens in the community, and, especially, to the children who attend the school.

Florida has increased funding to enhance Community Care for the Elderly (CCE). The CCE program has different supportive services that are available to older people. Some of the supportive services are help with house-keeping, meals-on-wheels, and personal care. Having these kinds of supportive services helps older people live in their own homes within the community for as long as possible.

Older Americans must be able to maintain a healthful, satisfying standard of living in the decades ahead. The elderly and their service providers have to develop and strengthen programs that help the elderly function as contributing resources to the community for as long as possible. Not only must the elderly remain independent for as long as possible, but they should continue as active members of their communities as much as possible.

The first step in obtaining this high level of functioning is for older people to develop solid communication and assertion skills. Skills that improve communication and action develop the individual and strengthen relationships. These skills become more important in the light of technological advances today, especially in the area of telecommunications.

People should be able to make contact with each other by giving and receiving clear messages. Formerly, social contact meant face-to-face interaction. Today, social contact may include human-to-machine transmitter interactions. Older people should be open to the changes in their lifestyles as a result of the continuous transition in society. They should be willing to enjoy the benefits and comforts of the changes.

TELECOMMUNICATIONS

Telecommunications may be defined simply as giving and/or receiving messages at a distance. The field of communications has come a long way since 1876 when Alexander Graham Bell spoke the first words, "Mr. Watson, come here. I want you," over a distance of several feet in Boston. Now telecommunication systems carry images and sounds over hundreds of thousands of miles.

Once considered to be intrusive to the privacy of the home during the 1930s and 1940s, telecommunication units now seem essential to the daily lives of most Americans. Some examples of telecommunication units that appear in most homes today are the radio, television, and telephone.

The developments of complex telecommunication systems contribute to the comfort of many older people today. As continued developments refine the telecommunication systems further, different machines in the systems will play an essential part in the future of older Americans who want to lead a full life.

The continued refinement of telecommunications technology is evident in the recent developments of the computer. In the United States the huge complex system of machines that made up the computer occupied 4000 to 5000 square feet of temperature-controlled space in the 1940s and 1950s. Today, the equipment that manages the same amount of work is about the size of a well-trimmed fingernail of an adult. This smaller sized unit is called the microprocessor.

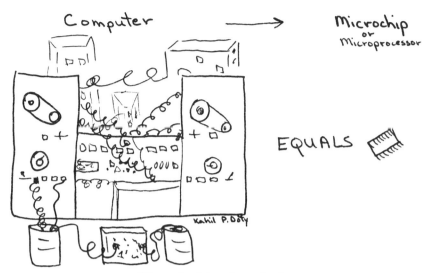

Mega-sized to micro-sized.

Research engineers discuss the computer of tomorrow in terms of the picoprocessor. The picoprocessor is described as a system that is too small to see with the naked eye. It is spoken of as being almost infinitely small. Although it will be small, it will have an incredibly large capacity to handle work.

Some engineers believe that the picoprocessor will be of great assistance to education. Engineers dream that a possible brain implant of the microscopically small picoprocessor may provide an individual with immediate access to all of the knowledge that exists in the world. A few of the engineers feel that the realization of this dream will occur in the twenty-first century. Looking ahead to such a dream and the continued developments of technology, there seems to be a great deal of promise for the lifestyles of older people in the future.

Today, some older people may be homebound because of a lack of transportation and personal physical limitations. They may limit their activities to daylight hours to guard against becoming the victim of a crime in the streets. They may avoid high risk areas of the community, such as the downtown area where the traffic is noisy, the crowds are pushy, and the restaurants are expensive.

In the future, older people will have many tools to help them be comfortable and satisfied during the later years of their lives. Many technological resources will become available to them to assist their material, physical, and emotional well-being.

The telecommunication systems will provide easy access to political meetings in the city; lectures at the community college; services at church or the synagogue; tours at the museums; and shopping at supermarkets and department stores. Machines will be available to speed up unpleasant chores of maintenance.

As a result of their willingness and ability to adapt, some older people will be able to maintain a high standard of living. They will be able to spend less time at daily chores and more of their time in activities that are fun and enrich life.

For instance, shopping at the supermarket or having medical check-ups at the hospital may be handled through a television at home. Taking care of material needs easily with the tools of modern technology, older people will have more time for leisure interests and fulfilling activities, such as meeting with friends, reading, or working on service projects in the community.

With friends.

Older people with strong personal skills that help them deal with the normal concerns of daily life will be able to adjust easily to the continuous changes in lifestyle that are suggested by the dreams and plans of scientists today. Older people who are able and willing to learn about new technology may use telephones that have adjustments for hearing and vision difficulties. For people who are eager to adapt to new technologies, electronic memory systems will make it easier for them to contact family members, friends, and emergency services.

Those people who enjoy the security of sameness may not welcome a new style of living. They may not be interested in thinking about a new idea, trying out a new garden tool, or a new food product. They may feel uncomfortable with new gimmicks. They may not want new machines invading the familiar furnishings of their homes. They may not wish to visit friends through the use of their television in the family room.

No new gimmicks.

They may choose to ignore change. Their choices to follow established, familiar ways may delay or decrease the opportunities to choose more enjoyable activities in their lives. They will not have access to resources that will lighten the hard labors of daily life, such as home maintenance and repair. As a result, they may be less comfortable and less satisfied in their lifestyles.

Tele-Tools

The communication system within society affects the development of its members. Using freedom of expression in an intelligent, assertive manner, the people may organize themselves more easily with modern "tele-tools," any of the new machines that improve communication over a distance. The better organization may result in social action that corrects social problems and improves the standard of living. Use of the mass media may help to connect a large social movement made up of people who are spread out geographically.

People are used to telephone conversations. They are accustomed to speaking to a person they do not see. Yet, after the conversation, they feel as if they have been together in the same room.

For example, they use the telephone to make appointments and keep in touch with family members. A person may talk with a real estate agent using a person-machine-person method of contact about the description of a home for sale, the costs, and the neighborhood setting. Other people use the same method of contact to visit with friends they have not seen for years.

Not distracted by the presence of the other person in the conversation, some business people prefer to negotiate contracts and settle conflicts on the telephone. In 1982 Muson studied behavior on the telephone and reported several interesting findings.

Muson noted that the telephone seems to have many advantages for some people. They work less efficiently in a face-to-face encounter. On the telephone, they seem less easily deceived and are able to convince other people more effectively.

People who express themselves with hand gestures are often frustrated by the inability of the telephone to carry the messages of the hand movements and facial expressions. People may use a tele-tool called the videophone to enrich their words with body actions that add to the spoken message.

The videophone, a telephone with a television screen, is an innovation in telecommunications that allows people to see each other while they are talking. It is used a great deal in the teleconference. The people arrange to use special equipment for a few hours in a local office. The teleconference allows people who are separated by great distances to stay in their home communities and meet together briefly to discuss important issues.

The videotex is another tele-tool. The videotex uses the telephone and the television together to provide printed information on the television screen. When a person places a telephone call to a business or service agency, the person is provided with information and pictures on the television screen. The consumer may shop at a supermarket, update a checking account, or read the news and weather report from home with the use of the videotex.

In looking at and making decisions about political issues, home viewers may use the television screen to observe closely the administrators of their communities. Currently, the standard television set in the homes of most average Americans is, in fact, a one-way video, telecommunication system.

Technology has introduced two-way television sets. Two-way sets are used primarily in the business world. They improve the security system in a bank. They improve health services in hospitals and clinics. The videophone, mentioned before, is a two-way unit that is used often for small business meetings.

The popularity of the two-way sets is spreading rapidly. In a few years, this type of two-way television communication will be more commonly available in the average home. Then the elderly will be able to participate directly in decision-making and the design of new policies at political meetings. Even people who are confined to bed may participate in the political decisions of their community. In this way, the experience of the older generations may contribute some direction to the development of the country.

For example, the silver-haired legislators may be able to receive input from citizens who are able to visit their planning sessions. The tele-technology of today permits messages to be carried into almost every home. In the comfort of their homes, people may be able to visit the local city and state legislative sessions. As members of the viewing audience, they may be able to respond to questions or to debate issues through their home telephones.

Participating.

When communication is closed, older people feel ignored. They lose their sense of value as contributors to the growth of the community. Instead of channels of communication being blocked between people and groups, the video screen opens channels into the living rooms of everyone. Then older people may continue to be productive contributors to society.

People may be able to observe, discuss, and contribute back to the leaders and the decision-makers of their organizations and communities. This type of feedback allows true grass-roots involvement to become a reality in the United States.

Telecommunications has made important strides in the areas of emergency care and security alerts. Receptors on a person's clothing, on a wheelchair, or in a home may be triggered by the voice of a person. The voice of the person works as a starter or key to unlock the system.

Using these kinds of receptors, older people who are in danger because of a health crisis, fire at home, burglary, or other emergency may request help quickly as long as they can talk. The special units for home security relay the request for help to security guards, the neighborhood fire station, the emergency health care team, or the community hospital.

When they receive the call, the emergency health care team comes quickly. Meanwhile, at the hospital, a machine quickly prints out a summary of the health status and special considerations of the individual. The older person who communicates well will benefit a great deal from the help of such systems.

Radio Pagers

Three developments are occurring today in radio pagers or beepers, as they are commonly known. Satellite systems, the first development, have provided the resources to develop nationwide paging. In other words, a person wearing a beeper may be reached anywhere in the country. Previously, persons wearing a beeper had to stay within the range of the tower that transmitted the messages.

The second development is the ability of radio pagers to show brief, oral messages and to print out written messages. Thus, the user may receive brief instructions that may consist of a few words and a diagram. This machine is a direct application of the saying, "a picture is worth a thousand words." A picture with words seems easier to follow than a message that consists of only printed words.

The third development in radio pagers concerns costs. As with most new technology, after the product has been marketed awhile, it is refined. Gradually, it becomes an improved, less expensive model. Not only are the "bugs" or errors worked out, but better methods of manufacturing reduce production costs.

For example, the cost of the first hand-calculators were sold to the average American consumer for $200 to $300. Three years later, they were available for about $25 and less. Current costs of radio pagers range from $150 to $300. Manufacturers predict that the costs will soon drop below $100.

Older people may like to take advantage of this type of one-way communication. Having the ability to speak in sure, confident words that communicate clearly, but briefly, the older person may use a radio pager that has voice sensitivity. This type of pager may be used to maintain a security system while the older person travels.

While vacationing throughout the country, the individual may travel almost anywhere. If someone wants to contact the traveler or if older travelers want to relay a message to a family member 3000 miles away, they may do it spontaneously. They will not have to wait until they find a telephone.

The national pager provides greater flexibility to security guards. They do not have to stay near an office or an automobile unit to be available for a call. The call is transmitted to them wherever they are located. An older person living in an independent home unit may use the pager to check in at prearranged times to confirm that "all is well." A check-in desk in the station of a security guard or the community police may be part of the telecommunications check for the general well-being of a neighborhood or village.

Thus, the older person with strengths in communication and assertiveness will be able to take advantage of many new tools to enhance the general quality of their lifestyle.

All is well.

ASSERTIVE COMMUNICATION FOR FULL LIVING

Practicing communication skills and selective assertiveness, older people may be more in charge of the direction of their lives. They will be able to participate actively in the decisions that affect their lives. The physicians who are concerned about physical wellness, the mental health professionals who are concerned with emotional wellness, the nutritionists who are concerned about health care through a good diet, the physical educators who are concerned about good mobility through exercise, etc., are all members of the health care team.

The most important member of the wellness team is the individual, the patient. The professionals on the team may serve the older population better when the older patients assert their rights to become, and are accepted as, members of the working team.

Wellness team.

Aging Americans should understand and try to adapt to changing technology. The increased reliance of society on machines frightens many. For those who adapt, however, there exists the potential for better comfort and easier access to resources.

The older person who communicates effectively is able to get in touch with feelings and needs below the surface of the manifested health problem. A person with good communication skills may control the amount of self-disclosure in counseling. The skills may be used to negotiate an individual treatment plan with the physician.

The nutritionist may listen to the asserter who insists clearly that foods must meet cultural requirements, budget allowances, personal tastes, as well as contain a high quality level of food value. The assertive older person may suggest to the physical education instructor some activities that complement the normal, daily routine of activities rather than add a new routine of strange exercises to well-established patterns of living.

As a result of assertive efforts, the older communicator may feel more in charge of interactions with others. Feeling in charge contributes to the ability of this person to continue a lifestyle of independence and self-sufficiency. Most older people state firmly: "I want to take care of myself." "I do not want to be a burden to anyone."

I do not want to be a burden to anyone.

I want to take care of myself.

Independence and self-sufficiency are the goals of most older people. These goals enhance their self-respect and feelings of significance. Stereotypes of the past begin to disappear. As they continue to age and change, older people can realize their potential in different ways. The following chapters in this book are an attempt to help older people develop some skills to help them realize all of their potential.

SUMMARY

The United States is now in the Communications Era. New technology has made life more comfortable for many. Older people who are willing to adapt to the changes may take care of their tasks easily with the "tele-tools" that are being made available. They will have more free time for fulfilling activities that lead to satisfaction in life. However, people must have good skills in communication and assertion to be able to take advantage of the technology that will enhance the activities in their daily living.

Suggestions for Further Reading

ARTIFICIAL INTELLIGENCE
Christiansen, J. (January, 1984). Grace Hopper boosts computers far and wide. *The Institute,* 8(1), 16.
Press, F. (1983). Commercializing new knowledge. *Educational Horizons,* 62(1), 3–4.

COMMUNICATION SKILLS
Wingate, A. (1983). Communicating with business. *Educational Horizons,* 62(1), 15–17.

DEMOGRAPHICS ON AGING
Kaasa, O. J. (April-May, 1982). What two years have meant to me. *Modern Maturity,* 25(2), 4.

ECONOMIC CONCERNS
Brickfield, C. F. (April-May, 1982). New federalism: Its promise and its dangers. *Modern Maturity,* 25(2), 4–5.
Schulz, D. (1980). *The Economics of Aging.* Belmont, CA: Wadsworth.

HOLISTIC HEALTH

Romano, J. L. (April, 1982). Biofeedback training and therapeutic gains: Clinical impressions. *The Personnel and Guidance Journal,* 60(8), 473–475.

Selye, H. (1976). *The Stress of Life* (Rev. ed.). New York: McGraw-Hill.

QUALITY OF LIFE FOR OLDER PERSONS

Brickfield, C. F. (April-May, 1982). New federalism: Its promise and its dangers. *Modern Maturity,* 25(2), 4–5.

Hughes, P. W. (April-May, 1982). How AARP will protect older Americans' rights. *Modern Maturity,* 25(2), 5.

Peterson, G. W., & Burck, H. D. (1982). A competency approach to accountability in human service programs. *The Personnel and Guidance Journal,* 60(8), 491–495.

TELE-COMMUNICATIONS

Gainesville Sun. (July 18, 1982). Soon the country will be pagerized. 107(12), 18F.

Iacobuzio, T. (1982). All alone by the high-tech phone. *Psychology Today,* 16(4), 46–47.

Muson, H. (1982). Getting the phone's number. *Psychology Today,* 16(4), 42–49.

9

Communication

To participate in relationships effectively and to develop a sense of belonging, people need solid communication skills. Learning assertive communication skills will help people to build a system of behavior that will lead to rewarding, fulfilling relationships.

The level of skill development in communication determines the level of quality that is developed in relationships. A lack of development in communication skills leads to misunderstanding. Frequent misunderstanding leads to distrust. Continued distrust fractures relationships.

Effective communication skills are necessary to resolve relationship difficulties. Individuals may learn how to be open and direct with each other. They may learn how to disagree in an agreeable manner. By explaining their viewpoints carefully and discussing their differences openly, people can come to a point of understanding. They can learn to respect each other. They will begin to accept their own and each other's individuality. A high level of quality interaction will lead to a high level of quality in relationships.

WHAT IS COMMUNICATION?

Communication is the exchange of information between people. It is the way in which people make contact with each other. Words, body movements, and hidden meanings are important parts of communication. Developing listening skills and understanding different types of communication help people to receive and transmit accurate information. In a general sense, communication includes all the methods by which the mind of one person is affected by the mind of another person.

The process of communication may include obvious behavior that points out a frank, clear message. An example of this is a traffic officer who blows a whistle, uses hand signals, and speaks out frequently to urge approaching drivers to bring their cars to a stop. The traffic officer is using different, direct signals to give a message to drivers. Hopefully, the drivers understand readily what is being communicated.

On the other hand, communication may involve subtle behavior that transmits a hidden message. For example, a guest stifling a yawn may be trying to hide his boredom and fatigue from an eager, talkative host. The guest is trying to act appreciative and interested. The host is trying to act hospitable and interesting. Neither person is communicating accurate messages to each other. Consequently, they will probably maintain a superficial relationship during their interaction. They are sending some messages to each other and hiding other messages. Deep, direct communication is being avoided.

People spend a large portion of their lives trying to communicate with each other. Some people estimate that 60 percent of the day is spent in communication, only 9 percent of which is spoken words. In other words, about 50 percent of communication is nonverbal.

Nonverbal communication involves body movements and concealed messages. The careful observer of a speaker's body movements, attitude, and hidden message will gain much more information from the speaker than the person who pays attention only to the words of the speaker. Nonverbal communication will be discussed later in this chapter.

Communication skills are very important in relationships. Transferring and receiving accurate messages from others communicates the needs and wants of a person in an effective way. Honest expectations and trust are created in the relationship.

This open type of interaction identifies and deals with problems. It builds relationships to a higher level. It leads to social support among family members and friends. Open communication enhances opportunities, such as meeting challenges in one's job or in relationships.

Not communicating, on the other hand, leads to misunderstanding and frustration. Not exchanging genuine messages may result in feelings of hurt and anger. One may be inclined to back off from the relationship. Sometimes older people feel a sense of helplessness and begin to avoid others when they sense that their attempts to communicate are patronized or ignored.

In 1981 Sobel did some research among the elderly in Britain and learned about their great frustrations in communicating. The professional staff and skilled helpers who worked with the elderly often ignored the messages of the older patients or clients and tried to quiet their fussy behavior.

Sometimes such frustration motivates older persons to assume the role of complainer. If that behavior is unsuccessful in gaining attention or help, there are other behaviors, such as not cooperating with routines—perhaps refusing to take a daily dose of medication. Sometimes their continued frustration results in their becoming the "sad one" or, often enough, the silent, withdrawn one.

Communication skills help people exert control over what they want to do. For example, a person, who must get around in a chair, may regulate life better by cooking on lowered kitchen counters, studying for a new job, and learning new team sports. As the ability to regulate normal, daily activities improves, the person feels more confident. A sense of adjustment, positive coping, and capability is experienced. The person, not the wheelchair, becomes in charge of the direction of life.

In the same way, people who are "too shy" to become involved with others should learn new ways of handling situations in their lives. They may learn different ways of putting together words. Changing the settings of activities may help them to feel more comfortable. They can learn how to change some of their body behavior when they are with other people. The changes will help them to be effective in getting across accurate messages to other people. As their ability to communicate improves, they will feel better in situations with others. They, not the shyness, will be in charge of their lives.

Changing levels of confidence often trigger the willingness for people to look at other areas that may be developed in their lives. They are ready to begin changing behavior in some of those other areas. An undeveloped area of skill or a hidden dream may be the next target of change.

For example, Settie, an older woman, has completed a series of continuing education classes in communication skills at the local junior college. Rather shy, she has been encouraged by classmates to sign up for a booth at the annual community arts festival to display her string art. Her classmates helped her to rehearse some of the situations she might face during the arts festival. She painted her booth table her favorite color.

During the "big day" she spoke clearly and comfortably to many strangers. She exchanged ideas with interesting folks. She was cheered occasionally by warm responses from some of her friends who attended the arts festival. By the end of the day, she decided she would act upon the wishes expressed by some of her friends. She would teach her craft in short, morning classes at the neighborhood recreation center.

Settie "wows them" at the festival.

Settie's increased skill in communication boosted her confidence. She took advantage of new opportunities. She developed new relationships and enhanced former ones. Further, she acted on her long-time dream of teaching.

Now she feels confident about standing up and speaking in front of others. Her sense of self-determination and independence are becoming stronger. With the extra income, she may fulfill another dream.

She has wanted to travel for a long time. Now she can start a special savings account for a trip. She would like to take a vacation tour of the American cities she has read so much about in history and travel books. At any rate, she is pleased about directing her own life, personal growth, and development.

WORDS

When people communicate, they tend to concentrate on the words that are spoken. Oral language, therefore, becomes an important part of communication. The people who are more adept at communication skills may use specific words to be straightforward and unpretentious. They may speak with fewer euphemisms and be more direct.

People should be aware of the vocabulary of the individuals with whom they work. The words of different groups of people often have different meanings in different parts of the country. Sometimes within one city, common ways of putting words together may vary from one neighborhood to the next.

The use of "y'all" in the southern United States is an example of combining words in a way that differs from other regions of the country. "Y'all," a contraction of "you all," refers to one or more people when it is used in the South. It is considered to be a warm, gracious way of addressing someone, such as in the statement, "Y'all come back now, y'hear." However, in the North, East, or West, y'all is considered to be poor grammar, a redundant phrase, and it is rarely used.

Language changes as the sociocultural aspects of civilization undergo change. The gerontologist should be aware of the words in the vocabulary of the elderly that have meanings reflecting their past decades of experiences. It is the responsibility of the gerontologist to maintain a vocabulary that is relevant to the older population.

Listening to the favorite radio and television programs of the elderly is a good way to learn their current vocabulary and special jargon. Soap operas and advertisements provide a good source of their current language. In addition, the gerontologist may use examples of program situations to help explain ideas or principles about healthy lifestyles. Integrating new information into what the elderly already know improves their comprehension and acceptance of the material.

It is a bit harder for the gerontologist to learn words that may no longer be part of the popular, everyday language. One way to learn them is by reading older literature. Another way is to listen to the stories of older persons. As the stories unfold, the gerontologist will discover a wealth of words and phrases that impact communication for the elderly. Also, the stories hold great entertainment for the listener. It is the experience of the author that older adults share readily when asked about the special meanings of vocabulary in their history.

For example, "heavy groceries," a term used commonly in the 1800s, now are called staples. Staples are items such as flour, sugar, and salt that are regularly stocked in one's home, but are not food items that may be grown in a garden.

In the early 1900s, the heavy groceries were stored in the larder. This area of the house was known later as the "pantry" or "butler's pantry." Many children today do not know the meaning of the word pantry. Today few (new) homes have such a room to store food and household supplies. Now a few shelves or cabinets in the kitchen area are supposed to take care of storage needs.

Awareness of the meaning of words used by other people facilitates the flow of accurate messages between people. It is important that older persons as well as gerontologists pay attention to special vocabulary. They should be alert to the confusion of the listener and be willing to clear up misunderstandings by filling in the gaps of information. Also, they should be willing to ask about unfamiliar terms in order to clear up their own confusion. Communication with older persons is enriched when all the parties involved understand the history of puzzling situations and words.

TRILEVEL COMMUNICATION

Communication occurs at different levels of sensory awareness. Some communication is verbal and some is nonverbal. Wrong messages or miscommunication results when one person does not pay attention to the way another person is speaking. There may be no awareness of the body movements associated with the spoken words. Thus, important information that would add to the spoken message is lost. To be in tune with the whole message, a listener should be skilled in trilevel communication.

The verbal message includes written and oral communication. As stated before, only the oral message is explored in this book. The oral message, what is actually spoken, is an important part of the information that is expressed. News and other topics may be communicated through the spoken word. Also, interest, sincerity, concern, love, disagreement, anger, and many other feelings may be transmitted through words.

In addition to the words that are heard, two kinds of nonverbal messages may be part of the information that travels from one person to another. Nonverbal language involves (1) body language and (2) the undercurrent language, often called the hidden message.

Body language or kinesics includes the body movements that accompany the oral message. Body language components enhance the communication. They provide additional information. The behavioral movements may confirm or be in conflict with the oral message.

By observing eye contact, a person may pick up extra information. Busy arm gestures may add excitement to the message. Or, they may indicate an attack. Watching body actions provides the careful observer with essential, accurate information.

The third level of communication involves the hidden meaning. Sometimes it is known as the concealed message or the undercurrent language. Through experience, one may pick up a "sixth sense" of what the speaker is trying to convey or conceal. In a way, the hidden message is felt. The hidden message may involve feelings or content. Hidden meanings are important to communication.

It is possible, though not easy, for people to receive and transmit clear messages on the three levels of communication. Just as the runner works hard to build up enough skill to try the 26-mile Boston Marathon, this level of skilled communication requires a great deal of work from the individual.

Specific techniques that enhance communication must be learned and practiced until the skills become part of the regular behavior style of the individual. For most people, achieving such a mature level of communication requires many months of effort, but hard work can result in small noticeable changes within just a few days.

Again this process can be compared to the development of the long distance runner. Daily workouts show a steady build up of strength and endurance. Gradually, short runs increase to longer runs until the distance is achieved. Gradually, occasional moments of clear messages increase to long intervals of effective communication. Understanding the types of communication and then practicing the techniques on the following pages can help a person begin the transformation of becoming a mature, effective communicator.

TYPES OF COMMUNICATION

Knowing the type and purpose of the communication may help the listener. Communication may be categorized into two major groups, informal or formal. An informal style of communication is a conversation that is light, such as small talk. Formal communication may be persuasive, informative, cathartic, or therapeutic. Each of these types of communication will be discussed in more detail in the following paragraphs.

Formal and Informal Communication

Informal communication is loose, unstructured, and casual. It involves the SOCIAL, LIGHT types of communication. Some examples are chatting on a telephone or in the ticket line of a theater. The listening is relaxed.

Formal communication is structured and goal-oriented. It involves the PERSUASIVE, INFORMATIVE, CATHARTIC, AND THERAPEUTIC methods of communication. Some examples are a public lecture (informative), a visit with an insurance salesperson (persuasive), telling a friend about the death of a spouse (cathartic), and a self-improvement group meeting (therapeutic). The listener should be alert to the oral and body language of the speaker in formal communication. Listening to hidden messages is important with PERSUASIVE and essential with CATHARTIC and THERAPEUTIC types of communication.

Being aware of the type of conversation or communication helps a person to determine the level of listening that is appropriate for the situation. Practicing good listening enables people to share genuinely in each other's lives.

SOCIAL OR LIGHT COMMUNICATION, SMALL TALK

Small talk is the friendly exchange of personal or impersonal information. Social conversation usually involves superficial, passing remarks. It may be light chatter, a courteous exchange of words, or brief comments to pass the time.

The interaction allows people to become acquainted and relax. It helps people to feel more free, less tense, and less restrained. It is a way to help people feel comfortable.

The style of listening is easy, relaxed, moderately active, not too intense. Generally, it is acceptable if only a small amount of the information under discussion is remembered afterward.

For example: telling jokes or short stories, daily greetings, casual party banter, discussing the weather, commenting on the immediate surroundings.

Light communication is one of the different levels of social interaction important to the psychological method of treatment called Reality Therapy. Reality Therapy was developed by David Glasser to help juvenile delinquents learn to act in ways that are more successful in society. This method has worked with other groups of people as well.

Reality Therapy increases skills that are important in the development of relationships. It is an approach used by many mental health counselors in working with people who are seeking help to understand and deal with their emotional problems. The social interaction seems to help a person to focus less on oneself, begin to think about someone else, and start up a relationship.

PERSUASIVE COMMUNICATION

Using persuasion, the speaker tries to influence others with urging, coaxing statements. The messages advise and direct the listener into specific activities. The words of the speaker are intense and convincing. The speaker seems to be absolutely correct and trustworthy.

The goal of the interaction is to produce action in the listener. The speaker is trying to convince the listener, or to change the mind, attitude, belief, or behavior of the listener. The speaker provides all the information to the listener. Typically, the speaker is active and emotional while the listener remains passive and quiet.

The style of listening may be attentive or inattentive. The listener may be in tune fully to the speaker. The listener may be captivated by what is being said. On the other hand, the listener may be turned off, not listening at all.

For example: "I want to sell you a car!" "You must have this . . . ," "You should . . . ," or "Why don't you . . ." statements.

"I want to sell you a car!"

INFORMATIVE COMMUNICATION

The speaker provides information about a person, place, object, or subject to the listener. Informative communication gives more knowledge to the listener. The information may involve an in-depth, lengthy explanation. It may include much detail, such as charts or lists. Or, the information may be brief and to the point.

The goal of the interaction is to give some knowledge or to share ideas with other people.

The style of listening is somewhat "active." The listener pays attention to the words and body language of the speaker. The listener makes an effort to retain the extra details that are being provided.

For example: describing the places visited during a recent trip to China, explaining the personal meaning of a poem, discussing specific facts about a research project, or talking about the details of a recipe.

CATHARTIC COMMUNICATION

Catharsis involves emotion-filled, intense communication. The words are spoken with sincerity. The period of time involved in the talking is usually long. It involves the deep sharing of experiences. The goal of the interaction is to allow some release of emotional pressure from feelings that have built up recently or over a long span of time. After a period of cathartic communication, the speaker feels a cleansing or emptying effect.

The style of listening is "active" with great attention to all three levels of communication, spoken words, body actions, and hidden messages. Both people involved are alert and in tune to the interaction.

For example: sharing feelings of anxiety, grief, painful memories, great happiness, or injury from an accident.

THERAPEUTIC COMMUNICATION

Usually therapeutic communication develops to a deep level. It involves the discussion of sensitive concerns and deep feelings. This type of communication usually occurs under the guidance of trained helpers. They are usually professional people, such as a mental health counselor, nurse, psychiatrist, psychologist, or social worker. They have some education, training, and experience in using this type of communication. Typically, in therapeutic communication the trained helper does more listening and the person who wants help does more talking.

Sometimes people feel burdened by stress. They may have a great deal of difficulty and function poorly in handling personal situations. A total physical-psychological examination will help to determine the amount of professional help that is needed. Some serious events or symptoms that show a strong need for therapeutic communication include:

1. Little awareness of the sense of oneself as an individual who is separate from other human beings.
2. A sudden change in relationships. The relationship may be under the stress of a serious misunderstanding or be broken off altogether.
3. Confused, disoriented, or fragmented thinking. The thinking seems to be mixed up. The ideas do not make sense in the regular way of thinking.
4. Memory loss.
5. Word scrambling or word salad. Words are put together in ways that do not make sense in the standard way that the language is spoken.

When people reach the point of feeling overwhelmed or unable to cope, they may benefit from the help of therapeutic communication. Talking and listening, the professional helper may uncover more information from the person in distress as well as from involved loved ones.

The professional helper will probably (1) ask for more information about specific concerns of the client; (2) evaluate what is needed by the client; (3) work with the client and a physician, when appropriate, to think out and to plan ways to improve the situation of stress in the life of the client; (4) help the client develop awareness and understanding; (5) encourage the client to continue behavior that deals with problems; (6) evaluate together with the client and the family of the client the ongoing progress of therapy; and (7) help the client lead a self-sufficient and independent lifestyle.

Therapeutic communication may involve working on simple, basic needs, such as is done with Reality Orientation. It should be pointed out that Reality Orientation is different from Reality Therapy, developed by Glasser.

In Reality Therapy, the professional person helps the client to accept the responsibility of caring for the personal needs of love and self-worth without depriving or hurting other people. A contract is often drawn up between the professional person and the client about goals and deadlines for changing behavior.

In Reality Orientation the professional helper talks in simple phrases that orient the person to his or her name, the time of day, the weather, and the immediate surroundings. The client is encouraged to focus on current circumstances. The communication involves the practice of simple words, memory activities, and repeating the basic information that orients the client to time, place, and activities.

Generally, Reality Orientation is practiced in an institution, such as a hospital or nursing home, because often a change in surroundings as a result of illness may be confusing to a patient. This confusion may be especially true of an older person, who may have slept in the same bedroom for over 50 years. Awakening briefly in the middle of the night in a strange room or hearing different sounds in a new environment, a person may become confused.

The goal of therapeutic communication may involve the development of the senses of sight, smell, taste, hearing, and touch. Older people who are institutionalized in order to receive health care may benefit from a therapeutic approach that stimulates all of the physical senses.

Some therapeutic approaches that are recommended for older persons are:

1. Increase time spent near or facing the activity of others, such as sitting with other people and other things, maybe even being with small pet.
2. Music therapy, such as listening to, humming with, or exercising to music.
3. Touch therapy, such as touching fabrics, woven reeds, the rough and smooth surfaces of foods, the hands of other people.
4. Exercise classes, such as chair exercises, relaxation techniques, and breathing exercises.
5. Describing foods and the preparation of foods, remembering odors, textures, and hand actions that were done in job or sports activities.
6. Going outdoors and experiencing the elements, such as the feel of sunshine or the sound and smell of rain.

The goal of therapeutic interaction is the improved well-being of the older person in need of help. The goals of the therapeutic relationship differ from the goals of friendship. The goals of friends are to continue to spend time together, to support and care for each other, and to know each other in deeper ways.

The goal of a therapeutic relationship is the eventual separation of the professional person and the client. The professional tries to help the client develop awareness, understanding, and self-respect. Then, the professional helps the client move in a direction that will help the client deal with issues in order to develop a more satisfying, independent lifestyle.

The therapeutic helper is reminded of the importance of acting as:

1. A caring person.
2. A listener.
3. A reflector of feelings.
4. An observer of hidden or subtle messages.
5. Someone who is willing to share one's personal self in an appropriate way.
6. A helper who is able to explore intimate, emotional issues.

LISTENING

Listening involves paying close attention to the messages of other people. Careful listening enables a person to be as close as possible to the meaning intended by the speaker. Each person has a different way of looking at a situation. The subjective view differs from person to person. It is important for people to overlap listening with the understanding of each other's messages. They should pay attention to what is being transmitted to them by other human beings.

When there is so much to be gained by really listening, why do people "half listen" to each other? Why do they continue to misunderstand, accuse, attack, anger, and hurt each other?

According to Dr. Lyman K. Steil at the University of Minnesota, studies show that the time spent in listening is high, but the levels of understanding are low. Test results show that after hearing a 10 minute presentation, the average listener keeps in 50 percent of what was said. Within two days the amount of information that is remembered drops to 25 percent.

Dr. Steil felt that "active listening" would improve listening skills and the ability to remember information. Paying "active" attention involves being aware of the words and body language of the speaker. Next, the listener should clarify or interpret what was heard.

Asking for feedback, the listener may use statements such as, "I think I heard you say . . ." OR "Did you mean to indicate. . . ." Then the speaker may confirm or make the original message clear for the benefit of the listener.

Attending.

ATTENDING

Attending is an important communication skill. It means really paying attention to what someone else is saying. It is a highly developed level of listening. Attending is alert and intense, a high level of "active" listening. A person may indicate attending behavior through two means (1) the environment and (2) personal actions.

The environment is the place or location of the interaction. The place may be the setting of a room, a central patio, or a bench outdoors in the backyard. Wherever the interaction occurs, a person may arrange the setting to let the speaker know that attention is being concentrated on the message of the speaker. When the setting is quiet, comfortable, and restful, then the setting contributes to the focus of other people onto the speaker.

Personal behavior is even more important in attending. By leaning forward a bit, by looking at the speaker, and by showing patience, respect, and open-mindedness about what is being said, the listener shows that she or he is paying attention.

She is involved with what the speaker is saying. Or, she is open-minded about what is being said. She continues to be alert to more information about the subject before making a decision.

He is not side-tracked by personal feelings and opinions. He concentrates on the information being given. He is in tune with the feelings of the speaker.

The next discussion exercise, ATTENDING TO YOU, helps the reader practice behaviors that indicate good listening skills.

DISCUSSION EXERCISE

Attending to You

DIRECTIONS FOR THE LEARNER: The class is divided into small groups of 4 to 6 members each.

STEP I: Each group talks for about 5 minutes about the various roles of people, in general, when the people are involved in any kind of group. Some examples of roles include leader, follower, questionner, caretaker, starter, and helpless. Roles are discussed at length in the previous chapter and may provide a good reference to stimulate discussion.

Try to think of other roles as the group develops its conversation. Write down some of the roles you observed in the space provided below.

STEP II: Each person stays in the small group, but writes down individually some words or phrases that most typically describe their role in a group. This will be shared within your small group as part of Step III.

It may be helpful to think for a moment about your behavior during the general discussion of Step I. In what ways was your behavior typical of how you perform in groups? In what ways did it differ? Take about 10 minutes to think about and write down in the following space some words or phrases that describe your behavior.

STEP III: Each individual, in turn, takes a few minutes to share the self-report with other members of the small group. While each individual is sharing personal information, the others are practicing attending to the speaker.

STEP IV: After everyone has shared the self-report, each group discusses the following questions.

1. While you were talking about yourself in front of other members of your group, what behaviors did you see that indicated people were listening to you?

2. What was the difference between the way people listened in Step I and Step III of this exercise?

3. *What did you experience when you attended to others? What did you experience when others attended to you?*

4. *How did it feel to have others concentrate their attention on you when you spoke?*

DIRECTIONS FOR THE LEADER: This exercise relies on interaction; therefore, it works better in a group. The purpose of the activity is to practice deep listening or attending behavior.

It is important for people to practice listening behaviors. When people experience (1) listening to others and then (2) being heard, they begin to understand the higher level of concentration needed to develop good attending skills.

Attending is hard work. It uses up a great deal of energy. After attending for a while, the individual should relax for a while. As in any physical exercise program, the participant should build up stamina and skills slowly. This slow build-up of skills applies to strengthening communication skills, also.

It takes about 30 minutes to complete this exercise.

MULTIPLE ATTENDING

Multiple attending focuses on a group of people as a unit. It moves from a single, one-to-one focus to a more general, overall focus. No longer is attention only on one individual. The leader is paying attention to the group which involves a total system. The leader is taking in more information at one time. The wider, group focus allows a quick assessment of each group member as well as the group as a whole unit.

Multiple attending involves skills in scanning and fluency in trilevel communication. The multiple attender should be able to involve everyone, develop group cohesiveness, and keep the group moving. It takes quite a bit of energy, discipline, and practice to maintain the concentration necessary to do multiple attending. It is appropriate to use for a casual conversation of two or three people or for a speech in front of an audience of 200 people. Working with larger groups, of course, requires a much higher level of skill than working with smaller groups.

Scanning is an important aspect of multiple attending. As one's eyes move across the group of people in a scan, one may compare differences within the group. The scanning registers the different behaviors and communications from group members. Observing a group of older people, the leader may observe that some people are bored or even asleep. Others may be frustrated, angry, eager to contribute, daydreaming, or withdrawn from all interaction.

Taking the group into account, the scanner may decide to change the pace of the presentation. The needs of group members may be accommodated by a livelier pace, an occasional "pregnant pause," or a five minute break for people to stretch out their legs and refresh themselves.

Scanning.

A person may begin multiple attending by becoming aware of the group system and by extending the scope of vision to include more than one group member at a time. To keep in tune with the attitude and behavior of the group, the leader should try to be aware of immediate activity.

It may help the leader to think in terms of the group process. In other words, what is the process that is occurring in the group? What is happening right now in the group? Are people listening to me? How are people feeling right now about what I am saying?

It may be helpful for the leader to stop talking for a while and ask the group members to discuss their immediate feelings. This kind of information from the group will help the speaker stay in tune with the group. In addition, the feedback will help the group members become more aware of their own feelings and more attentive to the speaker.

There are ways to increase one's ability to scan a group. A person may build up the number of people that are looked at within each glance. In a systematic way, the individual learns to observe more people at a time.

A person should first glance at one participant, then the next second, then the next, etc., until everyone has been scanned.

Scanning one.

Then the eyes of the leader move around in the group circle taking in two persons at a time.

Scanning two.

Then the scanner glances at three persons at a time.

Scanning three.

Some people scan in a circular pattern. Others use a back and forth motion that resembles the smooth swing of a pendulum.

With practice a person may learn to scan smoothly and quickly. Then the person is able to be alert to the behavior of a large group of people. Thus, a sensitive speaker may provide more accurate and more meaningful communication to large numbers of people.

For example, while teaching a class on home safety and security to 20 older people, Mrs. Kerin, the leader tries to practice multiple attending. She notices that two small clusters of people are commenting about something among themselves. She stops her speech and asks the group if they have any questions about what she is saying.

When no one responds to Mrs. Kerin's question, she asks people, "Right now, what are you feeling? What are you feeling as we talk about fixing the locks on windows and doors?"

One couple, Mr. and Mrs. Care, begin to tell about their fears during a recent robbery of their home. They were attacked and beaten. Their television and coffee-maker were stolen. Though not worth much, they could not replace them until all the hospital bills were paid. Their fear was overwhelming. They could not listen to anymore information about home safety because their memories and feelings were taking up all their attention.

A quick scan of the group notifies Mrs. Kerin that everyone is paying attention to the words of the couple. Mrs. Kerin takes some time to explore the feelings of different group members. Then she decides to teach the class in a different way.

She decides to have people share their experiences and to use the experiences as problem situations. Then, she will apply her teaching materials to the specific situations brought up by the class members. Multiple attending kept her in touch with her listeners and improved her teaching approach to the group.

CLOSED AND OPEN QUESTIONS

Closed and open questions vary in their purposes. By knowing how to phrase a question, a person may gather limited or extensive information. The person may stay at a light, superficial level of conversation or may enter a deeper, more intimate level of personal sharing. By applying the appropriate question, one may obtain the desired results in the process of communication.

Closed questions require short and simple answers. They may be easily answered by one or two words, such as yes, no, or a specific detail of information.

For Example:
1. Are you happy?   Yes.
2. Do you live on that street?   No.
3. Will you pay the utility bill?   Yes.
4. What is your name?   Jan.

Since the answers are brief, not much interaction occurs between the people. Thus, the relationship stays on a superficial level. The closed question works well when a person wants a quick answer to a question. Using this technique, people may cover quite a few subjects in a short period of time.

The closed question is helpful also when people are trying to move away from a deep, more emotionally intimate and intense dialogue. They are trying to be less intense. They want to relax for a while with a more superficial, more distant type of exchange. This type of communication is helpful when a person wants to end a conversation or interaction.

Open questions, on the other hand, encourage more information to be given. Open questions usually begin with the words, HOW, WHAT, or WHY. Usually the responses contain a great deal of information although there is no guarantee that this kind of response will occur.

For Example:
1. What did you eat for dinner yesterday?
2. How did you change the flat tire?
3. In what ways does the noise bother you?

Responses that give a great deal of information usually result in a deeper level of interaction. Long, involved responses open up the relationship and help people to feel closer to each other. Often much free information is provided. In other words, more information is given than was actually asked for in the question.

As a result of open questions and responses, the interaction becomes more intimate and more intense. This type of question works well when a person wants to explore a situation in more depth or become better acquainted with a person. It also works well when a person is trying to move from a light-hearted, casual conversation to deeper, more serious talk.

A deeper level of conversation is important when one person is trying to learn more about another person or subject. In addition, it helps to extend an interaction over a longer period of time.

The following discussion exercise, CLOSED AND OPEN QUESTIONS, provides practice in converting closed questions to open questions and then converting open questions to closed questions.

DISCUSSION EXERCISE

Closed and Open Questions

DIRECTIONS ABOUT CLOSED QUESTIONS FOR THE LEARNER: Change the following closed questions into open questions. In each space provided below, write down your response as an open question.

1. **Are you ill?**

2. **Did you attend her party?**

3. **Has he found his eyeglasses?**

4. **Would you like to go fishing this weekend?**

5. **At what time did you arrive home last night?**

DIRECTIONS ABOUT OPEN QUESTIONS FOR THE LEARNER: Change the following open questions into closed questions. In each space provided below, write down your response as a closed question.

1. **How did you relax after your speech to the Victory Club yesterday?**

2. In what ways do you find work as a reader to the blind to be satisfying?

3. What are the dangers of going downtown to the drugstore after 6:00 P.M.?

4. How do you prepare yourself to deal with the cold weather of the winter season?

5. What kind of garden are you putting in this year?

DIRECTIONS FOR THE LEADER: This exercise works well when written out as an individual homework assignment that is discussed briefly in the next class meeting. The purpose of the exercise is to clarify the differences between open and closed questions.

The total class should discuss briefly the differences between open and closed questions. The following questions may help the discussion.

Which style of question seems to be easier for you to use? Which style of question is used more frequently in your personal style of talking, such as when you are with family members or friends? What kinds of opportunities do you have in your normal, daily schedule to use open questions? What kinds of opportunities do you have in your normal, daily schedule to use closed questions?

During the discussion of the results, participants should be aware of the trilevel communication that occurs among participants. Also, they should remember positive feedback for their peers.

This activity takes about 20 minutes to complete.

REQUESTS

When a request is involved, how does a person know what to say and what to do? In certain situations, it seems difficult for some people to let others know exactly what they want. It is often easy for such people to do something for others. It is easy for them to give a gift to others. On the contrary, sometimes it is hard for them to ask others for something. It is often difficult or embarrassing for them to make their own wishes known to other people.

For some people, it is hard to request a favor or action from people who are close friends or relatives. Some people feel comfortable approaching acquaintances, but have great difficulty asking something of a distant acquaintance or a total stranger. For others, it is more difficult to make requests to people in positions of authority, such as a supervisor or the boss.

When a person feels self-confident and has a good sense of self-esteem, it seems easier for them to request a favor from others. When a request invites other people to reach out, to help, or to share in an activity, it is probably appropriate. When the request puts an unreasonable demand and burden on others, when it is hurtful, or when it is irresponsible, it is probably inappropriate. At any rate, the popular saying holds true: "You cannot hurt just by asking."

When making a request, it is often helpful to:

1. KEEP THE REQUEST SIMPLE. It is better to ask for only one thing at a time. This makes the request seem like a simple task, less overwhelming to the person who is trying to respond to the request.

    For Example:
    DO REQUEST: Would you baby-sit my parakeet while I am on vacation?

    DO NOT DEMAND: Would you run some errands, water the lawn, call the refrigerator repair service, and feed and exercise my parakeet while I am on vacation?

2. GIVE A DEFINITE TIME. It is helpful to state a specific time. The person responding to the request will probably feel more comfortable helping with a task that involves a limited amount of time.

    For Example:
    DO REQUEST: Would you send a card to Paul tomorrow? He is recovering from surgery on his kneecap.
    DO NOT DEMAND: Would you make sure that you keep in touch with Paul everyday? He is in the hospital. I am not sure how long he will be there. He will need lots of cheering up. I am busy with too many other things, so I am depending on you to take care of things.

3. BE SPECIFIC. When people do not understand exactly what the request involves, they are less willing to be of help.

   For Example:
   DO REQUEST: Would you help me change the oil on the old Ford tomorrow afternoon?
   DO NOT DEMAND: You have got to help me! That car is such a problem and I cannot do all that without someone who really knows what to do.

4. OFFER CHOICES. Many people like to be given some alternatives from which to choose when they are asked to help someone else. Making a choice about the time, the brand, or the method of work allows the potential helper to feel more respect from the requester. It also allows the helper to think ahead to accommodate personal plans.

   For Example:
   DO REQUEST: Will you pick up the refill on my medicine at the pharmacy this afternoon or tomorrow sometime?
   DO NOT DEMAND: I need for you to pick up my medicine at the drugstore now. They called to tell me that it is ready and I have to take the next dose in 30 minutes. Get that for me now, will you?

5. ASK. DO NOT COMMAND. A request involves asking a person for help. It differs from a command, a nagging comment, or a complaint that a job needs to be done.

   For Example:
   DO REQUEST: Will you be willing to chair the next meeting? Our president and vice-president will be on vacation during that week.
   DO NOT DEMAND: You must chair the next meeting. We never ask you to do more than the rest of us and it is your turn.

6. ABOVE ALL, REMEMBER TO ADD *PLEASE* AND *THANK YOU* TO EVERY REQUEST.

The following discussion exercises, MAKING A REQUEST and REQUESTS, provide some opportunities for the reader to learn better the differences between appropriate and inappropriate requests.

DISCUSSION EXERCISE

Making a Request

DIRECTIONS FOR THE LEARNER: Break up into small groups of 4 to 6 members. Each small group works through the seven situations described below. Within each group, individuals take turns to discuss a specific situation.

Each individual reads aloud the information about the situation and then responds in each of the five ways to the situation. The five ways are (1) a demand, (2) a request, (3) a passive response, (4) an aggressive response, and (5) an assertive response.

As the five ways to respond are discussed, the participant should try to act out the feelings and behavior that would be shown in the different types of responses. In other words, the responses should be demonstrated. The participant should try to become involved in the style of each response. Exaggerating the feelings and body language of each type of response will make the role playing more dramatic. The over-acting will increase the effectiveness of communication in the five different categories.

After each participant role plays the situation and the responses, the other individuals provide feedback about the effectiveness of the communication. What behaviors were used in the different types of responses? Was it evident to the other group members which response was being practiced? What words or behaviors left a feeling of doubt or confusion about the type of response being role played?

Situations:

1. You are at a museum lecture with about 200 other people. The program is interesting, but you barely can see the slides shown on the screen at the side of the room. You think that others are having some problems seeing in the crowded room. What happens next?

    1. a demand:

    2. a request:

    3. a passive response:

    4. an aggressive response:

   5. an assertive response:

2. The barber has finished trimming your beard. He is pretty pleased with the job he has just done. In fact, the barber thinks the trim looks perfect. You think it needs to be shaped more. What happens next?

   1. a demand:

   2. a request:

   3. a passive response:

   4. an aggressive response:

   5. an assertive response:

3. You purchased some fresh fruits and vegetables on your way to the annual potluck luncheon for all the volunteers at the city recreation center. As you unwrap the grapes in the kitchen at the center, you discover that the whole bottom layer is over-ripe and not fit to serve. What happens next?

   1. a demand:

   2. a request:

   3. a passive response:

4. an aggressive response:

5. an assertive response:

4. One of your team members has been coming late to practice. This month she missed two important business meetings concerning the team schedule for next year. What happens next?

    1. a demand:

    2. a request:

    3. a passive response:

    4. an aggressive response:

    5. an assertive response:

5. Based on the student evaluation results, a teacher in your department is not giving fair tests and is passing back homework assignments too late. What happens next?

    1. a demand:

    2. a request:

3. a passive response:

4. an aggressive response:

5. an assertive response:

6. Through a friend, you sold your antique wall hanging to a photo business downtown for $350. They have the wall hanging and you are concerned about their final payment on the rest of the balance. After three months, they still owe you $75. What happens next?

    1. a demand:

    2. a request:

    3. a passive response:

    4. an aggressive response:

    5. an assertive response:

7. This is the second time you have not received a raise. You receive a pension from twenty years of service in the military, but you feel you should be earning more in your current job. You have been working 18 months without any increase in salary or benefits. What happens next?

    1. a demand:

    2. a request:

    3. a passive response:

    4. an aggressive response:

    5. an assertive response:

DIRECTIONS FOR THE LEADER: This exercise requires a group to provide feedback to individuals who are demonstrating specific behaviors. The purpose of the exercise is to provide some practice in different styles of behavior.

The participants should be coached and encouraged to overplay the feelings and body behavior of the different types of responses. Feedback to the players should be positive and instructive. Feedback should not be attacking or critical in the negative sense.

Participants should be encouraged to consider the following questions as they discuss their answers to the seven situations above.

What different behaviors may be identified in the five different responses to each situation? As the five approaches were used, how did you feel? What trilevel communication did you observe? As you tried the five different responses, which response was the easiest for you to demonstrate? Which response was the hardest for you to demonstrate?

As you play out the roles of the five responses, what characteristics about yourself were confirmed? What new information did you learn about yourself?

It takes about 45 minutes to complete the exercise.

DISCUSSION EXERCISE

Requests

DIRECTIONS FOR THE LEARNER: Think of a time in the recent past that involved your making a request. Think about a situation in which your request was granted. Think about another situation in which your request was denied. Reflect on the two situations for a moment. Think about what you wanted, how you asked for it, and how people responded to you.

STEP I: In the space below, record briefly the two situations.

1.

2.

STEP II: In the space below, describe how you feel when you grant someone a request. What behaviors and words do you use when granting a request?

STEP III: Now describe how you feel when you deny someone else's request. What do you actually do when you deny a request?

DIRECTIONS FOR THE LEADER: This exercise works well with the total class unit. The purpose of the exercise is to strengthen the ability of people to make appropriate requests.

The participants should take a few moments to discuss the answers of group members. Include responses to some of the following questions in the class discussion.

In what ways did the two situations in Step I resemble each other? How were they different? What are some of your feelings that you experience now as you think about both of those past situations?

How may you change the situation described in STEP I, in which your request was denied, to get a favorable response if you should repeat that request in the future? How do others feel when you grant or deny a request? How do you actually DO that?

Be aware of trilevel communication as group members participate. Provide positive feedback to each other as personal information is shared.

It takes about 30 minutes to complete the exercise and discussion.

SUMMARY

Communication is the ability of information to get through from one person to another person. In a sense, it is a meeting of minds. It is how people share ideas, feelings, and experiences. Much of the time in the life of a person is spent with other people. Communication is important for the development of the individual and of friendships with others.

Though it may appear simple to do and easy to understand, communication is complicated. Giving out and receiving messages in an effective way requires skill. Communication involves language that changes with time. It involves listening and paying close attention to others.

Understanding whether the communication is formal or informal is important. Informal communication requires less work. The different types of formal communication, such as persuasive, informative, cathartic, or therapeutic, require more work.

Some of the specific techniques to improve communication were covered in the previous pages. They include using open or closed questions, making requests of others. Being aware of trilevel communication helps a person to be in touch with the total, accurate message from other people.

In touch.

Suggestions for Further Reading

ATTENDING

Allen, E. E. (1982). Multiple attending in therapy groups. *The Personnel and Guidance Journal,* 60(5), 318–320.

COMMUNICATION

Forbes, E. J., & Fitzsimons, V. M. (1981). *The Older Adult.* St. Louis, MO: The C. V. Mosby.

Romano, J. L. (April, 1982). Biofeedback training and therapeutic gains: Clinical impressions. *The Personnel and Guidance Journal,* 60(8), 473–475.

OPEN AND CLOSED QUESTIONS

Flowers, J. V., & Booraem, C. D. (1975). Assertion training: The training of trainers. *The Counseling Psychologist,* 5(4), 29–36.

REALITY ORIENTATION

Weiner, M. B., Brok, A. J., & Snadowsky, A. M. (1978). *Working With The Aged.* Englewood Cliffs, NJ: Prentice Hall.

REALITY THERAPY

Glasser, W. (1975). *Reality Therapy.* New York: Harper & Row.

STRESS (OVERWHELMING SYMPTOMS)

Coleman, J. C. (1976). *Abnormal Psychology and Modern Life* (5th ed.). Glenview, IL: Scott, Foresman and Co.

10

The Importance of Feelings in Communication

Over the years, families develop typical ways to handle feelings. These ways may be passed down from generation to generation and become deeply woven into the patterns of behavior of family members. The patterns of behavior may involve reaching out to other people, communicating honestly, being tender, and sharing. These behaviors are healthy, positive ways of dealing with feelings that have been passed down by older family members to the younger family members.

Sometimes the family style of behavior involves holding in feelings and trying to act unconcerned. Unresolved feelings and problems are allowed to build up. The person keeps emotional information inside. He may control feelings to the point of appearing untouched and uninvolved. Or, she may seem to keep people at a distance, to shut other people out. These types of behavior are less healthy than the open style of communication because they do not deal with problem situations and upset feelings.

Feelings are easily stirred. Some persons, however, try to control their feelings. They try to ignore their feelings and the problem that stirred them. Though they feel hurt, sad, or angry, they act unconcerned or uninvolved. The contradiction between the actual feelings and the unconcerned behavior will confuse or frustrate other people who have learned a different method of handling such matters.

Life may seem empty as a result of the person's maintaining the same even level of nonemotional behavior. After a while it may become difficult for the individual to know when good feelings or bad feelings are being experienced. Over a period of time, this kind of behavior may cause a great deal of stress. It may lead to mental health problems for the individual or for the family unit.

In some families, feelings are dealt with in an overemotional manner. Explosive outbursts are typical. Hurt feelings, tension, or anger build up until they burst forth. The outbursts of anger are often hurtful to the other family members.

The build-up of feelings may be compared to a pressure cooker. The valve on top of the pressure cooker gradually releases built-up steam. The release valve prevents an overload of pressure. As a result, there is no explosion from long-term, built-up pressure. The occasional slight spurt from the valve keeps the pressure cooker functioning well.

Following the example of the release valve on the pressure cooker, people may learn to release built-up emotional pressures in a healthy way. For example, they may set aside an hour to discuss the issue with a co-worker or have a family conference. They may set aside 30 minutes each day for exercise or time alone to help them relax from the tensions of the day. The continuous release of small amounts of pressure will keep the person functioning in a healthy, productive way.

The following discussion exercise, BLANK FACE FEELINGS, is an attempt to help the reader learn the importance of different actions in showing feelings.

DISCUSSION EXERCISE

Blank Face Feelings

DIRECTIONS FOR THE LEARNER: Divide into groups of 6 to 8 members each. Each member writes down a positive feeling and a negative one. The different feelings may be opposites, such as happy and sad. They may be different, such as happy and jealous.

Using body language, each member plays out only one of the two emotions in front of the small group. It does not matter whether the positive feeling or the negative feeling is played out first. It becomes more interesting when there is a mix of positive and then negative feelings as each person takes a turn. For example, the first demonstration may be a positive feeling and the second one or the third one may be a negative feeling.

After each member acts out an emotion, the other members of the small group try to identify that emotion from the actions they see. When the emotion is guessed, the next participant in the small group takes a turn.

After everyone has pantomimed the first feeling, each individual selects a paper bag big enough to put over his or her head to hide any facial expressions. A blank paper face mask may be made for this part of the exercise. People who do not like covering their heads or faces for this part of the exercise are encouraged to turn their backs to the other group members and role play from that position.

With the face hidden from other group members in some way, each individual acts out the second feeling they selected. While guessing the emotion being role played, the group members should try to become aware of which behaviors or actions would help to portray the emotion more accurately.

DIRECTIONS FOR THE LEADER: This exercise requires group participation. The purpose of the exercise is to strengthen communication through body actions.

After people have a chance to demonstrate the different feelings they chose, the small groups should discuss their perceptions of what they saw. Participants in the groups should remember to provide positive feedback to each "mimer." Also, they should discuss the behaviors that seemed more accurate and those behaviors that seemed less helpful in showing the identity of a specific feeling.

Group members should take some time to consider some of the following questions in their discussions. What was the difference in role playing when the player's head or facial expressions were hidden from view? Which parts of the body are most expressive in role playing activity? What did people feel as they tried to demonstrate each emotion? What did people experience as they observed the demonstration of each emotion?

It takes about 30 minutes to complete the exercise and discussion.

POSITIVE FEELINGS

Positive feelings provide comfort, support, strength, and caring. They help a person to feel good about the self. They contribute to the growth, development, fulfillment, and satisfaction in the life of a person. Positive feelings provide the motivation for activities and the zest for life.

For example, people who provide service to others are often energized by a kind word of appreciation. The teacher gains new zest from a student who says, "Thank you, I enjoyed your class."

"Thank you"

Expressing positive feelings.

Positive Feeling Words: caring, compassion, consideration, giving, honor, kind, loving, nice, respectful, sharing, sweet, tender.

INDIFFERENCE

Being indifferent means having feelings that are unconcerned or uninvolved in an issue. The feelings do not seem to be positive. Neither do the feelings seem to be negative. Indifference indicates an emptiness, a sense of apathy, nothing stirring within the self. The individual may not care in a positive or in a negative way.

When a person is intimately involved in a situation, apathy or a lack of obvious feelings usually is a disguise. Typically, underneath the disguise of apathy is a great deal of emotional turmoil.

In a realistic sense, people may feel indifferent only about others with whom they have no direct involvement. Or, they may feel indifferent about situations about which they have little or no information. In a relationship that has developed over a long period of time, indifference in the people may be a sign that misunderstandings and hurt feelings have been ignored.

For example, a couple may be having a conflict over where to spend their winter vacation. He knows that she does not want to visit his family in the Tennessee mountains. She knows that he does not want to visit her family in the Vermont mountains.

Every time they talk about the subject, they become angry. He tenses his jaw. She frowns. They tell each other that it makes no difference where the vacation is spent. They say that they have no feelings about Tennessee or Vermont.

After an hour of discussing their feelings of indifference, they both go off into different rooms in order to avoid an unpleasant scene. They both gain control over their stirred up feelings and get involved in the next activity of their daily routine.

They are used to getting stuck when feelings get stirred up and work hard to keep from being bothered by such things. They will probably solve the current conflict by trying to show more indifference. They may end up going nowhere for their vacation. Perhaps, they will go to Tennessee because she typically "gives in" or something came up, such as his parents becoming ill.

If either partner were actually indifferent, he or she would be willing to follow the invitation of the other person. There would be no strong positive or negative feelings involved. The attitude would be one of open willingness to pursue the interest expressed by the other person.

Indifference?!?

Words of Indifference: apathy, detachment, disinterest, empty, inconsequential, immaterial, uncaring, unconcerned.

NEGATIVE FEELINGS

Negative feelings are unpleasant feelings. They stimulate anxiety, fear, turmoil, and loneliness. They wear away or wear out the strength of a person and encourage the development of feelings of worthlessness and futility. Negative feelings are difficult to handle. As the years pass and the feelings become more negative, it becomes harder for people to deal with them.

When negative feelings are communicated in an open, respectful way, they will add to and help build a relationship. Talking about one's anger to a spouse, sharing a job disappointment with a friend, or discussing frustration over rude behavior with a child are some examples of healthy ways to deal with unpleasant feelings.

On the other hand, allowing feelings to build up and revealing them in an overemotional manner may be unhealthy. The overemotional behavior may harm others. If the explosive behavior is a typical way of responding, the other people involved may build up contempt, hostility, or fear in their relationships with the explosive person. The build-up may lead to a complicated system of unresolved turmoil. Over the years, this kind of turmoil may result in debilitating, destructive relationships.

Turmoil.

Negative Feeling Words: abandon, anxiety, brutality, courseness, discomfort, failure, fear, guilt, harsh, hate, helpless, jealous, loss, resentment, scorn, selfish, shame.

It is important to be aware of one's own personal feelings. A person should become aware of the feelings and try to deal with them. Feelings that are ignored or avoided may trigger unwise behavior and inappropriate decisions that may interfere rather than help in a situation. Well-being may improve once feelings are recognized, understood, accepted, and acted on in suitable ways.

Feelings range in level of intensity. When feelings are bottled up inside and not dealt with, behavior is affected. When feelings are aroused, reasonable actions and clear thinking decrease for most people.

A great deal of a person's energy is used to store up feelings, especially when the number of emotional issues builds up, as it is sure to do, over the years. Over the years, the weight of the burden affects the manner in which the person deals with the normal activities of everyday living.

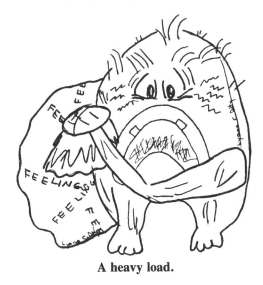

A heavy load.

Sometimes a crisis weakens the ability of a person to keep the burden in check or under control. Then the feelings of the past escape and add onto the turmoil of the current crisis. Old cares, guilts, anger, hurts, and joys may spill out. Weakness or confusion in dealing with them is experienced once more.

The following discussion exercise, LONELINESS TO LOVELINESS, compares unpleasant and pleasant feelings. It is an exercise that uses the imagination of the reader. It allows the reader to dip into some personal memories.

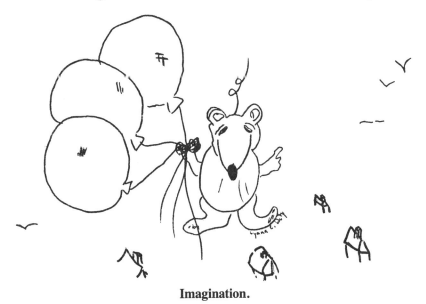

Imagination.

DISCUSSION EXERCISE

Loneliness to Loveliness

DIRECTIONS FOR THE LEARNER: This is an exercise in pretending. While you are feeling relatively relaxed, you will practice using your imagination.

A small amount of time will be spent thinking about some unpleasant feelings from the memory bank of your own experiences. The unpleasant feelings involve trying to experience being in a lonely place and feeling lonely.

After the experience of loneliness, you will be asked to spend a little time thinking about pleasant ideas and encouraging your imagination to develop some pleasant feelings and experiences for you. Then some time will be provided for sharing what has been experienced with other group members.

STEP I: GETTING READY (Directions for the Learner)

In the space provided below, write down the name of a pleasant, very happy place where you would like to visit for a short time. It could be a location you have visited before or a place you may have dreamed about. You may be with people who love you or you may be by yourself.

In this place that you choose, you will have a good time. You will enjoy yourself. As a part of this exercise in pretending, you are relieved of all worries or responsibilities concerning the place that you choose to visit. You may assume that the leader of the group will take care of those things. This will allow you to visit your special place in your imagination with no worry about obligations, etc.

STEP II: PRETENDING (Directions for the Leader)

First, the leader of the group talks about what is going to happen in this exercise of relaxation and pretending. It is important that group members read or be read the initial directions at the top of the page so that they have an understanding of what is going to happen. The following is a suggestion of how the leader might summarize the experience for the group members as the exercise is begun.

The leader should try to speak in a clear, soft, gentle voice. The pace of the speaking should be slow and relaxing, but not dull. The leader might say:

> *You are going to spend some time remembering or imagining an unpleasant experience. The unpleasant experience will allow you to feel an unpleasant situation, and to go through the emotions of that situation. Then, you will spend some time thinking about the pleasant, happy place that you have already identified. Afterwards, an opportunity will be provided for a discussion of the experiences. If you would like to share some of the feelings that are stirred by the remembering and the pretending, you are invited to do so during the discussion time. Each person is encouraged to share experiences. Remember, however, that the desire for privacy is respected.*

> *Also, it is important to remember that the feelings are important to the group discussion, not the details of the unpleasant or pleasant situations that are remembered or imagined.*

To begin the actual pretending or fantasy trip, the leader should speak slowly to help people feel more relaxed. Brief pauses between paragraphs will give some moments for people to use their imagination. The leader may go on with:

Now let's begin. Get settled in your chair. Try to be as comfortable as possible. It may help to loosen your shoelaces or necktie. Take a few deep breaths and get comfortable.

Now close your eyes. With your eyes closed, check to see if you can get more comfortable in your chair. Take some more slow, easy, deep breaths. For the next few minutes, try to set aside any worries that you may be carrying. Let your mind be free to share in the experience. Relax yourself. Relax your muscles a little more as you let yourself relax more into the chair. Breathe easy, slow, and relaxed.

As you are relaxed and enjoying the feeling of relaxation, think about being outdoors. You are breathing deeply, slowly. It is a warm, comfortable day. It is pleasant. There is a gentle wind that you can feel on your face. The trees are rustling slowly. You are alone. You move along enjoying the calmness of the day.

As you walk along a path, you see that the sky is getting gray. It is twilight. You are walking along. It is getting a little cool now. You are alone and feeling a bit lonely. It is getting late. You are concerned. You are walking along, but the path seems to be taking you the wrong way.

It is much darker now. The air is really cold. You are walking along the path trying to find your way. You begin to feel frightened. You cannot find your way. The wind is stronger now as you walk. You stop for a moment to decide what to do. Near you, by a tree, you see a gray, form. It is dark. It moves as the wind blows past. As you look carefully, you can see what it is. It is frightening. It is awful.

You move away quickly. As you run on the path, you turn around a corner and see, suddenly, the pleasant, happy place you remembered before. It is lovely. This is the place you wanted. This is the happy place you identified before we began to relax together. It is so happy. Here are the special things that mean so much to you. You can feel the joy. Be with that happy place. It feels so good. Enjoy it for a while.

The leader should give two to three minutes to the group to stay relaxed with their pleasant memories. After a while, the leader may ease them into finishing their experience with words, such as:

Begin to finish the pleasant, happy experience. Breathe in a relaxed way. Enjoy the good feelings you have. At your own pace, begin to come together with the group again. When you are ready, you may open your eyes. We will come together slowly as you are ready.

The leader should be especially patient with group members who "awaken" slowly. The leader should encourage people to breathe deeply to continue the feeling of relaxation. Then the leader may invite people to share some of their immediate feelings.

DIRECTIONS FOR THE LEADER: This exercise may be done with one individual or with a group. In both cases, a leader provides the story that guides the imagination of the participant(s). The group should not be larger than about 30 people unless the leader is very experienced in leading fantasy exercises. Sometimes intense emotion is experienced by the participant(s). The leader needs to be on the lookout for this kind of behavior to guide the participant along so that the resulting experiences will be successful.

The purposes of the exercise are to strengthen the ability to relax, to concentrate on some ideas, and to become aware of emotions. It is important that participants know what is going to happen before they close their eyes to begin the experience of pretending. If someone is unwilling to participate, that person may be invited to sit quietly with eyes closed and to listen with the rest of the participants.

The time spent discussing the experience is as important as the actual experience. The time of sharing should focus on the positive feelings first and then a comparison of the positive versus negative feelings.

Some of the following questions may be helpful to consider during the discussion. How does the pleasant experience feel? How does the happiness feel? What did you experience when you made the change to the pleasant, happy place? What did you feel when you were in the pleasant, happy place? How did the unpleasant experience feel? How did the loneliness feel?

Remember to discuss any sensory feelings, such as taste, smell, temperature changes in the air, colors, etc., that people experienced. How strong or weak were these sensations compared to sensations experienced in typical, daily activities? Was it hard or easy to participate in the exercise? Now that the exercise is finished, what are people feeling? As a result of the pretending, what physical and emotional sensations do you experience now?

It takes about 45 to 60 minutes to complete the exercise and discussion.

COMMUNICATING TO FEELINGS

Responses that promote the deepest level of communication are called the most facilitative responses. These responses ease communication. Facilitative responses are sensitive to the content, feeling, and meaning of the communication of the speaker. Good listening and attending skills are needed to be able to respond with sensitivity to the words of another person.

To respond skillfully to the speaker, the listener should be aware of the content and the feelings of the message just relayed. The content concerns the subject or topic, what was talked about. The feelings relate to the emotional experience of the speaker, how the person felt during the talking.

To provide a response that eases and encourages the flow of communication, the listener must be aware of nonverbal cues from the speaker and be open to the topic under discussion.

Empathy, not sympathy, is important to help the listener be in tune with the feelings that are discussed. The listener must also be able to put the other person in the center of concern and not be self-centered.

Quickly reviewed, empathy is seeing another person's point of view, understanding it, and being concerned without total emotional involvement. Sympathy is feeling immersed in the same emotional experiences of the other person.

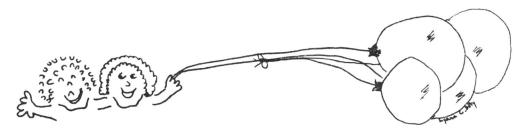

THE FACILITATIVE MODEL

The Facilitative Model helps a person to feel really heard. The model is comprised of six general kinds of responses to make to guide the communication. The six different kinds of responses include (1) reflection of feeling, (2) clarification or summary, (3) closed or open questions, (4) support or praise, (5) interpretation or analysis, and (6) advice or evaluation.

Although each of the responses has value, the responses that reflect feelings have a higher probability of centering in on the person. Reflective responses stimulate personal sharing. As the responses become more like advice, they become more focused on the problem and less centered on the person. The person in need feels helped, but experiences less caring from the listener.

All of the responses will be discussed with more emphasis placed on the reflection of feelings. The reflection of feelings makes a large impact on the person, who is talking about a personal concern or problem.

Reflection of Feelings

Reflection of feelings is a highly empathic response to someone who has just spoken. It focuses on the feelings of the speaker. Feelings determine how one perceives an event. Perception, in turn, determines behavior. Reflecting feelings back to the speaker shows that the listener really was paying attention to the speaker.

The listener tries to be sensitive to unstated feelings. The listener tries to respond to the stated feelings and include a message which indicates that a deeper message was heard. By using a more intense synonym for the feeling word that was expressed, the facilitative listener invites the speaker to share at a deeper level.

For example:
SPEAKER: I have so much time on my hands these days.
NONFACILITATIVE RESPONSE: Why don't you get outside more?
FACILITATIVE RESPONSE: You are bored.
SPEAKER: I am bored, but it is deeper than that.

NONFACILITATIVE RESPONSE: It is probably because the kids have moved out. Once you have grand-children, you will be as busy as ever.
FACILITATIVE RESPONSE: You are lonely.

Notice that the nonfacilitative responses seem to offer a quick solution to the concern and do not allow the speaker to explore deeper into the issue. The facilitative responses invite the speaker to share more about the difficulty being experienced. The speaker is also invited to share deeper, personal feelings, such as loneliness.

In another example:
SPEAKER: My youngest daughter is just driving us crazy. She has been in college for six years and still has not finished. She spent one semester hitchhiking across the country with this dude she fell in love with. We have not heard from her in six months. She has had problems with grades. The costs have drained us.
FACILITATOR: You are afraid your daughter may be in danger.

Notice that the facilitator hones right into the feeling of worry that this parent expresses indirectly. The parent probably will start sharing in a deeper, more personal way.

Some examples of phrases to reflect feelings are the following:

1. You feel . . . (angry, bored . . .)
2. It seems as if you are . . . (happy, sad . . .)
3. I am wondering if you feel . . . (eager, nervous . . .)
4. As you see it, you are . . . (stuck, frightened . . .)

The introductory phrase of the listener links to one of the speaker's words that identifies what the person was feeling. If the listener uses an inaccurate response, usually the speaker says, "No, I feel . . ." Then the speaker will continue to share at an intimate level.

The goal of the listener is to be empathic, respectful, and attentive. The listener is expected to try hard, but is not expected to have the perfect response every time. Even after a high level of skill is developed, the professional helper occasionally does not make the most facilitative response.

The goal of the facilitator is to help the speaker to communicate. Inaccurate or inappropriate responses from the facilitator may slow down the depth of the communication. However, inaccurate responses do not interfere with the process of communication when the speaker feels caring and support from the facilitator.

The following discussion exercise, REFLECTING FEELINGS, provides some practice in reflecting feelings to facilitate what a speaker is sharing.

DISCUSSION EXERCISE

Reflecting Feelings

DIRECTIONS FOR THE LEARNER: Break up into tryads, that is groups of three. Each person takes a separate role, SPEAKER, LISTENER, or OBSERVER.

The SPEAKER talks to the LISTENER about something that occurred in the last few months or years that involved helping someone else. The SPEAKER should talk for about three minutes.

Then the LISTENER reflects to the SPEAKER the feelings that were picked up in the story. The LISTENER uses reflective statements, such as, "You are happy," or "You were anxious." The SPEAKER provides feedback to the LISTENER concerning the accuracy of the reflective statements.

Next, the OBSERVER reports on the process of the interaction between the SPEAKER and the LISTENER. The OBSERVER discusses the attending behavior, the body language, and the undercurrent language that were noticed during the previous interaction.

After this feedback, the tryad members exchange roles and repeat the procedure. Everyone should have a turn at each role.

DIRECTIONS FOR THE LEADER: This exercise depends on group interaction. The purpose of the exercise is to practice trilevel communication as a speaker and as a listener.

After the exercise is completed, discuss the following questions. What speaking and listening skills were enhanced as a result of the exercise? How did the meanings of the experience in the memory of the SPEAKER change when the LISTENER reflected back feelings to the SPEAKER about the experience? How did the OBSERVER stay on task and not get distracted into the content or subject matter of each story?

It takes about 45 minutes to complete this discussion exercise.

Clarification or Summary of Contents

Clarification or a summary of the contents restates the words of the speaker in another way. It provides fresh words and new ideas. It usually makes the message more clear. Often it expresses the message more briefly and more to the point. It improves the communication, but usually it is less facilitative than reflection of feelings.

For example:

SPEAKER: I hated missing all those meetings, but so many things happened to my family this year. My husband was in the hospital. It has really taken all my strength. It is a wonder that we made it through the year. My son was drafted, so he went into the navy. My daughter had another miscarriage. My oldest grandchild dropped out of high school and cannot find a job.
RESPONSE OF SUMMARY OF CONTENTS: Family problems took up much of your time.

The listener has summarized clearly what the speaker is saying. The response targets in on family problems, the focus of the speaker's concern. This response will keep the conversation centered around that major theme. Otherwise, the speaker may be sidetracked on a minor point, such as being late to the current meeting. It should be pointed out, however, that the feelings of the speaker are being ignored completely with this kind of response.

Closed or Open Questions

Closed or open questions request further information. Closed questions require short responses and tend to limit communication. Open questions request a great deal of information and usually extend communication. Questions are less facilitative than Clarification or Summary of Content. Closed and Open Questions were discussed in more detail a few pages before.

For example:

1. Did you run your daily mile today? (The Closed Question will be answered with a brief "yes" or "no" answer.)
2. How was your mile-long run today? (The Open Question will probably be answered with quite a bit of information.)

Support and/or Praise

Words of support and praise provide comfort to an individual. They give positive words of encouragement or express approval of the individual actions. Support and praise are often helpful. Sometimes, however, they tend to cut off the flow of communication from the speaker. It is important for a person to be able to talk about inner feelings to someone who will really listen.

For example:

SPEAKER: I am so worried about Harry's visit to the doctor's office for a check-up.
RESPONSE OF SUPPORT: Harry is fine. He is a little overworked. There is nothing to worry about.

Notice how this caring comment that offers support to the speaker stops the sharing of deeper concerns. The speaker will probably be unsure or embarrassed about showing anxiety concerning the physical health of Harry.

Interpretation or Analysis

Interpretation or analysis often is used to provide a deeper level of information. It helps a person to understand the situation better. Sometimes the process uncovers more details or more accurate information about the circumstances.

Interpretation or analysis may cause defensive responses. It may limit the flow of communication and block a deeper level of communication about personal feelings.

For example:

SPEAKER: Sue is the best chauffer I have ever seen. She handles a limousine well in downtown traffic.
RESPONSE OF INTERPRETATION: You are impressed with Sue's skills and you want her to apply for that job.

Notice that the feelings of the speaker are ignored and the conversation is focused in a new direction. The new direction may indicate the direction of the thoughts of the speaker. The new direction of thought may concern job applications or general traffic problems in a big city instead of the immediate focus on skillful driving in the middle of traffic.

Advice or Evaluation

Advice or evaluation gives information and provides direction in approaching a problem or finding the correct solution. It helps open, exploring talk become a search for a quick solution. Sometimes this kind of communication seems to become defensive. The listener provides solutions and the speaker provides the excuses, reasons why all the solutions are unworkable. It seems to be the most frequently used response by those who are trying to help. It is the least facilitative response.

For example:
SPEAKER: I hate to leave a tennis match before it is over.
ADVISOR: Why don't you finish the game tomorrow?

The speaker is discouraged from personal sharing and is made to seem a little foolish by the suggested advice. The speaker will probably respond with a good excuse to which the advisor will provide another unhelpful and unwanted solution. The talking may continue for a long while in this manner, but the persons may never discover the real concerns of the speaker.

The following discussion exercise, FACILITATIVE RESPONSES, provides an opportunity for the reader to practice using the different responses of (1) reflection of feelings, (2) clarification or summary, (3) closed or open questions, (4) support or praise, (5) interpretation or analysis, and (6) advice or evaluation.

"You are happy that. . . ."

DISCUSSION EXERCISE

Facilitative Responses

DIRECTIONS FOR THE LEARNER: For each problem situation described below, develop six different ways of responding. The different responses should fit the categories of facilitative responses studied in the previous pages, they are (1) reflection of feelings, (2) clarification or summary, (3) closed or open questions, (4) support or praise, (5) interpretation or analysis, and (6) advice or evaluation.

Try to think of a response to each situation that helps the speaker feel as if the message is really getting through. What words could you say to help the speaker talk more about the stress being experienced? How may your response help the flow of communication? An example situation and responses follow the directions.

After reading the example, work on the situations given. Working by yourself, write your responses for each category in the spaces provided. Then take some time to share the answers with the other participants. It may be helpful to role play the different situations and responses. Remember to use body language to make the communication stronger.

EXAMPLE SITUATION:
You are having lunch with a friend. She is a full-time homemaker whose children have families of their own. She is restless and tense. As you eat and talk, she changes the subject of the conversation. She says, "Even though the robbery was two years ago, I still worry about someone breaking in and stealing all the things we have collected these last few years. I even hate to leave the house to take this time out for lunch."

What words would respond to the tense homemaker in a way that would strengthen the communication? What words may be used to show that the listener is sensitive to the concerns of the homemaker? What kind of response would encourage the homemaker to talk about the stress she was experiencing?

The following answers show different ways of talking that may be used to respond to the tense homemaker.

REFLECTION OF FEELINGS: "You are terrified someone may break in, even when you go out briefly for lunch."

CLARIFICATION OR SUMMARY: "You are concerned that someone will steal the things you care for so much." (This is a clarification.)

CLOSED OR OPEN QUESTIONS: "Are you worried that someone may be breaking into your house now, while we are eating lunch?" (This is a closed question.)

SUPPORT OR PRAISE: "Everything will be fine." (This is a statement of support.)
"You are so smart to protect your home with a new burglar alarm system." (This is a statement of praise.)

INTERPRETATION OR ANALYSIS: "I think you are afraid because you did not expect it to happen to you." (This is an interpretation of the worry expressed by the homemaker.)

ADVICE OR EVALUATION: "You should hire a security guard to protect your home." (This is advice.)
"You were careless to leave such expensive things in an unlocked house in that neighborhood." (This is an evaluation. It is negative and hurtful.)

SITUATION ONE:

You are waiting at the doctor's office for your annual physical examination. The nurse has just announced to everyone that the doctor has received an emergency call. The doctor will be delayed thirty minutes at the hospital. You decide to wait. You talk casually to the woman next to you.

Suddenly she says, "My daughter and two sons are putting so much pressure on me to come and live with one of them. Ever since my husband died seven years ago they have been after me."

"Would you believe I am 84 years old? I have my own apartment. I have friends and we go out to lunch every week."

"Now I am my own boss. I take care of myself. I have fun with my friends. I eat what I want and when I want. I go where I want. How can I tell that to my children? They will think that I did not love their father. I want to be a good mother."

You respond:

REFLECTION OF FEELINGS:

CLARIFICATION OR SUMMARY:

CLOSED OR OPEN QUESTIONS:

SUPPORT OR PRAISE:

INTERPRETATION OR ANALYSIS:

ADVICE OR EVALUATION:

SITUATION TWO:

A bus driver talks to you at your annual neighborhood street party: "I worked hard all my life and decided to retire early to go into cabinet making. The material cost so much that I had to go back to work part time to keep up with my bills. I hate driving that bus now. The traffic, rude passengers, stick-ups, . . . it was never like this before."

You respond to your friend:

REFLECTION OF FEELINGS:

CLARIFICATION OR SUMMARY:

CLOSED OR OPEN QUESTIONS:

SUPPORT OR PRAISE:

INTERPRETATION OR ANALYSIS:

ADVICE OR EVALUATION:

SITUATION THREE:
During a coffee break at work, your friend complains, "I dread the weekends. My wife's mother is such a pain. Every Sunday afternoon we pick her up to take her out to lunch and she acts so rude. She is never ready on time. She complains about the kids. She complains about the restaurants we go to. She says she wants to go out when we ask her, but she never seems to be happy when we are together. I hate the hassle."

You respond to your friend:

REFLECTION OF FEELINGS:

CLARIFICATION OR SUMMARY:

CLOSED OR OPEN QUESTIONS:

SUPPORT OR PRAISE:

INTERPRETATION OR ANALYSIS:

ADVICE OR EVALUATION:

DIRECTIONS FOR THE LEADER: This is a group exercise. The purposes of the exercise are to learn and to experience the effects of the six different responses. Take some time to discuss the feelings experienced by the speakers and listeners of the different situations. How do people react when they hear the use of each type of the six responses?

The following are some questions to consider in the progress of the discussion. What types of responses seem to show caring? What types of responses seem more objective or to be looking for more information than some of the other responses? What types of responses seem to be more critical than the others? What types of responses seem more sensitive to the needs of the person in the dilemma? What types of responses seem more sensitive to the listener who is trying to be helpful?

Remember to provide positive remarks in response to the efforts of other participants.

This exercise takes about 30 minutes to complete.

SUMMARY

Dealing with feelings helps to improve communication between people. Being able to use facilitative responses communicates respect, caring, and support to others.   .

The Facilitative Model has different responses, they are (1) reflection of feelings, (2) clarification or summary, (3) closed or open questions, (4) support or praise, (5) interpretation or analysis, and (6) advice or evaluation. Each response has a specific purpose in guiding the communication.

A person may use communication skills to take care of feelings in a positive way. These skills may involve personal awareness and the willingness to share candidly one's own feelings. Also, it may include listening with an open attitude to what other people have to say about their feelings.

Discussing and working out painful feelings and disagreements may result in mutual growth for both of the people involved. The interaction will strengthen the interpersonal relationship. The people will feel a sense of satisfaction in working together in a genuine, caring way.

Suggestions for Further Reading

FACILITATIVE RESPONSE

Carkhuff, R. R. (1973). *The Art of Helping.* Amherst, MA: Human Resource Development Press.

Egan, G. (1975). *The Skilled Helper.* Monterey, CA: Brooks/Cole.

Wittmer, J., & Myrick, R. D. (1980). *Facilitative Teaching* (2nd ed.). Minneapolis, MN: Educational Media Corp.

FEELINGS

Egan, G. (1975). *The Skilled Helper.* Monterey, CA: Brooks/Cole.

Gazda, G. M., et al. (1977). *Human Relations Development: A Manual for Educators* (2nd ed.). Boston, MA: Allyn & Bacon.

Passons, W. R. (1975). *Gestalt Approaches in Counseling.* New York: Holt, Rhinehart and Winston.

Silverstone, B., & Hyman, H. K. (1976). *You and Your Aging Parent.* New York: Pantheon.

Wittmer, J., & Myrick, R. D. (1980). *Facilitative Teaching* (2nd ed.). Minneapolis, MN: Educational Media Corp.

11

Selective Assertiveness

Assertiveness is the open expression of feelings, the willingness to make a choice, and the confidence to act upon one's rights as a human being. Selective assertiveness involves choosing the most desirable behavior for a given situation.

The purposes of selective assertiveness for people are twofold: (1) to improve and increase the ways of acting in different situations and (2) to be assertive as often as possible. An active assertive style of behavior rather than a waiting, passive style is important for the mental health and life satisfaction of older people.

Usually, assertiveness is the best path to follow because it provides a way to respect the rights of others. Sometimes, however, after looking over the facts of a situation and thinking about choices, a person may decide to act in a nonassertive way. That is, the person may decide to act in a passive or in an aggressive way. When the choice to be passive or aggressive is a careful one, it is considered to be selective assertiveness in this book. The choice has involved a sincere, open process of honest evaluation and decision making that has resulted in a passive or aggressive response.

The following paragraphs will briefly explore the three components of selective assertiveness: (1) passiveness, (2) aggressiveness, and (3) assertiveness.

PASSIVENESS

Passive people try to keep the real self hidden within themselves. They allow their rights to be violated by others. They allow other people to ignore them. They let others take advantage of them without protesting. They do not state their needs, wishes, or feelings. They control honest, spontaneous reactions.

Often they are as hurt, anxious, angry, or excited as other people, but they keep those feelings hidden within. Passive people limit closeness and emotional intimacy with others. Often other people view passive people as shy, awkward, frail, or incompetent.

An example of passive behavior is the following situation: When Mr. Dime goes outside the front door of his home to pick up the morning newspaper, he finds it on the curb, under the bushes, or in the low branches of the trees. Although he gets upset as he hunts for the newspaper every morning, he finds the paper, shakes his head, and resolves to ignore the problem. He tries to forget. He decides to avoid making a fuss about such a small problem.

AGGRESSIVENESS

Aggressive people stand up for their rights in a way that violates the rights of others. These people show a hostile, overemotional outburst of feelings and actions. Their behavior is hurtful to others. They attack the other person rather than the specific actions or words that upset them. They humiliate, dominate, attack, and put other people down with harsh words or punching fists.

The sudden, over-reaction of aggressors is usually explosive and then finished quickly. Their outburst is often the result of the building up of many feelings from past experiences that have left them angry.

An example of aggressive behavior is the following situation: Down the street from Mr. Dime, the passive newspaper customer in the previous example, is another customer, Mrs. Penny. When she stepped out to pick up her newspaper, she finally found it caught in a muddy bed of ivy. The newspaper was soaked with mud. She threw it into the trash barrel and stomped indoors.

Mrs. Penny phoned the newspaper delivery person immediately. She raged about the bad service and yelled that she would not pay the bill for the last month. Then Mrs. Penny slammed down the receiver.

ASSERTIVENESS

Assertive people act in a way that is open, honest, and respectful. Their speech and actions are appropriate. They communicate well. They express their feelings, beliefs, and opinions in an appropriate way. Their assertive behavior encourages interpersonal relationships. They stand up for their own rights without infringing upon the rights of others.

An example of assertive behavior is the following situation: Two streets from Mr. Dime is another customer, Mr. Bits, who receives newspapers from the same creative (or careless) delivery person. When Mr. Bits hunted for the newspaper that same morning, he found it perched on top of an empty birdhouse he had set out in the side yard last month. A shake of the branch on the tree loosened his newspaper.

Since he had already spoken to the delivery person about his daily difficulty in finding the newspaper, he decided to telephone the supervisor of the newspaper delivery service. Mr. Bits stated that he expected to receive the newspaper in an appropriate location, such as the front sidewalk or porch. The supervisor assured Mr. Bits the delivery person would be monitored for a week and then replaced if service did not improve.

As a result of the telephone call, the delivery person aimed the newspaper more carefully. Mr. Bits received the newspaper on his front porch steps every morning.

The same situation, poor delivery of the newspaper, resulted in behaviors that differed in Mr. Dime, Mrs. Penny, and Mr. Bits. The passive Mr. Dime did not upset anyone and did not create a stir. He did not solve the problem. The aggressive Mrs. Penny did create a stir, but also did not solve the problem. The assertive customer, Mr. Bits, spoke up in an appropriate way and solved the problem. He expressed his concerns in an open way. As a result, he took care of his personal needs and wishes and received a newspaper close by his front door.

The chart on the next page is provided to help the reader review specific differences between passiveness, aggressiveness, and assertiveness. The chart may be used as a guide for practicing different types of behavior in the next discussion exercise, HAPPINESS IS BEING SPECIAL.

Passiveness, Aggressiveness, and Assertiveness

	PASSIVE	AGGRESSIVE	ASSERTIVE
Communication	shy, closed, inhibited	pushy, loud, explosive	open, honest, direct, appropriate
Posture	stooped, sagging	stiff, towering, leans forward (threatening)	facing, upright, relaxed movements
Hands	fidget, flutter, clammy	clenched, abrupt, waving overgesture	relaxed, warm, smooth motions, caring gestures
Eyes	look down	stare, glare	friendly, relaxed
Face	frowning, timid, tense, controlled	rigid, tense, uncontrolled	relaxed, appropriate expression
Voice	quiet, whisper	loud, harsh, raspy	firm, relaxed, changing tones
Language	filled with excuses, hidden	accusing, attacking, angry words	clear messages, says what is wanted, honest
Emotions	low-key	high-key, hurtful	appropriate range, direct
Choices	follows others	forces choices upon others	chooses carefully for self
Personal Rights	violated	violates	respects, accepts
Benefits	avoids risks, stays safe	control over others	self-respect, high self-esteem, growth, pleasant activities
Results	frustration, sadness, unmet needs	frustration, anger, unmet needs	finishes tasks, met needs

---

DISCUSSION EXERCISE

Happiness Is Being Special

DIRECTIONS FOR THE LEARNER: You are a special person. Indeed, you are unique. There is no one else on the earth quite like you. Many factors, such as physical appearance, emotional make-up, interests in food or clothing, and hobbies, are responsible for your being different from everyone else.

Think for a moment about some of these factors. Think about what you like and don't like to do, how you act when alone, or in a group, or what you do for excitement or relaxation.

Think about a specific, recent event you have experienced that helped you to see how different and special you are.

Break up into small groups of 4 to 6 members. Each group member, in turn, will share the recent, special event in a style of passiveness, aggressiveness, or assertiveness. Each group member should choose one of these three styles of communication without telling anyone else which style has been chosen.

Group members should try to use the style of communication they find most different from their typical behavior. Or, they may find it helpful to try on a behavior that frustrates them in relationships. For example, a group member who is especially frustrated by people who behave in a passive way should accept the challenge of trying to act out passiveness. The learning will educate them about dealing with passive people in their lives.

As the group member shares the special event in the style of communication they have chosen, the other group members should listen and observe. After the member takes a couple of minutes to complete the personal story, the observing group members guess the style of behavior chosen. They tell the specific actions they observed to help them figure out the style of communication used. The speaker provides feedback concerning the group perceptions. The next member of the group has a turn.

DIRECTIONS FOR THE LEADER: This exercise needs at least two people and works best in a group, because of the need for feedback. The purpose of the exercise is to give the participant a chance to try out a new style of behavior, that is, one that is not often used by the participant.

Participants should be encouraged to discuss the feelings of each story and the messages communicated by the accompanying behavior. How did the behavior of each person add to or take away from the details of the story?

Some of the following questions should be considered in the discussion. How does a passive, aggressive, or assertive style feel when you try it out? Which style of communication feels the most comfortable to you? Which style of communication feels the least comfortable to you? How did it feel to be talking and acting in a way that was different from your typical style of behavior?

It may surprise some people to realize the amount of energy that goes into the three styles of behavior. Typically, people think that passive behavior takes no effort. They believe that assertion takes some effort and that aggressiveness takes a great deal of effort. What did the groups observe about the amount of effort used in acting out the three different styles of communication? Were people surprised to learn that passiveness requires a great deal of energy and work?

It takes about 30 minutes to complete this exercise.

BEING MORE ASSERTIVE

Many people behave assertively in most situations. They struggle only when they feel anxious, powerless, or in danger. Other people do not behave in an assertive way because they do not believe that they have the same rights or worth as other people.

It is important to be aware of one's own identity, one's style of relating to others, and the activities that one pursues to lead a more meaningful life. When a person is aware of these parts of themselves, they can start from that known foundation and then build new ways with which to lead a more fulfilling life.

Body Language Practice

A specific step to help a person be assertive more often is the practice of assertive body language. Working on one aspect of body language at a time, a person may appear to be acting in a more assertive way. A stronger, straighter body posture; a confident voice; a steady look in the eyes; and a relaxed, appropriate facial expression may send a new message of strength and capability to other people.

A timid posture gives the message, "I'm afraid to say this. You do not have to believe me. You probably should not bother to listen."

On the other hand, an aggressive posture gives the message, "I am going to get you. You had better listen to me or you will be hurt. You had better believe me if you know what is good for you."

However, an assertive appearance gives the message, "I have something worthwhile to say to you. Let's take some time to discuss it."

Sometimes belief precedes the behavior, but often, just the opposite occurs. As the person practices the new actions of assertion, the behavior will feel more comfortable. Getting used to the new behavior, the person will use it more often, and will increase assertive interactions with others. Then, after a while, the person will begin to believe in selective assertive behavior as a better way to live.

Hesitating

Sometimes it is helpful for people to admit their reluctance to respond or move ahead toward a goal. These people may be assertive in most situations. However, when under stress, they feel stuck and hesitate to make a move.

When people feel stuck, they should be able to admit it to themselves. Often the hesitancy or reluctance may be shared with others. It should be shared in a manner that shows careful thinking. The behavior should demonstrate that something different is being tried. The person is trying to be careful with or sensitive toward the feelings of the other individual. It is not helpful to act overly apologetic. The person should behave with confidence. For example: "This is hard for me to say . . ." or "I am a little unsure about saying this to you, so I want to be sure that I say it right . . ."

Then the speaker should go ahead with the response. For example, the grandmother may want to say, "This is hard for me to say. I appreciate all the help you gave me when I broke my hip last year, but I do not want to baby-sit the children every afternoon when they come home from school. I want to attend a history class at the junior college three afternoons a week. Perhaps we can work out a schedule with some of the neighbors who may be willing to help out."

Taking More Time

Sometimes when a person admits feeling unsure of the next words to say, a time delay technique may be used. For example, "It may take me a few minutes to think through a good answer to that . . ."

The time delay technique postpones the response for as much time as is stated. In the previous example, the delay of time is "a few minutes." The time may be a few seconds, one day, or more. Delaying the response gives a person time to relax and think through the issue. The extra time allows thoughts to be pulled together and an answer to be planned in a way that other people will understand. The extra time helps the person build up courage to say something that may be difficult, such as saying "No" to a request that has been made.

Some other examples of the technique to delay for more time are: "Wait a few seconds. I want to put together a couple of thoughts." "I'd like some time to think before I give you an answer. I will call you in a couple of days with my answer." "I will consider what you have said. Why don't you call me about it tomorrow?"

Asking for a little more time before giving an answer, the person who feels some pressure in the situation has a chance to relax. There is more time to think through an answer and perhaps to practice the words a few times. Then the actual answer may be given with a clear, more confident voice. Sometimes making introductory remarks shares some of your hesitancy with others, gives you additional time to gather some courage, and allows you to be honest.

The following example shows how a person may combine the technique of hesitating with the technique of taking more time. The purpose of the combination is twofold: (1) to be open about being careful and (2) to take more time to consider a response. The techniques work well in personal and business relationships.

"I'm a bit hesitant about answering right now. I am going to take a few minutes to think through the issue before I add anything." While thinking, the person may take a few sips of coffee or tea.

Sips for thinking.

Some people may find it helpful to leave the situation for a few minutes. Being out of the room or away from the location of the discussion may help them to relax. They may go to the restroom or go put on a new pot of coffee for everyone.

The following discussion exercise, ROLE PLAYING ASSERTION, will show the reader the differences among passive, aggressive, and assertive behaviors. The exercise provides some opportunities to act out the different behavior styles.

The sharing of roles with other group members in a relaxed setting helps everyone to learn assertive ways to improve relationship skills. The exercise has been useful in motivating people to increase the amount of assertive actions in their daily lives.

DISCUSSION EXERCISE

Role Playing Assertion

DIRECTIONS FOR THE LEARNER: Form small groups of 4 to 6 members. Work as a small group on the problem situations below.

First, think about how you would respond to the given situation. Develop a passive, aggressive, and assertive response to each situation. Some space is provided below each situation to allow you to write some brief notes about your different kinds of responses.

Act out the responses. Remember to use trilevel communication. Try to exaggerate the acting of the role playing. The feelings and the body movements should be overplayed to show clearly the communication style of the response.

SITUATION ONE:

You and a co-worker are competing for the office down the hall. It has more room than your current office. It has more comfortable working space. It even has a large window. During the past two weeks, the co-worker has taken your supervisor out to lunch twice and has told you several times, in so many words, to withdraw your request. What will you do?

Write down and then act out a passive, an aggressive, and an assertive response for this situation.

Passive:

Aggressive:

Assertive:

SITUATION TWO:
You and some friends are at lunch. The restaurant does not appear to be busy. The waitress is courteous. This is the second time, however, that she has brought a cold pot of tea to the table. You are almost finished with your meal. What will you do?

Write down and then act out a passive, an aggressive, and an assertive response for this situation.

Passive:

Aggressive:

Assertive:

SITUATION THREE:
The new neighbors across the street own a tomcat that keeps attacking your timid male cat. You talked to them once about it. They seemed unconcerned. They said that the cats will work it out on their own. Not a fighter, your cat has always enjoyed roaming around the neighborhood. Now, frequently, when he arrives at your front door, he is limping and his fur is torn up. What will you do?

Write down and then act out a passive, an aggressive, and an assertive response for this situation.

Passive:

Aggressive:

Assertive:

SITUATION FOUR:

A state government office is requesting proposals for a one-time-only grant of $100,000. You and two other agency directors are trying for the award. You have agreed to work together on a joint community proposal. Last week at a party, a friend remarked casually about the other two agencies working together on the proposal. The plan that the friend described seemed very different from your proposal. You begin to wonder, "Have the other two directors changed their minds and excluded me?" They have not called you in the past two weeks. The three of you were supposed to meet sometime this week. What will you do?

Write down and then act out a passive, an aggressive, and an assertive response for this situation.

Passive:

Aggressive:

Assertive:

SITUATION FIVE:

Your two teen-age children promised to try harder to bring up their school grades in order to get driving privileges for the family car. Their bedrooms look neater. You have noticed a real change in their behavior toward their nephews, the children of your oldest son. Grades just came out. Each of them improved in only one subject. They are crushed and are asking you to reconsider. What will you do?

Write down and then act out a passive, an aggressive, and an assertive response for this situation.

Passive:

Aggressive:

Assertive:

DIRECTIONS FOR THE LEADER: *This discussion exercise needs the interaction of a group. The purpose of the exercise is to provide practice in assertiveness.*

With the focus on role playing, people should be able to relax. Overplaying the feelings and body actions often helps people to loosen up and try out new behaviors that differ from their regular style of behavior.

Group members should be allowed to practice or rehearse assertive behaviors if they feel awkward in that role. The focus of the exercise is for people to learn assertion. Learning assertion involves being able to feel the difference in using passive, aggressive, and assertive behavior in various situations.

Acting out in a safe, supportive group of people provides the opportunity to learn and practice different behaviors. When the group members try out the new behaviors with people and in places outside the learning environment, they will automatically tone down what they did in the group. The resulting behavior will probably be closer to appropriate assertiveness than their original, frustrating, nonassertive behavior.

The leader may need to encourage people to get into the mood of the role playing situations. Sometimes it is helpful for people to change the details of the basic situation to give it more personal meaning. Often participants will adapt the situation in the exercise to a similar situation, one with which they are struggling in their own lives.

Everyone in the learning environment is a part of the group. They should be included in a direct or indirect way. People who are very uncomfortable play-acting may try out for an indirect role, such as a bystander. The bystander may play out the reaction of a person who responds at a distance to the interaction of the actual role players. The bystander may pretend to overhear the interaction as if in another room. Perhaps the bystander could pretend to be a pedestrian walking by as the interaction occurs.

It takes about 60 minutes to complete this discussion exercise.

GETTING ATTENTION

Sometimes as people enter their senior years, they have fewer relationships. Changes in the economic development of different parts of the country may result in the move of family members. They may have to move away quite a distance to obtain satisfactory employment. Changes in the interests of people may result in their moving away from lifelong friends. Or, having their friends move away from them.

For many people, developing new friendships is easy. They enjoy new situations and have fun reaching out to others and making new friends. For other people, developing new relationships is hard. As these people age and become more individual, the development of new friendships becomes even harder.

As the changes in society, in the local neighborhood, and in their organizations continue, some older people may feel lost in the midst of continually changing names and faces. They may feel frustrated with the loss of a sense of belonging to a familiar setting. They are angry about losing a sense of closeness and feeling comfortable with friends. They may feel overwhelmed with the new people and new ways of handling matters.

Sometimes this feeling of being overwhelmed results in the older person pulling away from contact with others. As the time spent away from others lengthens, loneliness begins. Some people cope by withdrawing further into themselves. The withdrawal may be considered a passive way of handling the situation.

Some older persons respond in a different way. In an effort to decrease their loneliness, they demand attention. They may become aggressive in their demands for attention. For example, they may demand that other people bring them things or take them places. They may live with adult children and demand that the family bring the newspaper, their glasses, dentures, shoes, etc., to them.

In a convalescent center or nursing home situation, older people who choose this method to decrease their loneliness may insist that the helpers adjust a pillow or their sitting position every few minutes.

Very often the demands are in the form of complaints, such as:

"I get so thirsty, I could die before someone gets me a drink of water."

"No one ever hears me! Quick, someone come to fix my shoulders before I fall out of the chair."

"The cooking is worthless. The food makes me gag."

"No one ever spends time with me. It is too much for them to visit and talk with their old, sick father."

These criticisms are often an attempt to reach out for an interaction. They are a cry for some kind of relationship. Some older persons prefer an unpleasant, grumbling, or defensive interaction to the unpleasant alternative of no interaction and isolation.

Instead of drawing attention to themselves and gaining enjoyable relationships, however, these types of nonassertive comments tend to decrease interactions. Relatives put off their visits to complaining family members until they feel ashamed. Then their feelings of guilt mount up and push them to go.

The visiting time, however, is not pleasant. Consequently, they resolve to avoid the next visit for as long as possible. The time between visits becomes longer and longer. All the people involved build up many unpleasant feelings as the time goes by.

Researchers have studied the importance of relationships to survival. In Chapter 13 the negative effect of loneliness on longevity and "sick roles" will be discussed.

Some people are lonely because of circumstances. Some, however, are lonely because they have taught others to ignore them. They may use passive and aggressive behavior to teach others to avoid their company. The passive behaviors may include acting helpless and dependent, closing out other relationships, wishing for the past, or trying to live in the future. The aggressive behaviors may include complaining, gossiping, or acting prejudiced. Both passive and aggressive behaviors may include concentrating on oneself and on things, rather than people.

In general, people prefer being with someone who is more pleasant. Getting attention is important to the physical survival as well as to the emotional well-being of a person. Assertive behavior helps a person to get the right kind of attention that is needed. Assertion promotes behaviors that lead to happy, fulfilling interactions during the time spent with other people.

Getting attention involves assertive, positive behaviors. Older people may use assertion to develop a different style of interacting with others. With assertive skills, they can gain confidence in themselves and reach out to others in a caring and sensitive way.

Assertive behavior in older people involves being open to new ways of dealing with old problems and living in the present. It involves caring more about people than about things. It means seeing through some actions to know what the real person within is trying to do or say.

Skilled helpers may encourage lonely older people to take on the responsibility of improving their ways of relating to others. The skilled helpers can show the older people how to reach out to others, how to listen, and how to respond in positive ways. It is easier for people to begin relationships of warmth and caring than to change poor, empty relationships. It is difficult to change bad habits in relationships. A great deal of hard work may be needed to change unpleasant habits into positive ways of interacting.

The following discussion exercise, ATTRACTING OR PUSHING AWAY OTHERS, provides an opportunity to clear up the difference between acting pleasant and unpleasant with other people.

DISCUSSION EXERCISE

Attracting or Pushing Away Others

DIRECTIONS FOR THE LEARNER: Label the following statements as "A" or "P". "A" indicates that the statement is a way to be attractive to people. In other words, they would be eager to pay attention to you or be with you. "P" indicates that the statement is a way to push away people. In other words, they would want to avoid your company.

In addition, write down whether each statement is an example of behavior that is passive, aggressive, or assertive.

_____   1.   *Why aren't you here when I need someone to help me?*

_____   2.   *You spend too much time on that car and not enough time on your family.*

_____   3.   *Even though I have to stay in bed now, I try to work each day to improve something within myself.*

_____   4.   *My medicine only makes me feel worse. I wish somebody would do something about it.*

_____   5.   *I go to visit Mrs. Ell every afternoon. It seems to cheer her up.*

_____   6.   *I make an effort to visit Mr. Ell every evening. I cannot understand why he ignores my advice. Why is he so forgetful?*

_____   7.   *I love to listen to the stories you tell about your children.*

_____   8.   *When the sign-up sheet for the weekly shopping tour comes around, I want to sign up Ms. Lake and myself.*

_____   9.   *When are people going to start helping each other. Things are so different now.*

_____   10.   *Do not bring me any flowers. They just clutter up the apartment.*

DIRECTIONS FOR THE LEADER: This exercise may be done on an individual or group basis. It works well as an individual homework assignment that is later discussed with the whole class. The purpose of the activity is to clarify the differences between messages that are sensitive/responsive and messages that are hurtful/rejectful.

The reader should think about the responses in each statement. The large group should discuss the different possible responses of listeners to the ten statements presented above.

The following questions should be considered as the reader reflects on this exercise. What are the feelings of the speaker in each statement? On a more personal level, how do you feel as you read each statement?

It may be helpful to take some time to rephrase the "P" statements into "A" statements. In other words, try to make the statements that may encourage people to avoid the speaker into statements that would encourage people to spend more time with or to like the speaker. In what ways do people agree or disagree about which statements are passive, aggressive, or assertive?

It takes about 20 minutes for the discussion of this exercise in a class. (Many people agree that the statements should be labeled as: (1) P; (2) P; (3) A; (4) P; (5) A; (6) P; (7) A; (8) A; (9) P; and (10) P.)

ANGER AND ASSERTION

Anger is a normal feeling. One should be able to express anger in a positive, honest, and assertive way. This will help the angry person as well as other people in the situation. It will provide an opportunity for solid communication and help people to be in contact with their real feelings.

Expressing anger in an open way does not involve hurting others. It does not involve hiding from the feelings within oneself. It does not involve thinking or saying "Forget it!" or "Let's just drop the whole thing!" Such comments are sure to leave people feeling frustrated, unsatisfied, and more angry.

When conflict with others has reached a point of strong angry feelings, an open, honest, and respectful expression of feelings may help to resolve the situation. Each person should take the responsibility for expressing personal feelings. The expression of personal feelings is aided with the use of "I" statements.

For example:

The Dore family just sat down to dinner. It has been a busy, frustrating, tiring day for everyone. The napkins are not on the table, the salad is soggy, and the potroast is burnt. Mr. Dore is angry. He is feeling more "burnt" than the potroast. Mr. Dore scolds in a loud, harsh voice, "I am angry that the dinner is burnt."

"I was so busy..."

Mrs. Dore responds, "I was so busy with the volunteer fund drive, I cooked the roast too long. I get so frightened when you yell that I can't even think straight."

He does not yell, "You always serve the worst meals. Why can't you cook like other women!"
She does not say, "You never appreciate a thing I do. You are always yelling off the top of your head!"

Their willingness to share personal feelings with the help of the communication tool, "I" statements, is the beginning of a two-way dialogue. They are on their way to uncovering the root of the tension and solving the conflict. Their sharing of feelings will help them sort out the objective facts from the opinions. The discussion may show them that the anger is covering up some hurt feelings.

In addition, they will be able to work out some common goals or methods of reaching a common goal. For instance, they may decide that the first person home in the evening starts to cook dinner and the next person to arrive becomes the helper. Or they may decide to treat themselves to dinner in a restaurant after a hectic day of work in the community.

Sometimes a form of negotiation is involved. If both people are willing to deal with the tension and conflict in an open way, they can decide on reasonable requests. Each person may have to give in on one or two details before reaching a point of compromise.

With assertive communication and understanding, cooperation may lead to a compromise that is acceptable to everyone involved. The compromise may result in a better decision than the original demands of either person. This may be demonstrated in the example of Mr. and Mrs. Dore, who have decided to share cooking duties on some busy days and avoid cooking duties on other busy days.

Killer Statements

Sometimes feelings of sadness, anger, or hostility are put into hurtful statements. In writing a book on personal awareness and communication skills, Canfield and Wells (1976) have called hurtful statements "killer statements."

Killer statements are negative comments that "kill" the feelings, thoughts, creative activities, and words of other people. The killer statements put down the achievements of other people. After being put down or insulted a few times, people may be reluctant to talk to or do anything for the insulter. They may fear taking another risk. They are sensitive about sharing a part of themselves. They are trying to avoid being hurt once again.

Some examples of killer statements are:
"Now what do you want."
"That is such a waste of paper."
"You never use tools the right way."
"How many times have I told you the way it should be done!"

Becoming aware of killer statements may involve some hard work. The killer statement is an intimate part of daily conversation. Identifying the harsh words and the hurt feelings are the first steps. Then the idea should be expressed in an assertive way. Putting the idea into words that are respectful and kind enhances communication. It fosters creative thinking and the growth of interpersonal relationships.

For example:
DO SAY: "I will be glad to answer your question after I finish this task."
DO NOT SAY: "Now what do you want."

In another example:
DO SAY: "I would like to show you the correct position for the saw. I know you are eager to finish cutting the pieces of wood for the new picnic table."
DO NOT SAY: "You never use tools the right way."

CRITICISM AND ASSERTION

Criticism includes the negative and positive comments that are made about a person, subject, or situation. Although in its full sense criticism is an evaluation that includes negative as well as positive comments, the negative aspect of criticism is discussed in this book. In other words, criticism is considered to mean finding fault with or judging someone in a harsh way.

People seem to criticize other people for various reasons. Often the critics feel they are being helpful to other people. They are trying to provide suggestions for improvement. They feel their advice is a way to help others do something in a better way.

For example, a neighbor may point out the patches of uncut grass that were missed by the hot, tired family who just finished working on their summer lawn. The neighbor feels friendly and helpful. The family probably is groaning with discouragement at the remarks. They are tired and hot. They would have preferred to use Saturday as a day of recreation rather than yard work.

Sometimes people criticize others because they are critical of themselves. The criticizers feel as if they are offering helpful suggestions that show love and caring. They do not think of their remarks as criticisms. They believe that they are only critical of themselves, never of other people.

These critics are eager to do their best. Their feelings about their own general inadequacies and their guilt put constant pressures on them to perform in better ways. Nothing they do is acceptable. Their own standards always put success one step out of reach. These types of people are often called advice-givers, perfectionists, or faultfinders. Sometimes they are given harsher names.

For example, the violinist who is a perfectionist may never feel good enough to give a public performance. The hours of practice increase. Family members listen, hope, and worry. The violinist, however, listens only to the faults. The two or three errors are heard. The beauty of the rest of the performance is ignored. The personal pressure of the violinist has created a great deal of tension among the members of the family.

Sometimes the faultfinders attempt to hide from their own sense of incompetency. The faultfinders may try to hide behind accusations directed toward other people. They may accuse others of being inconsiderate, inefficient, uncaring, clumsy, and careless. Assertiveness is an effective way to deal with faultfinders.

Finding fault with or blaming other people results in unmet goals and unhappiness. Typically, the giver and the receiver of the blame feel unhappy and anxious. Good communication skills help the faultfinder become aware of the personal factors that lead to the criticizing behavior. Understanding the factors, accepting the feelings involved, and then working to make some changes in the situation will begin the movement of the person toward more pleasant interactions.

Individuals who are at the receiving end of criticism may learn to deal with it in several ways. Controlling their own behavior, they may get what they want out of the situation by not responding to the criticism in a defensive or over-emotional way. They should remember that they are probably not the real source of the criticism. Typically, the faultfinder is upset about a sense of personal inadequacy.

People should think of criticism in terms of the task that needs to be done. They should try to move themselves away from feeling that they are the center of the attack. They should develop a sense of eagerness to approach the task at hand. If the faultfinder refuses to concentrate on the job or task at hand, the other person may handle the situation in an assertive way. Criticism does not need a response. The person who is the target of the criticism does not need to defend or deny the criticism.

When a person tries to guard against the accusations of criticism with anger and defensive remarks, the person has obviously lost some sense of control in the situation. The person may gain back the control by concentrating on the task. Some of the advanced-level, assertive coping techniques in the following section will help the person develop a sense of control and direction in dealing with criticism.

ADVANCED ASSERTIVE COPING TECHNIQUES

In the following section are some assertive techniques to help a person cope with criticism. They are advanced-level skills. They are to be used after much practice with more basic assertion techniques, such as body language skills. The advanced skills are to be used with great care, so that the rights of the individuals in the situation are respected. Used appropriately, the skills may encourage strong, growing relationships. When the skills are abused, relationships and individuals suffer.

The advanced skills in the following paragraphs are (1) "I" statements of feelings, (2) the broken record, (3) free information, (4) fogging, (5) negative inquiry, (6) negative assertion, and (7) clipping.

"I" Statements of Feeling

The "I" statement of feeling involves using "I" to begin a statement. The purpose of the statements are to express one's feelings when the faultfinder starts blaming or criticizing. The person who is being criticized does not think about the meaning of what is being said. Rather, the person concentrates on the general actions or the general category of the behavior of the criticizer. ("I" statements were discussed in Chapter 3.)

For example:
MOTHER: Dinner is such a big job in your house. (Mother is criticizing or finding fault with Nan.)
NAN: When you start fussing with the food on your plate and get that look on your face, you make me upset. (Nan is defensive and angry and starting to blame Mother.)
MOTHER: You go through too much effort to cook dinner. You make so much and nobody eats it.
NAN: I worry about trying to please you, so that you will be happy now that you are living with us. (Nan is using "I" statements of feeling.)
MOTHER: Maybe I could help out in the kitchen. I want to contribute to the family. I like to feel useful.

When the speakers use "I", they change from the blaming action of YOU statements to the personal, sharing action of "I" statements. As Mother and Nan start sharing personal feelings and concerns, the blaming kind of communication changes to an open dialogue. The tension in the setting becomes less. Both people begin to share feelings of concern. They develop new plans that point to a team approach for meal preparation. The resulting dialogue leaves both people feeling closer to each other.

The following discussion exercise, "I" STATEMENTS, provides direction in using "I" statements that give information about personal feelings.

DISCUSSION EXERCISE

"I" Statements

DIRECTIONS FOR THE LEARNER: *Be seated in a circle as one large group. Using "I" statements, people may take turns sharing some information about themselves concerning one of the suggested topics below.*

Some of the suggested topics are:

1. *When I feel good, I am . . .*
2. *When I am angry, I become . . .*
3. *I am afraid that I am . . .*
4. *I am worried that I feel . . .*
5. *If I could change one thing in my life, I would change my . . .*
6. *I was so excited when . . .*

DIRECTIONS FOR THE LEADER: *This exercise depends upon the interaction of a group of people. The purpose of the activity is to strengthen two skills, (1) sharing feelings and (2) looking for hidden messages.*

Participants should discuss the effort it took to stick to the purpose of this exercise, using "I" statements. Some questions to consider for discussion follow. What evidence of open, honest communication did you observe? In what ways was the information that was shared by each person personal or distant?

The group members should try to think beyond the details of the information that was shared in order to figure out the overall message that was shared by each speaker. The overall message should include a summary statement of the feelings and actions of the information that was shared.

What was the undercurrent message that was being communicated? In other words, what subtle or hidden meanings were being communicated as each person shared? Was there something the speaker was trying not to say? Was there something more than the expressed words that the speaker was trying to get across to the rest of the members of the group?

It is important to find out if the speaker had some hidden message, so that people may become sensitive to this level of communication. However, it is not important to find out the details of the hidden message. That is the private information of the speaker. In most groups that have done this exercise, the speaker is eager to share the hidden message when it is a pleasant one. When the speaker hesitates or does not want to share, the leader should encourage everyone to respect the freedom and right that people have to keep certain information private.

Group members should remember to provide encouragement and other forms of positive feedback to each other. It takes about 30 minutes to complete this exercise for a group of about eight members. A larger group may take longer, because the exercise invites people to share emotionally meaningful experiences.

Broken Record

The broken record technique involves saying the same words over and over again. The particular point that is being made or the answer that is being given is repeated in a firm, sincere manner. The words may be rephrased slightly. The message, however, is simple, clear, and repeated. It is important to focus on the message being repeated and to ignore all side issues that may develop.

The broken record technique may be used when making a request to others. Children who are two or three years old are natural experts at this technique. They are able to keep asking repeatedly for the forbidden cookie before mealtime. They remember to keep asking for the toy or library book that was promised long ago.

The broken record technique may be used as a response. Again looking at children who are two or three years old, a person will find the master of the answer, "No." The answer is firm, sincere, and constant, "No, no, no!"

The broken record technique is a good skill to use in a situation involving criticism. Application of the skill is shown in the following example.

WIFE: You never keep up with the maintenance problems around here. This kitchen door is going to fall apart if you do not repair it soon.
HUSBAND: When I buy the oil at the store next Wednesday, I will take care of the door.
WIFE: You always have time for your own hobbies and do not even care about the house.
HUSBAND: I will take care of the door when I buy some oil at the hardware store next Wednesday.

The repeating goes on until the wife indicates that she is getting the message. This will become evident in her words. Her words of criticism will begin to change to indicate that she has heard what the husband is saying. There will be a more relaxed tone to her voice and a note of compromise in her words. For example:

WIFE: I get so upset when things do not work right around the house. Wednesday seems so long away.
HUSBAND: I am trying to make fewer trips into town to save on fuel. Just a couple of more days and I will take care of the door.

The wife is talking about some of her feelings now. She is no longer finding fault with her husband. The attack of criticism has become a working dialogue. The communication shows strong evidence of ending in a solution that will satisfy both people.

Clipping

The technique of clipping involves cutting off extra words from the answer or response given to another person. All extra words are eliminated or clipped off. The response is a simple "yes," or "no," or the fewest words possible. A minimum of information is given out.

When a person feels under attack and is not sure about being right or wrong, the person should give the briefest answer possible until more information is given about the situation. The tactic is for the person to wait for more news or the progress of events. The information is used to clear up the details of the situation.

In general, people are sensitive to attacks and defend themselves quickly. There is no need for the person who is attacked to worry about the point of view of the criticizer. The person who is attacked should be patient until all the information has been gathered. Then, when all the information is in, the person may exercise assertiveness by looking at the issue carefully. Good communication may help clear up the points of confusion in the situation.

For example:
SECRETARY 1: The copying machine is not filled again this morning. You are the one who used it last.
SECRETARY 2: It needs more paper.
SECRETARY 1: I wish people would fill it when it is empty.
SECRETARY 2: Yes.

Secretary 2 provides no fuel to add to the fire of criticism from Secretary 1. Secretary 2 shows patience and self-confidence in her responses. The critical comments stay centered on the copying machine and do not become a personal attack on Secretary 2. Later events may show that there is no more paper at the office or that someone else was at fault. Meanwhile, Secretary 1 and Secretary 2 may continue their work with an attitude of mutual, professional respect.

Free Information

The technique of free information involves careful listening for any extra information that the speaker provides when answering a question or responding to a comment. The assertive listener follows the lead of the extra information by making a comment that encourages the speaker to talk more. The free information technique is a difficult one to learn. It requires the ability of people to learn by observation and practice. The technique may be used to begin and continue an interaction with another person.

To use this technique with skill, the assertive listener must know how to ask open questions which encourage a lengthy response. The reader may refer to the section, Closed and Open Questions, in Chapter 9 for additional information.

An easy way for an assertive listener to learn the technique of open questions is through observing interviews. The newspaper, radio, and television frequently use the interview format. The interviewer uses open questions to obtain more information from the guest. Then the interviewer focuses on specific points of the free information that may interest the viewing audience. The interview may move further in that direction with the aid of more open questions.

For example:
INTERVIEWER: What is your title in the group you represent?
GUEST: I am President of the Older Overachievers Organization and have been on the board for five years.
INTERVIEWER: How did you become involved as a board member five years ago?

Then the guest discusses this point at length. The beginning of the talk focused on the title of the organization. Now the subject is the personal experience of the board member.

A health care worker may apply the same interview style to encourage a patient to share some anxieties about returning home after an illness at a convalescent center.

For example:
HEALTH AIDE: How was your lunch this afternoon?
PATIENT: I could barely touch it. My hip has been aching today. I am probably not healing as quickly as the doctor thinks I am. It is going to be really hard when I leave you wonderful people next week.
HEALTH AIDE: When you go home, how will you handle things while your hip is still healing?

By focusing on the extra information that the patient reveals, the health care worker is helping the patient talk about underlying feelings. The conversation may help direct the patient from worry and anxiety to thinking and planning.

In a situation of criticism, the scene of a health care worker and a patient may be used in the following example.

PATIENT: The lunch was so horrible I could not touch it. Everyday the food gets worse. If you cannot make my hip feel better, the least you people could do is to make the food taste better.
HEALTH AIDE: What kind of difficulty are you having with your hip today?
PATIENT: I have been in pain all morning and the doctor wants me to go home next week. He does not care about someone my age. How could he possibly understand what it is like to be alone and helpless?
HEALTH AIDE: You are worried about being alone at home. Perhaps we can talk to the Homemaker and Health Service people and arrange for some help at your home.

The health aide has focused on the free information of the patient. The health aide has turned the attack of criticism into an investigation of the concerns and feelings of the patient. The direction of the conversation will probably go into planning to help the patient feel capable and comfortable upon returning to an independent lifestyle in the community.

Fogging

The technique of fogging involves focusing on the important point of the communication and then trying to ignore or cloud over the rest of what is said. Action is taken to pay full attention to the matter of concern and to ignore all the extra comments, especially the harsh emotional words.

Fogging is a communication skill of a very high level. It is to be used with great care. The purpose of fogging is to improve communication. The focus is on maintaining a good interaction. It is important to focus on important points in the communication and to ignore the distraction of stirred-up emotions and words that hurt.

Fogging is useful in heated discussions that seem to be moving away from the central subject of concern. In this type of situation, fogging helps the skilled communicator to keep the talk centered on the important elements. It weakens the power of words that hurt, attack, or do not relate to the central topic. The technique of fogging is a way of showing respect to both people in the discussion. It helps the progress of the communication through moments of confusion. It helps people bypass the points or moments that block the resolution. It helps people to finish the point of the discussion.

The technique of fogging has three components. Each component may be used alone. When a person starts to use the technique of fogging, it is easier to work on one of the fogging techniques at a time. A person who communicates at a high level of skill may try to combine the three techniques. However, this is very difficult and should be practiced before it is used in a serious discussion.

The three fogging techniques are explained in the following paragraphs. The techniques are (1) the bit of truth, (2) the principle, and (3) "may be right."

THE BIT OF TRUTH

The first fogging technique, the bit of truth, involves finding a bit of truth in the criticism and then agreeing only with that specific point. The rest of the comments are ignored. No response is made to the other information.

For example:
GEORGE: This cole slaw tastes bad enough to kill someone. You did not even bother to chop the onions right.
HARRY: Smaller pieces of onion would be better.

By centering in on one part of what was said, Harry shows that he is listening and that he respects George. Harry, however, is not agreeing that the cole slaw is bad. Harry is saying only that he thinks smaller bits of onion would be better. Harry is avoiding the emotional impact of George's words. Thus, the hurtful impact of the comments of George is weakened.

Fogging.

THE PRINCIPLE

The second fogging technique, the principle, involves agreeing with the principle of what was said. The value, principle, code of etiquette, or essence of what has been said should be determined first. Then the assertive responder agrees only with the value or principle, etc., and does not become concerned with the rest of the message. The rest of the message is considered to be irrelevant.

For example:
DONNA: How dare you drive off like that! You do not know what you are doing when you get inside a car. Don't you realize that this is an old car. You are going to ruin the engine.
DON: What you say makes sense. The car needs a moment to warm up.

Don has focused on a principle about the proper use of a car, letting the engine warm up before driving on the road. Don avoids any reference to his actions, driving skills, or any of the other details of his companion's comments. The result is that Donna feels he has agreed with her. As a result, she stops the criticism and off they drive into the sunset.

"MAY BE RIGHT"

The third fogging technique is called "may be right." It involves agreeing with the POSSIBILITY that the criticizer could be right. The asserter is not saying that the criticizer is right or wrong. In addition, the asserter is not claiming to be right or wrong.

The asserter is saying only that there exists the possibility that the other person may be correct. In this way, the asserter manages to weaken the power of the other person's critical statement. Weakening the power of the statement also breaks up the influence that the other person is trying to gain over the asserter.

For example:
SUE: You let that meeting get out of control last night. If you would tell people to quiet down once in awhile, someone else would have a chance to contribute.
MARY: There may have been another way of handling last night's meeting. People were certainly concerned about what was happening.

Mary is suggesting that there is a possibility that what Sue is saying is correct. Mary is not saying that Sue is right or wrong. Mary is not admitting that she was wrong. Mary is keeping open the channels of communication. She is talking in a way that is open-minded and respectful of the opinion of other people.

Negative Inquiry

The technique of negative inquiry involves asking for more information. The criticized person who is assertive asks for more details about the criticism that is made. The faultfinder is asked for more facts about the negative comments that were made.

The asserter acts as if the criticism is not upsetting. In other words, the asserter acts as if the purpose of the criticism is to present new goals or directions for personal development.

The technique of negative inquiry is another technique for people with highly developed communication skills. It is a sophisticated technique that requires a great deal of practice in order to be used correctly.

Negative inquiry weakens the effect of criticism. It decreases the strength of the criticism from another person by requesting more information about the negative comments. With the use of negative inquiry, people may change a situation of criticism into an opportunity for education and growth.

As a result of this kind of approach, the faultfinder usually gives information that is more thoughtful. The invitation to the faultfinder provides a way for the critic to relieve some stress. The invitation may encourage the venting of feelings that have built up over a long period of time.

This kind of talk between the asserter and the faultfinder results in constructive dialogue. Instead of acting in the role of an attacker, the faultfinder becomes a helper. Both people may end up discussing areas in the relationship that may benefit from further development.

For example:
OSCAR: You were awful yesterday. I do not like the way you act at baseball games.
OLIVER: What upset you about my behavior yesterday?
OSCAR: You were fine during the first couple of innings. When that man on second base struck out during the third inning, you lost it. I mean, you were swearing and dropping coke all over everyone.

OLIVER: I really like baseball. I get so involved in what is going on. Do you remember what happened when, as you say, "I lost it?"

OSCAR: I like going to games with you. I don't think I have ever seen you that upset before.

OLIVER: Tell me more about what you saw happen during that inning.

The criticism becomes an exchange of information between friends. They are exploring and learning together. Both people feel heard and respected. Their relationship is strengthened by their open, caring communication.

Negative Assertion

The technique of negative assertion involves agreeing with the truth that has been stated and then moving on to provide a positive picture of oneself. After making the appropriate apology or admitting the mistake, assertive people move on quickly to a positive point about themselves. After allowing for the error, the next course of action is a move to provide other people with a positive view of oneself.

Little time should be spent dwelling on mistakes. Mistakes do not need to be defended. They do not merit a great deal of extra attention. The time should be spent on positive points.

Personal awareness is important for growth and development. It is important for people to be able to see their own mistakes. They should be willing to admit their errors. Admitting a mistake shows how human they are.

There is one caution in using negative assertion. It is to be used in social situations, but not in physical or legal conflicts. Admitting a mistake in a social situation shows how human a person is. Sometimes admitting a mistake in a physical conflict or a legal dispute encourages the other person to strike harder to bring one to defeat.

An example of negative assertion in a social situation is the following example:

SALESMAN: You should not have lost your temper with that last customer.

SALESWOMAN: You are right. That was a foolish thing to say. She is one of our good customers and I enjoy waiting on her. I usually manage to sell her just what she is looking for.

The saleswoman has turned an event that centers on her faults to an event that centers on her professional skills.

SUMMARY OF ADVANCED ASSERTIVE COPING TECHNIQUES

The six advanced assertive techniques have been explained and then described in simple example situations. The following example repeats the basic situation of the last example, a salesperson under stress. However, the following example shows how the six assertion techniques may be combined. Terms to identify each technique will be provided in parentheses as the drama of the situation unfolds.

The example:

SALESMAN: How could you say such a thing to that customer! You are the only one who makes the cash register get jammed. You are always pressing the wrong code keys when you ring things up.

SALESWOMAN: It is important to be patient with the customers. (This is a fogging statement. The fogging focuses on the principle of being patient with customers.)

SALESMAN: You should not have lost your temper with that last customer. You are always in such a hurry.

SALESWOMAN: Patience is important. (This repeated emphasis on patience is the beginning of broken records technique.)

SALESMAN: How can you do that and risk your job? The pressure gets to everyone. We cannot afford to lose customers.

SALESWOMAN: Yes. (This is a clipping statement.)

SALESMAN: You should not let the customers get to you, especially when we are working under so much pressure.

SALESWOMAN: You are right. That was a foolish thing for me to say to her. I am usually in top form and handle the customers well on the days we have special sales. (This is negative assertion.) What did you notice was going on before I lost my temper? (This is an example of negative inquiry. Notice how "what" introduces the open question.)

SALESMAN: Maybe it had to do with the cash register. I have noticed that every time the computer is down and the cash register does not work, you seem to get upset. And it always seems to happen at the busiest time of day. (This last statement is free information. The saleswoman may choose to develop the point if it seems to be interesting or important to her.)

SALESWOMAN: I am so glad that you were willing to tell me that. (This is an "I" statement of feeling.) Maybe I will go through the computer manual again and review the section on how to run the register. That will be a big help. Mrs. Tress is one of our steady customers and I enjoy waiting on her. I usually manage to sell her just what she is looking for.

SALESMAN: That is true. She seems to prefer that you wait on her.

Using many different, advanced-level, assertive coping techniques, the saleswoman has turned an event of criticism into a situation that focuses on growth and development and her success as a skilled salesperson.

The following discussion exercise, ASSERTING AND SUPPORTING, provides an opportunity for people to practice using the advanced-level, assertive coping techniques.

DISCUSSION EXERCISE

Asserting and Supporting

DIRECTIONS FOR THE LEARNER AND LEADER: *The purposes of this exercise are (1) to provide an opportunity for group members to practice some assertion skills and (2) to become aware of and share some feelings.*

The leader of the group selects four volunteers at a time to perform this exercise. The four volunteers do some role playing in front of the rest of the group members, who may sit in a semicircle around the four role players. The four roles are one SPEAKER, one ASSERTER, and two SUPPORTERS.

The SPEAKER will team up with one SUPPORTER and the ASSERTER will team up with the other SUPPORTER. The SPEAKER and the ASSERTER will have a discussion. The SUPPORTERS will provide comfort and assistance to their partners during the discussion. More specific directions are provided for the role players in the later paragraphs.

The discussion is finished when the SPEAKER and the ASSERTER have reached an agreement or compromise. Then the role players and the rest of the group members spend some time discussing the interaction.

If the four role players are interested, they may want to switch roles, choose a new word, and start a new interaction.

It may be helpful to the role players, however, to think about their experiences for a while and to give four different volunteers a chance to act out roles and practice skills. Typically, the role players are tired after one round of this exercise.

A fresh set of role players will generate a different creative direction for the next round of interaction. They will bring out a different type of conflict and manner of interacting. Changing role players provides a chance for group members, first, to become directly involved in active learning and, then, to unwind while participating indirectly as observers in the next round of role playing. It seems to be helpful to the total group to have a short recess between each round of interaction.

SPECIFIC DIRECTIONS FOR THE SPEAKER: *The speaker thinks of a personal incident or makes up a situation that centers around the theme of a word that has been chosen from the next paragraph.*

The speaker chooses a word from the following list:

fear	*failure*	*loneliness*	*anxiety*
hate	*selfishness*	*restlessness*	*hurt*
jealousy	*rejection*	*anger*	*sadness*

The speaker's role in the discussion exercise is to blame the asserter for being the cause or problem maker in the incident or situation. The speaker and asserter sit down facing each other in some way.

SPECIFIC DIRECTIONS FOR THE ASSERTER: *The asserter listens to the speaker and uses various advanced-level, assertive coping techniques to try to deal with the speaker. The asserter is trying to calm down the speaker. The asserter may try whatever coping techniques seem to be appropriate in an effort to avoid, deal with, or escape the critical attacks of the speaker.*

The asserter and the speaker should become intensely involved in an exchange of words as the drama unfolds.

SPECIFIC DIRECTIONS FOR THE TWO SUPPORTERS: Each of the supporters gives support and care to an assigned partner during the role playing. One supporter is assigned to the speaker and the other supporter is assigned to the asserter. Each supporter stands or sits near the person receiving the support. Thus, the speaker has a supporter close by and the asserter has a supporter close by.

The supporters take care of the emotional well-being of their partners. They try to empathize with their partners. They care about the stress their partners are experiencing and try to be helpful.

Occasionally one of the supporters may choose to call a "time out" in order to give a pep talk to the partner. The pep talk may be helpful when the partner seems anxious, confused, losing ground, or unsure of the progress of the role playing.

The supporters may contribute to the interaction between the speaker and the asserter when given permission by the partner. However, the supporters should limit their contributions to words that clarify or reinforce the feelings or statements of their partners. It should be the responsibility of the speaker and the asserter to add new ideas to the communication.

The roles of the supporters are to offer comfort and to help strengthen their partners whether the partners are right, wrong, justified, or unjustified in what they say. Sometimes the supporters may find that appropriate touching on the arms or shoulders of their team member is helpful.

SPECIFIC DIRECTIONS FOR THE LEADER: This exercise is for a group of people who are sophisticated in communication skills. The leader of the total group should be experienced in group behavior and facilitating feelings. Anticipating the intense, high level of interaction that may occur in this exercise is essential to promote a positive learning experience for participants.

The exercise requires a leader who remains in the background of the role playing, but yet is sensitive to the needs of the players. Emotions may become heated during the exchange. It is important to remember that the purpose of the exercise is to develop and practice an advanced-level of assertion techniques in communication. Actually the purposes are twofold: (1) to practice skills and (2) to get in touch with feelings.

The leaders should have skill in slowing down or interrupting the interaction to keep people oriented to the objectives of the exercise. Occasional, brief time-outs may help people to reflect on the activity that is occurring and predict the direction of the immediate issue.

The total group should discuss the progress of developments in the exercise. They should spend some time considering the following questions:

What trilevel communication did you observe? How did people use body language to help their spoken words? As the role playing progressed more deeply into the issue, how did the body language change?

Thinking in terms of assertive, aggressive, and passive, how would you label the general behaviors of the speaker, the asserter, and the two supporters? Which of the assertive coping techniques seemed easier to use than the others? Which of the assertive coping techniques seemed to be more effective than the others? Which communication technique was the most useful in helping to resolve the conflict?

How did the speaker and the asserter work with their supporters? What was the experience of the members of the group who were not in the active roles? How did you feel playing your role? How did it feel to be working with a partner? Which role, speaker, asserter, or supporter, would you have preferred to play? Of the role that you prefer, what factors in the role seem to be interesting or appealing?

As part of the group discussion, participants should remember to provide positive feedback and words of appreciation to the players. The positive remarks should highlight specific parts of the role playing. It is important to talk about sensitive issues, to build up the positive feelings, and to strengthen the cohesiveness of the group before the discussion is completed. Otherwise, the intensity of the exercise may result in people feeling emotionally exposed, dangling, and hurt.

The exercise requires 45 to 60 minutes to complete one round of the role playing and discussion.

SUMMARY

Selective assertiveness is a need basic to emotional and physical well being. Being able to make a selection from available alternatives helps a person to choose the best way to lead a satisfying life. Many techniques on assertiveness are available to help a person gain appropriate attention, cope with criticism, and communicate openly.

Passiveness and aggressiveness do not work in a healthful way to achieve goals and solve problems in normal, everyday living. A person should not wait passively with the hope that others eventually will see their needs and respond spontaneously. In most situations people should not be aggressive. In the long run, people feel dissatisfied and unfulfilled when they choose behaviors that ignore or disrespect the rights of other people.

Selective assertiveness helps older people develop pleasant relationships. It helps them to act upon their rights of personal freedom. Though difficult to enact, the asserter knows that assertive behavior values each person and builds relationships. Assertive people function as whole human beings.

Suggestions for Further Reading

ANGER

Canfield, J., & Wells, H. C. (1976). *100 Ways to Enhance Self-Concept in the Classroom.* Englewood Cliffs, NJ: Prentice-Hall.

Egan, G. (1975). *The Skilled Helper.* Monterey, CA: Brooks/Cole.

Rathus, S. A. (1975). Principles and practices of assertive training: An eclectic overview. *The Counseling Psychologist,* 5(4), 9–20.

ASSERTION SKILLS

Alberti, R. E., & Emmons, M. L. (1974). *Your Perfect Right.* San Luis Obispo, CA: Impact.

Barkan, B. (September-October, 1981). The Live Oak regenerative community. *Aging,* (321–322), 2–7.

Butler, P. (1976). Assertive training: Teaching women not to discriminate against themselves. *Psychotherapy: Theory, Research and Practice,* 13(1), 56–60.

Corby, N. (1975). Assertion training with aged populations. *The Counseling Psychologist,* 5(4), 60–74.

Donnelly, G. F. (1981). Freeing the nurse to practice. In E. J. Forbes & V. M. Fitzsimons, *The Older Adult.* St. Louis, MO: The C. V. Mosby Co., 128–129.

Flowers, J. V., & Booraem, C. D. (1975). Assertion training: The training of trainers. *The Counseling Psychologist,* 5(4), 29–36.

Hamachek, D. E. (1971). *Encounters with the Self.* New York: Holt, Rinehart and Winston.

Rathus, S. A. (1975). Principles and practices of assertive training: An eclectic overview. *The Counseling Psychologist,* 5(4), 9–20.

INTERACTION

Lowenthal, M. F., & Haven, C. (1968). Interaction and adaptation: Intimacy as a critical variable. *American Sociologist Review,* 33(1), 20–30.

PASSIVENESS/AGGRESSION

Alberti, R. E., & Emmons, M. L. (1975). *Stand Up, Speak Out, Talk Back!* San Luis Obispo, CA: Impact.

Smith, M. J. (1975). *When I Say No, I Feel Guilty.* New York: Dial Press.

Sobel, M. (September-October, 1981). Growing old in Britain. *Aging,* (321–322), 8–16.

12

Transition in Life

As the events of life unfold day after day and year after year, a person becomes aware of the constant change that is an integral part of the life process. The unfolding of life involves the natural development of young, simple structures to mature, complex systems involving different amounts of time.

In nature, a seed becomes a full, petaled flower within a few weeks. A seedling becomes a giant pine tree after several years. Volcanic ash and coral reefs in the Pacific Ocean near Equador, South America, formed the Galapagos Islands after several centuries.

What is the process that involves the ongoing development of human life? How does the richness of change occur?

A baby who explores with great curiosity grows into a restless adolescent. The adolescent questions, learns, and challenges the established way of doing things. After a few years, the adolescent becomes a stable, civic-minded adult.

As the years continue to pass, the adult becomes a senior, who teaches others good business techniques, home-making skills, and relationship skills. In a few more years, the adult may become a grandparent, who enjoys watching the grandchildren explore everything within the reach of the sensory system of sight, sound, touch, smell, and taste.

Similar to the metamorphosis of the seed that grows into a flower, the human being develops from a simple being to a complex, resourceful, adult person. The human being may take pleasure in personal change and growth. Humans are enriched further with the pleasure of being able to participate in and enjoy the development of others.

ADULT DEVELOPMENT

Adult development includes physical, emotional, social, intellectual, philosophical, and spiritual areas. After going through the successive stages of childhood, a person passes through a series of adult stages. Typical behavior has been researched, defined, and described for the first two decades of human life. However, the identification of normal patterns of development during the middle years of the human life span are still in the process of being verified by scientific studies. The late decades of mature adult development are still in the beginning stages of being identified.

Many studies point out that genetic inheritance as well as environmental influences contribute to how a person ages. Biological, psychological, sociological, philosophical, and religious factors are interrelated. They work together to influence aging in subtle ways.

Dr. Paul T. Costa, Jr., chief psychologist at the research center of the National Institute on Aging in Baltimore believes that personality may contribute indirectly to longevity, the length of life. People who have a warm, outgoing personality and are assertive seem to be able to handle the stress associated with aging better than people who are somewhat depressed and withdrawn from others.

Some theorists have attempted to describe the adult stages of growth. The descriptions and theories of adult development vary widely. Often one theory contradicts another. Historical trends, cultural patterns, differences in professional training, and inconsistent attitudes toward aging are reflected in most of the developmental theories of middle and older adult life.

For example, personality and behavior have been explained in different ways as the thinking of psychologists changed throughout the twentieth century. In psychoanalysis, the popular model of aging from the late nineteenth century, Freud discussed instinct and different levels of consciousness as being responsible for behavior. A student of Freud, Carl Jung talked about the expansion of the personality to be more wholistic as a person becomes older.

Later, humanistic psychologists, such as Carl Rogers and Eric Erikson, focused on the basic worth of human beings. Rogers felt that the individual needed to learn how to function fully as an independent person. Openness to new, daily experiences, making choices that help one grow, and realizing the full possibilities in one's life lead to a healthy existence.

Erikson, on the other hand, focused on the virtues of love, caring for others, and wisdom. Erikson felt that the challenge of the later years of life was (1) to resolve and accept the purpose and meaning of life, (2) to realize one's potential and limitations, and (3) to resolve despair with wisdom. As they mature, adults undergo multiple biological and psychological changes that contribute to the process of aging.

Physical well being is determined by proper exercise, good nutrition, and adequate rest. Vocational as well as avocational development are also important to physical well being. Vocational is related to work. Avocational is related to hobbies or special interests.

Factors that contribute to emotional well being are feeling worthwhile, often called self-worth or self-esteem, being productive, having control in making decisions, feeling useful, having activities or roles that are satisfying, and having at least one close relationship.

Successful aging is defined by some researchers as a combination of several factors, physical and emotional health, comfort, longevity, and satisfaction. Successful aging is the result of physical and emotional wellness over many years of living.

THE BALANCE OF VARIETY

According to many research reports, mature adults consider a happy life to include the following:

1. Material well being.
2. Physical well being.
3. Emotional well being.
4. Keeping informed.
5. Learning new things.
6. Having useful work.
7. Relations with family members (this appears to be more important to younger adults).
8. Relations with friends (this appears to be more important to older adults).
9. Helping.
10. Socializing with other people.

Various factors work together to make up human beings who function in healthy ways. It is important for people to contribute to their own health by having variety and flexibility in their lives. Maintaining variation and adaptability in the activities that fill their lives will contribute to feelings of well being.

Some people have a hard time providing variation, flexibility, and balance in their lives. For example, the work ethic is still a powerful driving force as a motivator for people. In looking at their daily schedules, some people may find variety and balance in a schedule such as the following situation.

The following schedule represents a typical day for Millie:

1. Work at the office for 9 hours.
2. Catch up on extra work from the office at home for 3 hours.
3. Spend time with the family for 2 hours.
4. Play tennis for 1 hour.
5. Community zoning board meeting for 2 hours.
6. Read for 1 hour.
7. Sleep for 6 hours.

A closer look, however, may reveal that the total schedule is a working schedule. Not only is the job-related time of 9 hours spent in work, but a driving, competitive attitude turns the family time of 2 hours and the recreation time of 2 hours at tennis and reading into work. In reality there is no variation, flexibility, and adaptability in the life of Millie. Every task and relationship is interpreted and used as a situation for some kind of work.

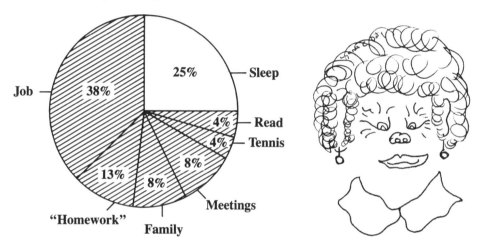

Millie's day: 75% of the day spent at some kind of work.
▨ Time that is work-related;   ☐ Time that is not work-related.

Another type of person may be able to measure a great deal of time spent with others and almost no time spent alone. People may be happy doing things the same way they learned at first. They may become quite upset with new machines and methods.

These people prefer to use the scrub board and the hand-powered lawn mower instead of the automatic washing machine and gas- or electric-powered mower. They refuse to consider that the new equipment provides the opportunity to exchange tasks of long drudgery for some extra time to enjoy relationships and creative interests.

Some people have a small number of activities that interest them. Developing other interests that give a balance to a person's life may be a hard challenge for them. A person, such as Mack, for example, may enjoy his life as a single person. He enjoys his work as a cook. His only hobby is hunting alone with his beagle. Mack likes to hunt wild game to use in different recipes that he has created.

Mack seems uninterested in trying out any other activities. To such invitations, he says that he does not want to waste his time. He considers the company of one or more people to be a bothersome crowd. As a lifelong loner, Mack will probably feel satisfied with his well-established lifestyle for many years.

If, however, he can no longer cook or go hunting, he may have great difficulty finding other activities that bring him a sense of satisfaction. He may not be able to deal with the changes in his life.

Since Mack did not develop much variety in his earlier style of living, his inability to deal with changes in activities may have serious consequences. Mack may become depressed. He may not have enough resources to take care of the normal, daily needs of living. He may not have enough income during retirement to pay for food, shelter, and utilities. He does not have anyone other than his faithful beagle to help him take care of himself.

In general, people need different kinds of activities in which they participate (1) in group or team as well as individual activities; (2) in active and sedentary, or more quiet, calming, and restful interests; (3) in self-fulfilling activities and activities that provide service to others; (4) in short-term and long-term projects; (5) in familiar and new experiences; (6) in activities that involve rational thinking and activities involving creative thinking; and (7) in extrospection as well as introspection.

Group and Individual Activities

Group or team activities, such as baseball or tennis, provide interaction and social support. It is important to know how to perform in activities that involve a large number of people, such as baseball. However, it is also important to know how to participate in activities that involve smaller numbers of people, such as tennis. Some activities, such as bowling or horseshoes, have flexibility in that they may involve large or small numbers of people.

Individual activities are also important. Individual activities help a person to develop a separate sense of the self. Activities, such as walking, gardening, or playing a musical instrument, may provide special pleasure. The activities allow a person to enjoy being alone. Relaxing in an outdoor setting, a woman may take some time to think through her plans for the day. Sitting on the sunporch, a man could relax and reflect on personal concerns.

Active and Sedentary Interests

Tennis and playing the piano are examples of complementary activities. Tennis is an active game. It requires high levels of energy and quick decisions. On the other hand, playing the piano is a more sedentary interest. It involves a more even, restful level of energy.

Tennis provides a great deal of physical exercise. Playing the piano may be more restful, although some music is intense and provides great emotional exercise. The way a person participates often follows the mood of the music, the interpretation of the player, or a combination of both.

Self-Fulfillment and Service

Working on hobbies may provide the opportunity for self-fulfillment as well as service to others. A carpenter may build a bookcase for his or her home or donate it to furnish the community center.

In a similar way, a person who makes quilts feels fulfilled and productive. A quiltmaker uses practical and artistic talents. Quilts are wonderful gifts that provide an important service of warmth to others during cold winter nights.

Short-Term and Long-Term Projects

Working on short-term and long-term projects help a person to organize time and to feel productive. An example of a short-term project may be planning the next weekly breakfast for the Rotary Club. The project requires a small investment of time. The reward, the good feeling of a job well done, comes in a few days when the breakfast meeting is completed.

Examples of long-term projects are (1) organizing a new system to keep income tax information and receipts and (2) redecorating the study. These projects require a larger investment of time and energy. In addition, they provide a sense of continuity over a longer period of time. The rewards of a long-term goal may add a great deal to the self-concept and esteem of an individual.

Familiar and New Experiences

Familiar activities provide a pleasant sense of relaxation and security. However, even though they may bring on stress, learning new activities may stimulate growth. Hidden talents and skills may be uncovered in the process.

A familiar activity, such as painting the house may provide a person with the sense of relaxation and productivity. Trying to develop a new interest or using skills in a different way, the painter may try to work at an easel.

Struggling with different tools and new techniques, the painter may experience a great deal of frustration before hidden talents emerge in the picture of a beautiful landscape or a still life of fruit. The new painting on the canvas is the result of unleashed creativity which fills the artist with a new excitement.

Something new.

Rational and Creative Thinking

Rational, organized thinking may be balanced by spontaneous, creative thinking. Rational thinking involves ideas that unfold in a step-by-step manner that is controlled and logical. A person may use the method of organized thinking to review the figures in a bank book.

At first, creative thinking may seem confusing and disorganized as ideas take on different forms and directions. Later, the ideas may come together in a different way. The ideas may give new insight to a plan. Or, they may refresh the spirit of the person watching a lonely flower unfold in a meadow as the sun rises in the morning sky.

Sometimes rational thinking and creative thinking may be used together. For example, creative thinking helps a person develop a feeling into an artistic form. The artwork may be expressed in music, a painting, or the theater. Rational, organized thinking helps the person refine the rough edges of the artwork until it is ready to share with the public.

Extrospection and Introspection

A balance of extrospection and introspection are important to healthy living. It seems as if society associates extrospection with young and middle-age adults. Introspection seems to be associated with older adults.

Extrospection is a concern about matters outside of oneself. Through extrospection a person stays in contact with the demands of the practical parts of daily life. These practical elements may involve rearing a family, paying off the mortgage, being involved with a crime watch program in the neighborhood, or improving the system of traffic lights for the roads downtown.

Introspection is a concern about the person within. The process of introspection involves reflection about oneself, finding the real nature of oneself. As a person looks within, parts of his or her life may take on new meaning. As a result of finding new meanings in parts of the self, a person may develop a new attitude to life in general. Usually personal beliefs, especially religious beliefs, play a large part in the insight and wisdom that results from this kind of "inside" thinking.

Often people become introspective after they have experienced a major change in life. Retirement from a career in the military, graduation from school, and marriage after many years of widowhood involve major changes in a person's lifestyle. Major milestones such as these may be accompanied by a great deal of introspection.

Perhaps, younger adults are more eager "to do" because they are eager to act, to finish jobs, and to move ahead. Perhaps, older people spend more time thinking through a situation because they have a larger "savings account" in their bank of experiences to consider before they move ahead.

Variety in the life of an individual is important. The following discussion exercise, LIFE STYLE, is an attempt to help readers explore the variety in their own lives. The exercise encourages readers to think about and look at their personal lifestyles.

Looking at the kinds of activities that fill up a day or a week, readers will find a picture of their interests, choices, and lifestyles. The exercise will show what parts or what activities contribute to the specific lifestyle of each individual.

DISCUSSION EXERCISE

Life Style

DIRECTIONS FOR THE LEARNER: Work through the discussion exercise on an individual basis and then discuss the results with other participants.

Think about your own life for a little while. How do you spend your time? For a few minutes, think about the usual things you do with your time and energy. Your activities may be related to work, recreation, relatives, or strangers. Your activities may be boring or dreary. Or, they may be fun. They may involve daydreaming, trying to fulfill the wishes of your imagination. The activities may be actual things that you do.

STEP I: In the space provided below, make up a list of all the different kinds of activities that take up your time during a typical day or a typical week. Which time would be more meaningful to you, (1) to think in terms of one typical day or (2) to think in terms of one typical week. Consider what would be the most sensible way for you to do this exercise. What would give you the best information about yourself?

If you choose TYPICAL DAY, outline in the large space below the day as (1) morning, (2) afternoon, and (3) evening. Then fill in the activities. This is an example of a chart for a TYPICAL DAY:

MORNING	AFTERNOON	EVENING

If you choose TYPICAL WEEK, outline in the large space below the days of the week. Then fill in your activities. This is an example of a chart for a TYPICAL WEEK:

SUNDAY _____

MONDAY _____

TUESDAY _____

WEDNESDAY _____

THURSDAY _____

FRIDAY _____

SATURDAY _____

If the space provided below for your chart is not large enough to include all the things that you do, please add enough extra sheets to take care of your particular situation. Some people may need less than the following space; others may need one or two extra sheets of paper.

CHART OF TYPICAL _____ *(DAY OR WEEK)*

STEP II: Look over your list of different activities in the space above. Think about each activity in terms of which category or categories explained below describe each of your activities. The five categories are:

1. *R for RECREATION—This includes leisure time, hobbies, sports, etc. The activities are for fun, pleasure, relaxation, or goofing-off.*

2. *C for CAREER—This includes work for pay, or volunteer work for no pay. The activities help one to be self-supporting or to feel productive. This may be a job with specific expectations or a contract that exchanges your services for certain resources. If you are a homemaker, then it may be a bit difficult to separate the activities that relate to your career as a homemaker from the activities that relate to recreation.*

3. *G for GROUP—This involves time or activities spent directly with other people. Some type of social exchange or interaction occurs during this time. The people may be family members or friends.*

4. *S for SOLITARY—This involves time spent alone, by yourself. The activity may be related to work or recreation.*

5. *M for MISCELLANEOUS—This category is open to any of your activities that do not belong to any one of the categories just listed. Some of your categories may fall into a group that you may want to identify, such as O for OUTDOOR activities or I for INDOOR activities. Other categories of interest may be SELF for SELF-FULFILLMENT or SELF-DEVELOPMENT or SERV for SERVICE TO OTHERS.*

Go back over the items in your list of TYPICAL DAY or TYPICAL WEEK. What category does each item fall into? First, does each activity fall into the category of RECREATION or CAREER? Put an "R" before each activity that is a form of RECREATION for you. Then put a "C" for a career- or job-related activity.

Then go over the whole list again. Decide whether each activity belongs to the category of GROUP or SOLITARY. Label each activity with either a "G" for group activity or an "S" for solitary activity.

For example, if the listed activity is . . . play the piano. This activity may be labeled as "C" for career and "S" for solitary if you are a professional pianist who performs concertos or solo pieces. Even though you may play occasionally with a band or orchestra, you usually play alone on the stage. Your activity would be labeled like this:

Play the piano   C   S

DIRECTIONS FOR THE LEADER: This exercise may be done on an individual or group basis. The purpose of the exercise is for people to evaluate the quality and quantity of activities in their daily lives.

This activity works well as a homework assignment that is evaluated on an individual basis or is discussed later with the group. Participants may find it helpful to consider the following comments and questions as they think through or discuss their results.

Look over your list of labeled activities. How do the R, C, G, S, etc., categories balance out? Are you "all work and no play" or just the opposite? According to your list of activities, how do you mix the need to be alone with the need for interactions with others? How does your list satisfy you? How does it dissatisfy you? How would you like the list to differ?

Some people almost never think about how they spend their time during a typical day or week. It may be quite a struggle for them to figure out the details of a daily schedule.

For example, they may think that a daily schedule has only two activities, work and dinner time. It may be hard for them to think about the details of different, daily activities, such as carpooling to work with a friend or stopping at the supermarket for groceries on the way home. Their general category of work may include nonwork activities, such as lunch with friends or a meeting in the community. It may take these people a while to realize the details of their lives that they usually take for granted.

Some people feel discouraged when their lists contain only a few activities while the lists of other people are long. Participants may need to be reminded that individuals have different ways of living a comfortable, rewarding lifestyle. After participating in the group discussion, some group members may want to think about the exercise again. It may be helpful to them to make up a new list of activities in a TYPICAL DAY or a TYPICAL WEEK.

Developing the list requires about 20 minutes of thinking time. This activity works well as a homework assignment. Then during the next meeting, the participants may take about 20 minutes to exchange information about their lists. Otherwise, it takes about 40 minutes to complete the exercise and discussion together.

AGING

As people get older, they experience the process of aging in different ways. Adults seem to become more different from one another as they age. After the passage of many years, the different backgrounds, educational levels, the socio-economic status, beliefs, and values have transformed each older person into a unique individual.

In a group of older people, the variation among the people is obvious immediately. They look different. Their styles of talking vary. The older adult functions in ways that are different from a young adult who is just beginning the adventures of life.

Getting to know the individuals by listening to the stories they share, an observer may become even more aware of the variety that makes up the complex history of each life. Each person has a unique personality that has been enriched with a special set of past and present circumstances. As the years of experience increase the person becomes richer with perspectives.

Story-telling time.

Aging has been described as a time of growth, minimal stress, happiness, health, continued development, and meaningful friendships. Although many think of aging as a process involving positive growth during the ongoing experience of life, many others think of aging with a negative attitude.

Some experts in psychology, such as Buehler, Havighurst, and Super, considered the life of normal people, 60 years of age and over, to be filled with decline, regression, despair, and deprivation. In *Childhood and Society* (1963), and more recently in *Life Cycle Completed* (1982), Erik H. Erikson, however, believes that older people continue to develop. Erikson suggested that wisdom may be achieved by older people. When older adults work on self-acceptance and a personal evaluation of their life experiences, they may draw new meaning from the significance of their lives.

DEMOGRAPHICS

Currently, older persons represent 11% of the total U.S. population. By the year 2000 they will represent 16% of the U.S. population.

Based on the 1980 United States Census, more people than ever before have celebrated their 65th birthdays. During the 1970s, the number of people 65 years of age or over increased by 5 million. It is predicted that by the year 2000 the number will increase by 7 million people.

Every day approximately 5,000 Americans celebrate being 65 years of age. More than 25.5 million people have celebrated that event. This represents an increase of 27.9% more than the number of people 65 years of age in 1970. By the year 2000 a total of 32 million people will be 65 years of age or more. Of those 32 million people, 6 million will be over 85 years of age.

In the United States, some 3% of all older people, 60 to 65 years of age and older, are institutionalized in long-term care facilities. Currently, about 20% or 1.2 million people, 85 years of age and older, require long-term care in nursing homes. It is anticipated that in the year 2000, about 300,000 people will need long-term care.

Aging, however, is not a synonym for deterioration or loss. Even though 6 million disabled older people live in the United States, this number becomes more meaningful when specific categories of ability are considered.

First of all, most of the elderly are highly mobile. For example, 86.2% of older Americans go outside their homes without any difficulty. They are independent and take care of all their normal, daily needs for comfortable living.

Only 5.4% of older people must exert some effort to go outside their homes. They need some kind of assistance. They require some special equipment or the help of another person to move about in their communities.

About 6% of older Americans are confined to their rooms or homes. They maintain a somewhat independent level of living with the assistance of relatives or part-time helpers. In addition, of course, are the approximately 3% of older people who receive skilled nursing care in long-term care institutions.

In other words, almost 92% of older people are independent, active, and in charge of their own lives. In contrast to this, only a small number of older people, about 3%, are highly dependent on the skilled care of others for their survival.

Median Age

Median age is used to indicate the general age of a population. In other words, 50% of the general population are older and 50% of the general population are younger than the median figure. The median age is in the center of all the other figures. A median age in the young 20's indicates that the population of a country is young. A median age of over 30 years indicates that a country has an old population.

In the United States, the median age of the general population has changed from 28 years old in 1970 to 30 years old in 1980. Experts in statistics predict that the median age will continue to increase in the decades ahead.

Descriptions of the Older American

The new entrants into the category of older persons differ from those who were elderly two or three decades ago. Their life histories, experiences, interests, resources, and attitudes are much more varied than that of their elders.

Older people today are healthier and more active. They are better educated. They are more likely to speak out to others and to try to change the rules that govern them.

The influence of older Americans today is being felt throughout the country. Older Americans made an impact on state and national legislative assemblies. Their needs have been the subject of advocacy groups. Organized groups of older Americans have been members and leaders of committees that have resulted in hundreds of bills being enacted into law.

Despite this new "gray wave" of activity sweeping over the nation, the stereotypes of the old are still deeply imbedded in society. A great effort must be made to continue the search for accurate information about the older population. Aging must be defined in terms that mirror the true process of the total development of the human being.

The following discussion exercise, AGING VOCABULARY, allows readers to expand their vocabulary of words that relate to aging. Then a second discussion exercise, OLDER PEOPLE, provides an opportunity for readers to develop an awareness of some older people who play important parts in the life of the community and country.

DISCUSSION EXERCISE

Aging Vocabulary

DIRECTIONS FOR THE LEARNER: Add to this list of words other words and terms you may think of that describe the positive aspects of aging.

accepting	*heterogeneous*	*sage*
ambitious	*humorous*	*sensible*
candid	*independent*	*sensuous*
capricious	*keen*	*sharing*
cheerful	*kind*	*smiling*
concerned	*loving*	*stubborn*
creative	*mentor*	*supportive*
doting	*motivated*	*sweet*
eager	*nice*	*teacher*
emotional	*patient*	*thoughtful*
empathic	*perceptive*	*understanding*
energetic	*persistent*	*unique*
fighters	*principled*	*volunteer*
frisky	*resilient*	*willing*
giving	*respectful*	*wise*
grandparent	*role model*	*zealous*

DIRECTIONS FOR THE LEADER: This exercise may be used as an individual or group activity. The purpose of the exercise is to help people think more about the positive aspects of aging.

First, the participants should take a few moments to add vocabulary words to the list above. It may be helpful to think about the images or feelings that are experienced as people read through the list of words. In a group situation, as people think of more words that relate to aging, they may share their own words with other participants.

Typically, as people work on this activity, they start thinking in more objective terms, such as aging in general. Then they start thinking in more subjective terms, that of becoming or being old themselves.

Memories begin to unravel. The memories may be accompanied by physical sensations. There may be a flood of images, ideas, special sounds, fragrances, or nostalgic experiences. The participants may remember about an older person who was or is still part of their lives. The person may be a close relative, such as a grandparent, or a temporary acquaintance, such as a grade-school teacher.

If people are willing, they should be encouraged to share some of the memories and sensations they experience. And more positive aging words should be drawn from this sharing.

Positive feedback should be provided to participants who are willing to share. Appreciation should be given for their willingness and their efforts to contribute to the learning of other participants.

It takes about 15 minutes to complete the exercise and discussion.

DISCUSSION EXERCISE

Older People

DIRECTIONS FOR THE LEARNER: *On an individual basis think about older people who have played important parts in your personal life, the life of your community, or the progress of your country. The older people may be relatives, friends, or persons that you know as a result of information from the television, the radio, the newspapers, or magazines.*

Look below at the list of older people and add other names that come to your mind. Then use the vocabulary list in the previous discussion exercise to help you describe the characteristics of the special people listed below. Some descriptive words have been added already to some of the names to help you get started.

George Burns—cheerful, humorous

Jimmy Carter—

Kathryn Hepburn—energetic

Maggie Kuhn—persistent

Art Linkletter—

Representative Claude Pepper—

The (current) Pope Pius—

The Queen Mother of England—

Chancellor Helmidt Schmidt—ambitious, patient

Barbara Stanwick—dignified

DIRECTIONS FOR THE LEADER: *This exercise may be done on an individual or group basis. The purpose of the exercise is to focus in on the strengths of older, well known people who are or have been leaders in society.*

Take some time in class to discuss your answers. Begin to become aware of older persons in your community and in the limelight of the daily news. What are they telling or showing you about the ways of older persons? What strengths and talents are they contributing to the development of your local organizations, churches, temples, community, and the world?

It takes about 20 minutes to complete this discussion exercise.

AGISM

Agism is thinking or believing in a negative manner about the process of becoming old or about old people. Although agism may involve attitudes toward persons of any age, it is typically used with older persons.

The attitude of agism in many people is heard in words that distort and restrict the abilities and resources of people who are getting older. Agism is a part of the meaning of words that refer to aging in diminishing terms. Some examples of these words with negative meanings are deterioration, disease, disability, distance, disengagement, and dependence.

Generally speaking, agism may be seen almost everywhere in the U.S. The aged are devalued in society. Some think that old age is considered to be a condition that should be dreaded, avoided, prevented, or even reversed.

Not only do people of all ages have negative attitudes toward the elderly, but the attitude is especially strong among older people. Thus, the younger generations observe and learn from the older ones. They, in turn, teach their attitudes to the upcoming generations. Agism may be divided into two categories, age distortion and age restrictiveness.

Age Distortion

The first category, age distortion misrepresents the ability of people in relationship to their numerical age. It distorts the real ability of the individual person. It relies on the number of years a person has lived, known as the numerical or chronological age, to determine ability. In other words, people should or should not be doing something because they are a certain number of years old.

An example of age distortion is the thinking that a 70 year old man should not travel alone on the bus to go shopping, that it is too risky for someone his age. Another example is expecting or demanding that a person retire at the age of 65 because it is commonly believed that is the time when people should retire. This attitude of agism ignores the specific abilities, needs, and interests of the people who are involved in the situations.

Age Restrictiveness

The second category of agism is age restrictiveness. This category concerns limiting the behavior of a person because the person is considered to be too old to do certain activities. In other words, the years of age or chronological age is the deciding factor used to gauge the behavior. Again, the actual interests, needs, or abilities of the individual are not used or considered.

An example of age restrictiveness is the thinking that Henry Fonda and Kathryn Hepburn were too old to star in the movie, "On Golden Pond." The movie was about an elderly couple. The couple were dealing with the issues of getting old during their annual summer stay at a lakeside cottage in New England.

In this situation, the quality of work by Mr. Fonda and Ms. Hepburn shattered the feelings of agism. Their performances won the attention and respect of actors and viewers everywhere. The Oscar Awards they received as a result were symbols of the high level of respect paid to them by their professional peers.

Feeling Disconnected and Useless

Many people think of aging as a process of disconnection. They see it as disconnection from the self, from experience, from independence, and from productivity. As they age, they feel an increase in distance from the ongoing activities of life. This results in their feeling useless.

The feelings of uselessness among older people may be seen in the discouraged faces of the many who rest in idleness for hours on benches that are set out in public places. They feel out of step, out of place, and out of the pulsebeat of life. They look downcast and discouraged. They seem to have nothing to do and no one to be with. In their final years, they wait only for life to finish.

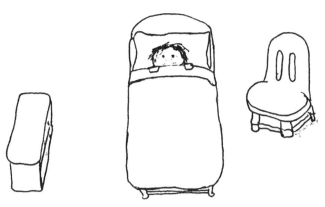

Waiting with emptiness.

CHANGES IN AGISM

People, however, are beginning to become sensitive to the needs of the aging. The youth-oriented culture is extending itself slowly to include the older generations of human beings. As attention begins to focus on them, often the older generations are viewed at first with agism. Then, as people in the media become more comfortable with and accepting of them, older people are shown as individuals with special personalities and skills.

For example, formerly, Grandmother was portrayed frequently on television as a person having bad breath or stained dentures. However, more recent portrayals of Grandmother show her as a person of responsibility and skills. She is seen as a person who has time to speak to family members who are homesick. She is willing to share recipes and cooking techniques, and business expertise with the younger generations.

Teaching the next generation.

At first, Grandfather was depicted on the porch rocker, as being critical of the younger generation or telling boring jokes. More recent portrayals, however, show him as a good listener or creative storyteller. Sometimes he is shown as the only one who takes time to fix special toys for his grandchildren or the youngsters in the neighborhood.

The next discussion exercise, AGING AND AGISM, provides practice in determining the difference between aging and agism.

DISCUSSION EXERCISE

Aging and Agism

DIRECTIONS FOR THE LEARNER: In the columns of AGING and AGISM below, there are some statements. What are the feelings or attitudes that are expressed in each statement? Write below each statement, some words or phrases that describe the feelings or attitudes expressed toward older people or the aging process. Try to describe the differences in the ways each of the AGING statements addresses the same topic of each AGISM statement.

For your assistance, the author has filled in some words and phrases under the first statements in the AGING and AGISM columns.

AGING	AGISM
1. Adults of any age may fall in love and want to be married. open to new experiences, relationships, taking a risk, loving is living, happy	1. It is silly for 80-year-old people to be married. close-minded, puts down 80 year olds, suggests life is finished at 80 years of age, hurt
2. Hardening of the heart ages people more quickly than hardening of the arteries.	2. Old age is like winter, the season of losses.
3. Retired people may plan new activities to fill their expanded leisure time.	3. Retired people just sit and rock their lives away.
4. Tennis is a game of careful strategy.	4. Tennis is only for those with lots of quick energy.
5. Sometimes a hobby brings in some income during retirement.	5. Old people should not take away jobs from the young people.

DIRECTIONS FOR THE LEADER: This exercise may be done on an individual or group basis. The purpose of the exercise is to examine agism in specific statements commonly believed by people to be true.

Participants should take a few moments to think about or discuss their responses to the statements above in terms of the following questions.

What role do people over 50 years of age play in your life? What role do people over 75 years of age play in your life? In which locations of your daily activities do you see the elderly? In what kinds of activities are they involved?

What do the older people in your life think about? What do they say to you? How do you act when you are with older persons?

What feelings did you experience as you filled in your responses to some of the statements in the exercise above? Were you aware that you had some of these feelings? Did some of these feelings surprise you?

It takes about 30 minutes for a group to complete the exercise and discussion.

AGING AND AGISM IN RESEARCH

Aging and agism were defined and discussed in more detail on previous pages. Aging is the growth and development of people as they become older. Agism is the negative attitude toward old age and old persons. Not only is agism a problem in the general population, but also, it is a problem in the work of the experts in aging. This is especially true of the people who study and do research on the different aspects of aging.

Scientists are becoming more aware of the overlap of aging and agism in their work. They are beginning to look at their studies on aging for evidence of agism. They are more careful to avoid distortion and oversights in the designs of their research studies. They search in their results for evidence of agism that may be due to prejudice within themselves or their field of work.

Some published studies will be discussed in this section in an attempt to see how an awareness of agism may result in different research conclusions. When the researcher pays careful attention to oversights, misperceptions, or distortions that result from attitudes of agism, their conclusions become different.

Standards for Good Health

From the scientific point of view, there appears to be no age cut-off for disease. Disease may affect the newborn who is just starting life, the young adult in the middle of life, or the older adult who is completing life.

Recent research discoveries are showing clearly that aging differs from disease. What is normal for a young adult differs from what is normal for an older adult. Levels of activity vary greatly from one older person to the next. For the older adult, individual functioning is very important. Moving muscles more slowly or showing a different capacity to breathe in a certain amount of oxygen does not mean that an older person is diseased. Further examination of the older person may result in a conclusion of normal functioning for the lifestyle chosen by the individual.

Studies are beginning to show conclusions that a wide range of different levels of chemicals in the blood and the mechanical functioning of muscles and bones differ for healthy old people. Different levels of functioning are well within the ranges of health for different older adults. Within the older population, healthy values of chemical balances in the body vary greatly. For younger adults, the same ranges of chemicals in the blood, muscle movement, or bone functioning may indicate illness.

For example, people around 60 years of age often appear to have diabetes when their blood sugar level is tested in the laboratory. Richard Greuflick, the scientific director at the Baltimore Center of the National Institute of Aging, has reported that the use of glucose by the human body changes as people become older. Glucose is a form of sugar after it has been digested by the body. Older people gradually lose their ability to absorb glucose into the body. A 60 year old does not seem to metabolize sugar in the same way as that of a 40 year old.

This difference in using sugar seems to be a factor of change that can be related to the numerical age. It is not disease. It should not be considered as a disability related to the "loss" of youth. This action of the body appears to be a normal change related to normal aging.

Memory

In tests of memory, there exists a wide range of individual differences. Previous research indicated that memory loss was a part of aging. Older people scored lower on tests than younger people. The lower scores were interpreted as a signpost of memory loss.

In recent studies scientists have tried to eliminate agism from the method of research. The researchers distinguished the differences between the speed of recall and the amount of information recalled. As a result, some people, who were 60 years of age and older, showed modest recall. Other people in the same age categories showed no memory losses when tested.

In dealing with the flow of information into and out of their minds, some elderly seem to work more slowly than younger people. However, most of the elderly have maintained the level of their skills of intelligence. Some of the elderly showed an increase in intellectual skills as a result of being older.

In 1975, Sokoloff demonstrated that healthy men, who averaged 72 years of age, exhibited rates of blood flow in their brains and oxygen use in their lungs that were similar to men in their 20's. The older men showed a minimal amount of difference in thinking, sensing, and psychological abilities.

The results indicated that numerical age by itself is not necessarily associated with less ability. This is especially true in the areas of intelligence. When exploring the issue of less ability, other factors, such as diet, exercise, companionship, interest, and the personal need should be considered.

Ability to Perform

In a different type of study, some adults were asked to rate old people as opposed to young people. The adult raters became trapped by their own agism. The adult raters ranked the performance of people in imaginary problem situations according to numerical age. They rated the young people at a high level and the old people at a low level.

When the adult raters were given a chance to look at cohorts, their behavior changed. Cohorts, of course, are peers, people that were born and grew up around the same period of time in history.

When they looked at pictures of cohorts, the adult raters thought that the specific qualities of the individuals made a difference in their performance in the examples of problem situations. Thus, when the age differences were not extreme, such as when comparing the very young with the very old, adult raters evaluated older persons based on the specific qualities that they saw in photographs.

Attitudes on Aging

Other researchers have studied the attitudes of people toward aging in terms of (1) perceived age and (2) chronological age. Perceived age refers to how old a person seems to be. Chronological age, as discussed before, is numerical age, the number of years a person has lived. Adults seem to feel that being young is related to success. They feel that being old is related to failure.

According to one study, age was the factor considered by many to be responsible for the success or failure of doing a task. Adults in the study rated the success at doing a task to be a result of young age. They evaluated made-up situations involving both young adults and old adults failing at a task. Only the old were accused of failing the task as a result of their age.

Surprisingly, when the older people pictured in the made-up examples were described as being successful, people decided that the success was not related to numerical age. The raters looked at the qualities of the young adults when relating them to the examples. As a result of their study, the scientists Banziger and Drevenstedt reported their conclusions in 1982, that numerical age rather than the actual ability is the deciding factor in considering the ability of a person to do a task.

Although they came to a definite conclusion regarding the ability of people, the scientists Banziger and Drevenstedt did not include the factor of ability in the study. They did not study the different parts of the factor of ability. Yet, they used ability to help them decide upon the meaning of the results of their study. If they had developed more tasks to test the levels of ability in the problem situations presented to the adult raters Banziger and Drevenstedt would have increased the accuracy in the conclusions of the study.

In 1982 Goebel reported on a study of older adults, 61 to 89 years of age. She found something different from most other studies on attitudes toward aging and the aged. She found that older adults preferred relationships with middle- and older-aged individuals.

In Goebel's study, adult raters, 42 to 89 years of age, were given an opportunity to choose adults of different ages in a variety of examples of activities. The adult raters considered which people in the examples of activities would add to their life satisfaction. The adult raters chose the young adults as the group they preferred the least. The older adult raters preferred the middle- and older-aged people according to the sex and the attractiveness of the persons in the examples. Numerical age was not important.

In the beginning states of developing her study, Goebel considered age and the possibilities of agism. She had noted that many studies contrasted very young adults with very old adults. The studies did not examine a wide range of adults of all ages. Goebel provided photographs of adults of all ages for the raters to select in their responses to each problem situation.

Having adults of all ages from which to select rather than only two groups with sharp age differences seemed to influence the use of other criteria for making choices. Consequently, Goebel found a difference between the responses of her subjects and those of Banziger and Drevenstedt. The adult raters in the Goebel study used qualities, such as personality characteristics or probable ability, to help them choose friends.

SUMMARY

Aging and adult development involve changes. The changes include physical, emotional, social, intellectual, philosophical, and spiritual factors. Although the stages of childhood have been fully described, the stages of later adult life are still being identified and defined. Much inconsistency is seen in the theories and research results concerning older persons.

Agism, the prejudice toward old age and old people, is a problem in society. Scientists are beginning to be more careful about the distorting effects of agism in their research projects. As better information about aging becomes more widespread, agism will decrease. New opportunities will be made available for a better quality of life in the later years.

Moving Forward

People of all ages must be provided opportunities to contribute to the development of each other's lives. To unleash the latent power available in the more than 30 million older Americans in the population, society needs to move away from the trap of agism. Society must learn the truth about the process of aging in order to develop cultural values that respect and support the worth of the older person.

Communities must plan activities that provide active roles for older persons. The resources of the elderly must be included in the development of the community. Policy and legislation must provide for the freedom to choose and act on a lifestyle of quality.

To understand the dynamics of aging, one should look within oneself to become aware of the many aspects of one's own aging process. First, the individual should think in personal terms about aging. Then, the person becomes more sensitive toward the process of aging in others.

The following questions may help people to think about what they really expect in terms of their own aging. Am I growing now? Am I changing in ways that I like and respect? Am I willing to continue to grow as an individual? Am I willing to accept new challenges to change my ways of behaving with other people? Am I willing to deal with the frustrations of change? How important is it to me to improve the quality of life for myself and others?

As one becomes more willing to accept personal change and aging, one begins to walk along the path of positive development. Then, the person reaches out easily and spontaneously to others to help them do the same.

The willingness to move ahead toward quality in life begins the movement toward an age-irrelevant society. Then the negative attitude of agism will be less. New perspectives will unfold as people enjoy the life events of today and anticipate the promises of tomorrow.

Looking Ahead

As a person looks at specific aspects of the aging and developing person, some obvious needs emerge. A person begins to realize the need to be in tune with oneself and to be able to make genuine contact with others. A person should be alert to personal change. Being aware of oneself is the first step to being able to make genuine contact with others. In an effort to explore this area in more depth, Chapter 13 provides a discussion of ROLES AND RELATIONSHIPS.

Suggestions for Further Reading

AGING AND ADULT STAGES

Alpaugh, P., & Haney, M. (1979). *Counseling the Older Adult.* Los Angeles, CA: The Ethel Percy Andrus Gerontology Center.

Barkan, B. (1981). The Live Oak regenerative community. *Aging,* (321–322), 2–7.

Birren, J. E. (1964). The psychology of aging in relation to development. In J. E. Birren (Ed.), *Relations of Development and Aging.* Springfield, IL: Charles C Thomas.

Butler, R. (1975). *Why Survive? Being Old in America.* New York: Harper & Row.

Butler, R. N., & Lewis, M. I. (1973). *Aging and Mental Health.* St. Louis, MO: The C. V. Mosby Co.

Erikson, E. H. (1963). *Childhood and Society* (2nd ed.). New York: W. W. Norton.

Erikson, E. H. (1982). *The Life Cycle Completed.* New York: W. W. Norton.

Flanagan, J. C. (1978). A research approach to improving our quality of life. *American Psychologist, 33,* 138–147.

Helms, F. C. (1965). An inside look at retirement. In selected papers of the Fifth Annual National Conference of State Executives on Aging. Washington, D. C.: U.S. Department of Public Health, Education, & Welfare, 69–70. (OA No. 123).

Kaasa, O. J. (April–May, 1982). What two years have meant to me. *Modern Maturity,* 25(2), 4.

Kalish, R. A. (1975). *Late Adulthood: Perspectives on Human Development.* Belmont, CA: Wadsworth.

Levinson, D. et al. (1978). *The Seasons of a Man's Life.* New York: Alfred A. Knopf.

Palmore, E. B. (1979). Predictors of successful aging. *The Gerontologist,* 19(5), 427–431.

Super, D. E. (1957). *The Psychology of Careers.* New York: Harper & Row.

Troll, L. E., Miller, S. J., & Atchley, R. C. (1979). *Families in Later Life.* Belmont, CA: Wadsworth.

White, R. W. (1966). *Lives in Progress: A Study of the Natural Growth of Personality* (2nd ed.). New York: Holt, Rinehart & Winston.

AGISM IN GENERAL

Atchley, R. C. (1980). *The Social Forces in Later Life.* Belmont, CA: Wadsworth.

Axelrod, S., & Eisdorfer, C. (1961). Attitudes toward older people. *Journal of Gerontology,* 16, 75–80.

Carlson, E. (May–June, 1982). Gaining on the fountain of youth. *Dynamic Years,* 17(3), 48–54.

Reigel, K. F., & Reigel, R. (1960). A study on changes of attitudes and interests during later years of life. *Vita Humana,* 3, 177–206.

Spencer, M. E. (1979). *Truth About Aging.* Washington, D.C.: NRTA–AARP.

Tibbets, C. (1979). Can we invalidate negative stereotypes of aging? *The Gerontologist,* 19, 10–20.

Tuckman, J., & Lorge, I. (1958). Attitude toward aging of individuals with experience with the aged. *Journal of Genetic Psychology,* 92, 199–204.

AGISM IN RESEARCH

Banziger, G., & Drevenstedt, J. (1982). Achievement attributions by young and old judges as a function of the perceived age of stimulus person. *Journal of Gerontology,* 37(4), 468–474.

Birren, J. E. (1964). The psychology of aging in relation to development. In J. E. Birren (Ed.), *Relations of Development and Aging.* Springfield, IL: Charles C Thomas.

Birren, J. E., & Schaie, K. W. (Eds.). (1977). *Handbook of the Psychology of Aging.* New York: Van Nostrand Reinhold.

Carlson, E. (May–June, 1982). Gaining on the fountain of youth. *Dynamic Years,* 17(3), 48–54.

Goebel, B. L. (1982). Age preferences of older adults in relationships important to their life satisfaction. *Journal of Gerontology,* 37(4), 461–467.

Kalish, R. A. (1977). Social values and the elderly. In R. A. Kalish (Ed.), *The Later Years: Social Applications of Gerontology.* Monterey, CA: Brooks/Cole Pub. Co., pp. 64–68.

Sobel, M. (September–October, 1981). Growing old in Britain. *Aging,* (321–322), 8–16.

Wingard, J. A., Heath, R., & Himelstein, S. A. (1982). The effects of contextural variations on attitudes toward the elderly. *Journal of Gerontology,* 37(4), 475–482.

COPING WITH STRESS

Carlson, E. (1982). Gaining on the fountain of youth. *Dynamic Years,* 17(3), 48–54.

DEMOGRAPHICS ABOUT THE AGED

Aging America (2nd printing). (1984). Washington, D.C.: U.S. Senate Special Committee on Aging & American Association of Retired Persons.

Jackson, J. J. (1980). *Minorities and Aging.* Belmont, CA: Wadsworth.

Special Committee on Aging. (July 26, 1982). *Long-Term Health Care for the Elderly.* Washington, D.C.: U.S. Government Printing Office.

PERSONALITY STAGES

Erikson, E. H. (1959). Identity and the life cycle. *Psychological Issues,* Monograph 1.

Erikson, E. H. (1964). *Insight and Responsibility.* New York: W. W. Norton and Co.

Rychlak, J. F. (1973). *Introduction to Personality and Psychotherapy.* Boston, MA: Houghton Mifflin.

Schultz, D. (1977). *Growth Psychology.* New York: Van Nostrand Reinhold.

QUALITY OF LIFE

Doty, L. (1981). Planning and preparation for the new life. *Resources in Education.* ERIC/CAPS Clearinghouse (ED 198408).

Flanagan, J. C. (1978). A research approach to improving our quality of life. *American Psychologist,* 33, 138–147.

Larson, R. (1978). Thirty years of research on the subjective well being of older Americans. *Journal of Gerontology,* 33(1), 109–125.

Special Committee on Aging. (1982). *Long-Term Health Care for the Elderly.* Washington, D.C.: U.S. Government Printing Office.

13

Roles and Relationships

Roles and relationships are important. Roles provide different ways of functioning and give people the opportunity to feel independent and useful. Relationships help people feel that they belong. The interactions provide support and caring. Roles and relationships help people to feel alive and to strive to meet their potential in life.

How many people do all that they are capable of doing as they become older? How many people realize their potential as they approach their senior years? To consider the possibility of living as full a life as possible as an older person, people should understand the importance of roles and relationships in the lives of older citizens.

All of the activities and relationships in a person's life may be thought of in terms of a painting. First to be seen in the picture as the center of focus is the person. All around the person are the activities and involvements of the person. They spread out from the individual to include other people, places, and objects. As the person changes throughout life, the picture changes. The person matures. The involvements change.

People have different levels of involvement. They may barely know some people and may be deeply committed to others. They may be active or inactive when they are with others. People seem to behave in different ways as their roles in life change. Knowing something about the activities and involvements, or roles and relationships, of a person gives some information about who that person is. Knowing this information provides clues as to how a person may change parts of a life to improve the quality of life.

When people know each other better, they understand and accept each other more easily. When people understand how others function, they see how their various activities and relationships fit together. They are able to strengthen a network that provides satisfaction, intimacy, emotional support, and a special sense of belonging. These factors are essential to emotional well being.

For example, when a new family moves into his neighborhood, Mr. Lowe tries to become acquainted with them about one week later. He tries to exchange information with them about hobbies, career experiences, personal interests, and involvement in the community.

The friendly talk provides information to the newcomers about resources to help them adjust to and begin building a meaningful life in the community. The exchange provides information to Mr. Lowe about ways he may help others and maintain a friendly, caring attitude among the neighbors.

Sometimes it is helpful to look at what is happening in the outside setting to find out about the inside make-up of a person. What a person does and with whom it is done give a great deal of information about the identity of the individual. The roles and relationships of a person provide a beginning glimpse of the panorama or total picture of the identity of the person.

In considering the panorama of the current life of a person, it may be helpful to explore first in this chapter how individuals see themselves. Next, relationships will be examined. The traditional manner of developing relationships in families and with friends seems to be changing. Openness to modern lifestyles and substitutes for family relationships offer new choices in the development of meaningful relationships.

Then, it may be helpful to look at the different activities or roles that are part of the person's lifestyle. Some roles, such as librarian, plumber, or sales clerk, are productive and promote personal growth. Other roles, such as the "sick role," seem to be nonproductive and lead to unhappiness.

Going through the successive stages of development, acquiring skills, meeting with success, and growing through experiences of failure, the maturing adult becomes individualized. The mature adult, however, never reaches a permanent plateau of sameness. Life circumstances continue to be an influence, sometimes positive and sometimes negative.

In 1963, Havighurst looked at several psychological factors that influenced success in growing older. He determined that satisfaction in life could be measured in the older adult. He considered a zest for present life, resolution, fortitude, the congruence of goals and achievements, a positive mood, and a positive self-concept as the relevant parts of successful aging. Other researchers have identified similar factors and included longevity as a contributor to success and satisfaction in aging.

The following discussion exercise, WHO I AM, will help readers develop some awareness of the more personal parts of themselves. The exercise will provide some specific information to them about the various components that weave together to make up the fabric of their lives.

DISCUSSION EXERCISE

Who I Am

Before reading the next section of Chapter 13, ROLES AND RELATIONSHIPS, please take some time to follow the directions below regarding the discussion exercise, WHO I AM.

DIRECTIONS FOR THE LEARNER: List 15 words or phrases that identify who you are. Think about how you see yourself as a person. What parts of your personality or actions in your life give information about who you are?

Answer as if you were giving the information to yourself. Do not worry about your responses "making sense." Do not try to organize what you write. Just write down your ideas as they come to you. Think about what has meaning for you. Use symbols to represent any information you prefer to keep private.

1.

2.

3.

4.

5.

6.

7.

8.

9.

10.

11.

12.

13.

14.

15.

DIRECTIONS FOR THE LEADER: This exercise is designed for the individual as a homework exercise. The purpose of the exercise is to focus on the various parts of one's identity.

In private the participant should reflect briefly on the following questions. How hard did you have to work to write down 15 identifying remarks about yourself? How do some of your responses give you some new information about how you see yourself? Which responses came to mind quickly? Which responses took a great deal of thought before they came to your attention?

The information from this exercise will be explored in more depth after people have read and worked through the rest of this chapter. After spending some time on this particular exercise, readers generally study the rest of this chapter more seriously. They bring personal focus to the ideas that are explored.

THE SELF

The sense of self develops in early life. It continues to become more complex as a person experiences more of life. The sense of self forms through the independent actions of the individual and through interactions with others.

As people develop, they increase their skills of observation, understanding, and the ability to act. They are able to think through ideas. They can form opinions about themselves that may differ from the opinions of others. They have access to their private thoughts and feelings which have more information about their own meaning of themselves.

Many people gain their sense of self or self-meaning from interactions with others. For some people, the views of others contribute a small amount to their own meaning or definition of themselves. For others, the sense of self seems to be formed almost completely by the opinions of others.

For example, the infant spends a great deal of time responding to others. In social situations the infant behaves spontaneously, at first. Then, the infant becomes more careful as people begin to give back information to the youngster about who she or he is. People may comment:

"You ate all your lunch. What a good child!"

"Picking up all your toys. What a helper you are!"

Hearing comments such as these the child will develop a positive view of the self. The meaning of the self to the child will probably grow to be stable, predictable, and strong. As the definition of self continues to develop, the feeling of being confirmed and cared for by others will be accompanied by a growing sense of confidence.

"What a good child!"

On the other hand, people may comment to the child:

"You are always making a mess."

"Do not touch the books. You will tear the pages."

As a result of hearing such comments, the child will attach negative words to such actions. Then the child will associate the negative words with his or her developing sense of self. When more negative remarks and feelings are expressed to the child than positive remarks, the child begins to feel unsure, incapable, and disliked.

"You always make a mess!"
(The child is hearing, "You always are a mess!")

As the sense of self continues to develop, it may continue to be contradicted and devalued by others. Feeling clumsy as a result of criticism from others, the growing child experiences frustration, a lack of self confidence, and then anger. This may lead to a lack of trust in oneself. It often results in the development of a poor self-concept.

SELF–CONCEPT

Self-concept may be defined as how one looks at oneself. It is a person's own idea or feeling of who he or she really is. Sometimes self-concept is referred to as self-image, the picture one has of oneself. People who have a strong self-concept feel more positive about who they are. They are considered to have a high level of self-esteem.

People with a strong self-concept are more confident about their own basic worth. They show more confidence in their abilities and behaviors. They are able to maintain a longer sense of independence and self-sufficiency. They worry less about the opinion and approval of others.

One way of thinking about self-concept is to consider it to be made up of four different parts. In this sense, the self-concept is comprised of objective facts and subjective opinions. Also included are the feelings and activities which a person experiences.

The different parts of self-concept are demonstrated in the following examples. The part of each example that illustrates the specific aspect of self-concept is highlighted with capital letters.

1. Objective Facts in Self-Concept: "I AM A SKILLED TENNIS PLAYER. I have competed in world matches for the last two years."

    The comment in capital letters is a statement of fact that reflects how the person views himself or herself. The statement may be verified by a check of tennis scores or by challenging the player to a game of tennis. Also, objective facts are given in the second statement, "competed in world matches . . . last two years." However, they describe action, not the meaning or sense of the self.

2. Subjective Opinion in Self-Concept: "I AM THOUGHTFUL, especially to people who are my friends, although I try to be respectful to everyone." Or, "I AM RESPONSIBLE because I like to finish jobs that I start."

    The comments in capital letters are subjective remarks. They are the opinions of the speaker. They represent the attitudes or beliefs of the speaker.

3. Feelings in Self-Concept: "I AM ALWAYS AFRAID that I will forget what I have to say when I have to stand up in front of a group of people."

    The comment in capital letters reflects the feeling of the speaker. The speaker perceives the self to be tense and fearful when in a specific kind of situation.

4. Activity in Self-Concept: "USUALLY I RUSH AROUND at the last minute when getting ready for a long trip."

   The comment in capital letters indicates the activity level that is part of the sense of self. The speaker may be expressing behavior associated with trips or feeling incompetent about the general ability to organize for special events.

In 1957, Dr. Donald Super described the self-concept in another way. He felt that the total self-concept is complex. It is actually a self-concept system. The self-concept system involves many simple self-concepts combined together to form a belief about the self.

The self-concept system begins to develop during the early years of life. During the interactions of infancy, self-concepts are developing. As time passes, the simple self-concepts of the young mature into a complex self-concept system.

For example, the remarks: "I am an excellent repairwoman around the house, but never can help people with personal problems."

The simple self-concepts form the building blocks of a detailed self-concept system.

1. I am a woman. (This is a simple concept of the self.)

2. I repair. (In other words, I do repair work. This is a simple concept of the self.)

3. I repair at home. (This simple concept of self includes more information or details about "I repair," the previous statement.)

4. I repair at a level of excellence. (These are two simple concepts of the self. The first concept is "I repair." The second concept is "excellence." In other words, "I perform in an excellent way.")

5. I deal poorly with personal problems. (These are two simple concepts of the self. The first concept is "I help people with personal problems." The second concept is "I help" poorly.)

6. I fail at helping other people with personal problems. (There is much more detail added to the basic concept of helping.)

There are probably many other simple and complex concepts of the self that make up the whole self-concept system of this woman. The part of the self-concept system that is described here is: "I am an excellent repairwoman around the house, but never can help people with personal problems."

Another example of a part of a whole self-concept system may be seen in the following statements: "I enjoy being involved rearing my four children. I am really challenged as president of the PTA, but I do not have the skills or patience to supervise a group of teen-agers on a soccer team."

The simple self-concepts of parenting: PTA membership, leadership as President, lack of skills in soccer, lack of patience with children, etc., build up to a detailed self-concept system.

In both examples, the people show a sense of self-meaning, who they are, and what they will do. They show that they recognize their capabilities and respect their limitations.

The self-concept is fostered, maintained, adapted, and even protected through different kinds of relationships. The relationships start within simple family interactions. As the individual grows, the relationships extend to include friends in the neighborhood and, then, in the community. Traveling across the country or to different continents may bring even more relationships into a person's life. As relationships and experiences expand, roles become different.

Thus, the self-concept system of a person becomes more complex through independent exploration within oneself and through the activities and relationships in one's life.

RELATIONSHIPS

Proximity and similarity play an important role in relationships. People form deeper relationships with those who live nearby. Sharing similar interests are important to the growth of deeper relationships. People who share interests in similar hobbies, for example, are likely to spend a great deal of time with each other.

A civic-minded adult will probably have a great many interactions with the neighbor next door who is concerned about the social service issues and the town budget. They may increase their time together by planning to share rides to the town hall meetings that are being held to debate the issues.

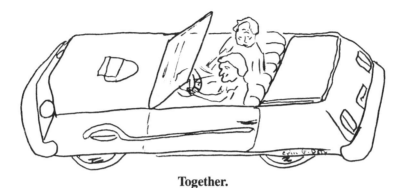

Together.

These two adults will probably have fewer interactions with other neighbors who live far away or former classmates, who have moved out of state. As time passes, if the interests of the two adults become different or their values conflict, they will probably spend little to no time with each other. Spending no time with each other will affect the development and the depth of their relationship.

In general, people interact most often with the members of their family. The family interactions also form the deepest relationships. For the young child, family interactions provide their most intimate level of relationships. The young adult may interact most intimately on an emotional level with peers. Typically, after marriage older adults interact most intimately with a spouse or a companion who is very close.

The Family

The family may be known by many different names. It is often made up of several, different kinds of groups. The family acts in different ways to help its members.

Some of the names given to families are nuclear family, family of origin, and the conjugal family. The nuclear family is made up of parents and their children, who are siblings. The nuclear family into which a person is born is known as the family of origin or the family of orientation. The nuclear family that is established through one's own marriage is known as the conjugal family, the family of procreation, or the created family.

Extended family is the term used to include all of a person's relatives. Often the extended family includes more than one nuclear family living in a single home unit. This home unit may be made up of one or more buildings. Sometimes a leader or "father figure" is elected or self-selected to provide direction to the members of the nuclear unit.

Family members play the most significant role in the development of the self because they interact so frequently. Their interactions tend to be more spontaneous. On an emotional level, their interactions are very intimate.

Family members care for and support one another. The support system helps each person to adjust to change inside and outside the family. The family system has a great impact on the development of the identity of its members.

With the emerging isolation of the nuclear family in the highly mobile, industrialized society of today, older people have become estranged from the mainstream of life and from close interpersonal relationships. Therefore, it becomes more important than ever for the older people of today to develop strong emotional ties between cohorts and friends. The ties may provide a substitute for genetic kinship.

Close ties between members of the older generation may serve as a major social, emotional support system. These close relationships may be necessary for healthful, human survival in the future. In 1968, two scientists, Lowenthal and Haven, reported that having a close friendship with at least one other person may strengthen greatly older adults who are threatened with a crisis.

In another study of 7,000 California residents, Dr. L. Syme, University of California at Berkeley, reported that loneliness shortens the lifespan. He studied people isolated from others. Their death rate was twice as high as those who have frequent human contact.

Surrogate Family

Family members and close friends are often referred to as significant others. They have relationships that are deep and meaningful. Friendships that last many years may develop a level of intimacy that seems as close as the intimacy of a nuclear family.

As they age, older persons may find that new ways of developing friendships seem risky and undesirable. By accepting the risks of making personal and interpersonal change, older people may enjoy the adventures of new and exciting roles that are introduced by the new relationships.

Such close friendships may be very important to people, 80 years of age and older, especially those who may have outlived all their family members. The friends may become as close as a family. They may become a substitute for the family that no longer exists. They may become a surrogate family.

The surrogate family may be the new way of providing emotional support to the elderly. It can help the older person remain self-determined and independent for as long as possible. It has sufficient flexibility to fulfill the functions met in previous years by the nuclear and extended families.

A major benefit of the surrogate family is its flexibility. The surrogate family may change according to the needs of the ever-changing older adult. It has flexibility in membership, which changes as the depth of the relationships change. It has mobility in that it may be defined by the location of its members. A person may develop a surrogate family from neighbors. In other words, people on the same floor of an apartment building may become close companions and feel like a family. A move to a new residence opens the opportunity for the development of a new surrogate family.

People Pleasers

Significant others may contribute greatly to the ongoing development of the individual. The relationships may provide mutual trust. They may provide the opportunity for exchanges that are free of barriers, such as economic status or educational differences. Sometimes people try to be sensitive to and conform to the expectations of the significant others in their lives. Sometimes they achieve great skill at pleasing others with their conforming behavior.

Occasionally the conforming behavior interferes with the ability of the person to make choices in life. Busy obeying and conforming to the demands of others, they never develop their own sense of individuality and independence. They become "people pleasers."

The loss of significant others results in great confusion among "people pleasers" who are 70 or 80 years of age or more. They flounder. They feel lost because their regular behavior no longer works. They do not know how to relate in a meaningful way to the current situation.

They worked hard for many years to do what their family, religion, career, or society expected of them. Now they do not know how to cook for themselves because they obeyed the "rule" that men should not be in the kitchen. Now they do not know how to write out checks because they obeyed the "rule" that women should not have to fuss over figures and paying the bills.

They spent a lifetime being careful, responsive, and obedient to social rules and expectations. They did what was expected of them.

In this current age of liberation where some men choose to be homemakers and some women enter military academies, how may the elderly figure out the new "rules" of behavior? How can they learn which expectations of society they must obey? Even more critical, how may the elderly survive in the midst of such changes in their personal life and in society? How will they be able to deal with the confusion of continuous transition?

Older persons must begin the struggle of looking inside themselves to discover their own expectations and wishes. They must begin to develop personal awareness. They must begin to decide what they want to do in life in terms of their own interests. They must find out what has importance and meaning to them. They must start to walk on the lifepath of self-determination.

Changing one's lifestyle in this direction is difficult, but it is not impossible. Learning self-determination becomes an invigorating experience. The energy that was so carefully controlled in order to follow the expectations of others for so many years may now be unleashed.

The unleashing may result in a new surge of energy that helps the person put personal affairs in order. It may help the person to move in a creative direction, such a developing a new kind of living for people who want to share space, expenses, and friendships. The discovery of new potential within oneself may help the individual to become all that is possible in a full life.

ROLES

The roles of a person may be explained as the functions, behaviors, and ways that the person performs. Roles contribute to the pool of information that helps define who a person is. Sex, age, kinship, race or ethnic group, occupation, and socioeconomic class provide a basis for role definitions. Special functions, such as manual skills, and ways of behaving, such as revealing a good memory for dates in a conversation, contribute information to role definitions. Knowing the roles of a person supplies more detail to the picture of the person's identity.

For example, a man may introduce himself to new friends at a picnic as, "I am Joe, the guy everyone calls when their television acts up." Or, in another example, a woman may define herself as the 57-year-old sister of the new city mayor, for whom she campaigned vigorously. The specific roles help supply more information about who the person is and the kinds of activities in the person's life.

Roles are varied. They have different purposes. As the member of a family, a person may function in the role of parent, spouse, child, sibling, cousin, aunt, or uncle. Roles in a family provide stable relationships and provide intimate affection. The career role may stimulate intellectual development and provide economic security. In the role of friend, a person may provide stimulating conversation or emotional support to someone in a crisis.

People may take on roles, such as helper or team player, that are appreciated and respected by others. Other people may choose roles, such as explorer or single person, that are not as easily accepted in society. This lack of acceptance is felt strongly toward roles that differ greatly from the typical lifestyle of the major part of the population.

A role may contribute to a person's sense of significance and level of status. An example of this is the career role. Career roles often contribute to one's self-perception. Success in developing a satisfying career results in someone feeling good about personal abilities and skills.

Failure at a job may be shattering to a person. This may be especially critical to someone who uses the job role to make up a major portion of the person's definition of significance and worth. If the job has little status in the culture, the individual may feel a sense of incompetence and failure despite a high level of quality in performance at work.

Falling apart.

Many people who are ending the work role at the time of retirement feel a restlessness and loss of meaningful activity in their new lifestyles as retirees. They feel as if the whole sense of who they are has fallen apart. Their identity is in fragments.

For others, retirement seems to open up opportunities. In retirement they may explore avocational interests, such as gardening, education, or traveling. Some activities may be pursued for pleasure and relaxation. Other activities may bring in some cash earnings.

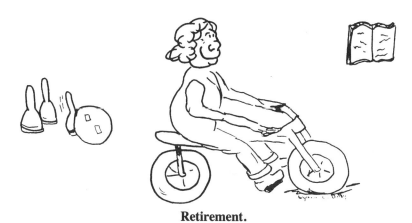

Retirement.

Many roles are complementary and provide mutuality. The role of lover may be complemented in the role of spouse. Both the role of lover and the role of spouse will flourish when the needs of the two people in the relationship are satisfied.

Roles may be helpful to or interfere with the ability of people to lead a happy, meaningful life. The role of a leader in a group may bring satisfaction. Developing the behavior of a "sick role" may lead to sadness and loneliness.

The study of roles covers a great deal of material. The following sections will focus on four major topics, (1) roles of group members, (2) leadership roles, (3) reference groups, and (4) the sick role.

Roles of Group Members

A group will be defined here as three or more people gathered together. They may have been brought together by chance or for a purpose. The members of the group may be part of a family, business, task force, worship group, book club, or counseling group.

Several roles are available to people who participate in a group. Some people have a standard way of behaving whenever they are with others. They take on the same role each time they are part of a group. Other people combine different roles in creative ways, such as a leader who occasionally acts as a questionner or as the helpless one.

Some people change roles or behavior in different groups depending on their current feelings or mood. They adapt their behavior to the kind of group. They may act in a more formal, controlled way when they are meeting in the shop with their coworkers. They may act more patient, quiet, and "spiritual" in a religious gathering.

Some of the roles that people assume in group activities will be identified briefly in the following paragraphs. An attempt has been made to use simple terms that name the roles in ways that identify the function of each role. For this reason, the names of roles that are used in this text may differ from names used by other authors.

The roles are not meant to be interpreted as labels for tagging the identity of people. Rather, the roles are meant to be discussed briefly to help people gain some understanding of their own behavior and that of other people. The roles to be discussed are LEADER, FOLLOWER, DEBATER, QUESTIONNER, INFORMATION–GIVER, JOB–FINISHER, CARETAKER, NOISEMAKER, STARTER, REJECTOR, NONJOINER, SILENT ONE, CUSTODIAN, and HELPLESS.

Whether self-selected or elected by others, the LEADER of a group emerges as the director of the activities in the group. Generally, reluctant to provide direction for any decisions or activities, the FOLLOWER goes along with the choices of the leader and other members of the group.

Unlike the easy-going follower, the DEBATER always wants to explore fully both sides of an issue. The debater wants to discuss all other possible points of the issue before coming to a conclusion or moving on a decision.

Sometimes helpful, the QUESTIONNER wonders and asks about omitted information or alternatives. The INFORMATION–GIVER fills in the gaps of information with opinions, facts, and, often, references.

Despite challenges, hurdles, or inadequacies, the JOB–FINISHER pushes through to finish the job or to meet the purposes of the group. On the other hand, the CARETAKER prefers to attend to the comfort and satisfaction of the people in the group. The caretaker is much less concerned than the job-finisher about meeting goals or completing the task.

The NOISEMAKER gains significance in the group by creating harmonious or discordant sounds. The noise-maker may tell jokes, sing songs, whistle, bang furniture, or make other creative noises that interfere with the smooth progress of the group.

The STARTER always seems to have new ideas for the group to pursue. Even when the group seems to be finishing up a task with success, the starter will encourage the group to take on a new challenge or to move in a new direction. These suggestions, however, are usually criticized and/or turned down by the REJECTOR.

The NONJOINER may also move against the suggestions of the starter by not participating. The nonjoiner tries to keep separate from the group unit. The nonjoiner does not seem to belong to and does not seem content with any of the activities. The SILENT ONE, on the other hand, often appears to be listening to and following the activities, but is usually quiet and makes no remarks to the members of the group.

The CUSTODIAN is always working to keep things as they are. The custodian seems to be committed to maintaining the status quo. The custodian believes that matters should stay as they have always been and always should be.

The HELPLESS seem unable to do anything. The helpless one expresses incompetence in skills, lack of motivation, and a need for resources. The helpless person seems weighed down by the inability to think, say, or do anything.

These roles describe some of the typical behaviors that people assume when they are in groups. The next discussion exercise, ROLES IN A FISHBOWL, allows the reader to interact or participate with others in some natural, spontaneous roles within a group setting.

Roles in a Fishbowl

DIRECTIONS FOR THE LEARNER: The whole group is divided into two smaller groups, the TALKERS and the LISTENERS.

STEP 1: At first the TALKERS sit comfortably in a circle in the middle of the room. The LISTENERS are seated in a circle that surrounds the outside of the circle of TALKERS.

All of the TALKERS discuss informally a topic of interest for about five minutes. Topic subjects may be (1) a family member who did something special for me long ago (or recently), (2) a special tradition in my family, or (3) older people that have been important to me. As a group, the TALKERS should select one of the suggested topics on which everyone can share some personal information.

While the TALKERS are discussing, the LISTENERS observe. Then the LISTENERS provide feedback to the TALKERS about the trilevel communication that was demonstrated during the five minute discussion.

NOTE TO LISTENERS: As LISTENERS, try to focus on the activity or behavior you see in each person, or in the activity that occurs between people. Try to avoid being distracted by the topic under discussion. You are trying to focus on watching. Remember to keep your comments constructive and encouraging.

LISTENERS may find it helpful to use the TRILEVEL COMMUNICATION CHART at the end of this exercise for assistance. It may be helpful to write down some brief notes on the chart about communication that is observed. Remember to use POSITIVE FEEDBACK in all comments of feedback to each other. (Refer to CHAPTER 4, BASIC COMMUNICATION SKILLS, for more information on positive feedback).

STEP 2: The second part of the exercise is an exchange of roles. The TALKERS and the LISTENERS swap places. Now the new TALKERS sit in the inside circle and talk for about five minutes on any of the three topics suggested before.

This time, however, the new LISTENERS will observe two levels of behavior. The new LISTENERS will observe the trilevel communication going on. In addition, the new LISTENERS will observe the roles that people naturally assume during the discussion.

As discussed in the previous section of the text, roles that people take on in a group may include leader, follower, debater, questionner, information-giver, job-finisher, caretaker, noisemaker, starter, rejector, nonjoiner, silent one, custodian, and helpless.

As you watch behavior during the discussion, you may see other kinds of roles being acted out during the discussion. Remember to make note of them to add to your information about roles.

TRILEVEL COMMUNICATION CHECKLIST

LEVEL I: ORAL SPEECH

LEVEL II: BODY LANGUAGE

1. **Eye Contact:**

2. **Look on Face:**

3. **Voice:**

4. **Posture:**

5. **Arm Gestures:**

6. **Personal Space:**

7. **Timing:**

   Interrupts:

   Too Late:

LEVEL III: HIDDEN MEANINGS OR UNDERCURRENT MESSAGES

DIRECTIONS FOR THE LEADER: The exercise depends upon group interaction. The purpose of the exercise is to develop an awareness of some of the informal roles assumed by oneself and others.

Participants should take some time after the exercise to discuss the following questions with the other members of the group.

How were speaking and listening skills enhanced through the exercise? What feelings of the speakers became evident during the course of the conversation? How were these feelings demonstrated to those who were listening and observing?

What kinds of feelings did you experience in the role of LISTENER as you worked to observe the behavior of others? How did some of your own feelings affect your job as a LISTENER? In your role as LISTENER, what undercurrent messages did you pick up?

What kinds of behaviors indicated that a person was acting in a specific role during the exercise? Is this specific role (or roles) typical of that person in their regular life activities outside of this particular group situation?

As has been mentioned before in previous exercises, it is difficult to divert the attention of the LISTENER from the topic or story in the conversation to the activity of the speakers. In other words, it is difficult to watch HOW a person is speaking. Watching the speaking behavior of others on the three levels of communication helps participants to become more aware of their own style of trilevel communication.

Even more difficult, however, is to watch trilevel communication and the roles that people are assuming. More effort is expended by the LISTENERS than the TALKERS in this exercise.

It takes about 45 minutes to complete this exercise and discussion.

LEADERSHIP ROLES

People become leaders for different reasons. In a factory setting, the supervisor, who has worked for years in the same department, may have earned the position of leadership because of a background that is strong in practical experience.

When a family member dies, often the oldest woman in the family is appointed to make plans regarding burial services. It is assumed that she will know the religious and social customs for the situation.

In a different kind of situation, a task force to raise funds for a daycare center may elect their leader by default. No one who attended the meeting wanted the responsibility and he was the only person who missed the meeting.

Often older people are the leaders of groups because of their accumulated experience, their development of a sense of authority, or their willingness to give time to carry out important tasks. Sometimes, however, the older person is not the leader or considered to be an authority. Often, it is the older person who is struggling under the leadership of a younger person. This is evident, especially in the health care system where the patients are older people and the providers of care are younger people.

The manner in which people carry out their roles as leaders varies in different people. Roles within a group depend upon a person's interests, abilities, and self-esteem.

People with a sense of high self-esteem will lead a group in the style that they value the most. As leaders they will feel comfortable being less intimately involved with and less accepted by other group members. Their sense of confidence in their ability as group leaders will provide enough strength to enable them to do the job well. They seem to respond more to the value of their own standards, ideals, and goals than to the individual demands from the group.

The style of leadership varies according to the individual characteristics of each leader, the behavior of members within the group, and the purposes of the group. A leader may decide to take on the position of control and authority. This type of leader tries to direct others to act in a certain way.

Another type of leader may give most of the authority to the members of the group. Sometimes a leader prefers to act on the same level as other members. This kind of leader prefers a position of authority that is equal to the positions of other group members.

Leaders who focus primarily on meeting goals and finishing jobs are often called task-oriented. These leaders may be willing to lose some popularity with the members of the group in order to lead them in a meaningful direction.

Task- or job-directed leadership.

On the other hand, some leaders feel that the happiness of group members has priority over meeting a goal or finishing a task. These leaders assume the role of caretaker. Leaders, who act in the style of caretakers, focus on taking care of or helping the members of the group to feel comfortable. These leaders provide support to the other group members and are interested in their well-being.

Caretaker leadership.

Understanding the style used by a leader will help other group members to understand the progress of the group. Then group members will be in a better position to decide if they want to follow, change, or leave the progress of the group meetings.

For example, Mr. Copper has been selected as the leader of the Newsletter Task force. The purpose of the task force is to research the idea of a quarterly newsletter, regarding federal and state taxes on investments.

Concerned about meeting the goal of a published newsletter, Mr. Copper directs the committee with efficiency. Within one month, a publication staff is selected and the first newsletter is printed. Mr. Copper praises the task force about how well they performed. He ignores the tense remarks from group members. He tells them not to worry about anything and to enjoy the newsletter.

The style of leadership used by Mr. Copper may be called task-oriented or goal-centered. In his eagerness to finish the task, Mr. Copper may have neglected completely the needs of the other members of the group. If Ms. Hefel had been a member of the task force, she may have been able to help some of the other members of the group.

Ms. Hefel, who is a consultant on styles of leadership and management, may have presented several suggestions at the meetings. She may have helped other people in the group to express their ideas or feelings.

She may have asked for a special session to brainstorm, to discuss everyone's ideas without making any decisions about specific plans. As feelings seemed to become tense, she may have invited people to share what they were thinking. She may have provided positive comments to the contributions of people in order to keep a positive setting during the meetings. With special responses, she may have shown respect for people who suggested different ideas.

Ms. Hefel may have met with the leader and helped him become more sensitive to the needs of other members in the group. Working together, Mr. Copper and Ms. Hefel may have been able to meet the goal of the task force as well as to be supportive of group members.

REFERENCE GROUPS

Reference groups are groups of people to which individuals refer as they are developing their identities. The individuals depend upon the behavior of the group to teach them the appropriate ways of behaving. The reference group defines the values, standards, dress, languages, etc., of these individuals. In some cases, the reference group is used by people to help define their self-concept, self-esteem, and roles.

For example, joggers have a special way of dressing, talking, and expressing their values. These behaviors identify them as specific members of the reference group of joggers.

Professional people wear dark, pin-striped suits, ties, and briefcases to identify themselves as a separate group. Their reference group of lawyers or people in business may establish standards of behavior that include subscriptions to special magazines and memberships in certain clubs.

Which reference group?

Sometimes it is difficult for older persons to find an appropriate reference group. They may have to work hard to link with people of similar interests, standards, and self-concepts. Having reference groups provides older people with a sense of peer support, mutual help, and "we-ness", the sense of belonging.

The following two discussion exercises, A UNIT and THE IMAGE, should be done as a sequence. The first exercise, A UNIT, provides a good introduction to the second exercise, THE IMAGE.

A UNIT allows people to form a small group with some other people. No directions are provided by the group leader or teacher. On their own, the members choose the people with whom they will form a group.

THE IMAGE provides an opportunity to think about how the appearance of people gives information about their self-view, reference group, and roles.

DISCUSSION EXERCISE

A Unit

DIRECTIONS FOR THE LEARNER: Everyone in the class stands up together as a large group. They walk casually in no special order. They amble around the room for a little while. The leader of the class asks everyone to stop wherever they are for a few seconds while directions for the discussion exercise are given.

The only directions given are that participants are requested to form groups of four people each. No other specific instructions are given to them about how to form the groups. It is up to each participant to decide how to form a group with three other people.

After the groups are formed, people may sit down together. As a unit, each group takes a turn to tell everyone else how the group was formed. In whatever way they decide, the members of each of the groups report on how they got together.

DIRECTIONS FOR THE LEADER: This is a group exercise. The purpose of this exercise is to aid participants in taking initiative or becoming more independent.

Allowing participants to form their own groups introduces a higher level of involvement for class members. After this experience, instead of awaiting the teacher's or leader's directions, participants begin to take more initiative in group activities and discussion. They become less structured, reluctant, and dependent on the direction of the leader. They are more spontaneous about joining activities and are more willing to learn new behaviors.

This is a good warm-up exercise to use before doing another, more complex, discussion exercise. It takes about 15 minutes to complete this exercise.

DISCUSSION EXERCISE

The Image

DIRECTIONS FOR THE LEARNER: Use the previous discussion exercise, A UNIT, to make small groups, each consisting of four members. Within the small groups, each member chooses a person as a partner to describe. The following directions in STEP 1 should be used for the description.

STEP 1: In terms of what you see before you, write in the spaces provided below a description of the person who is your partner. Write down your thoughts or evaluation of the (1) identity of the person, (2) how they see themselves, (3) some roles they may have, and (4) to what reference group they belong.

DO NOT ASK YOUR PARTNER FOR THE INFORMATION. Try to determine some of the values of your partner by using only what you see to give you clues. Remember to keep your comments positive.

1. **Identity:**

2. **Self-view:**

3. **Roles:**

4. **Reference Group:**

STEP 2: Each person, in turn, shares the evaluation with the partner. Then the partner provides feedback about the accuracy of the description and evaluation. Remember to keep comments positive.

DIRECTIONS FOR THE LEADER: This exercise requires group interaction. The purpose of the exercise is to learn how appearance gives information about the identity (and roles) of a person.

Participants should take time to discuss the accuracy of the comments and the different feelings involved at STEP 1 and then STEP 2. The following questions may help guide the discussion.

How comfortable were you when you knew someone was watching you carefully? How did you feel about sharing your comments? What new information did you learn about your ability to assess other people? What new information did you learn about how others see you? How does someone else's view of you differ from your own view of yourself?

It takes about 30 minutes to complete this discussion exercise.

ROLE CONFLICTS

Sometimes the roles of a person seem to overlap or to be in conflict. For example, Ms. Free, a businesswoman, is the owner of a construction company. She has just been elected for her first four year term as mayor of the city. Her two career roles, in business and in community politics, may result in a conflict of interests when bids for the construction of city government offices are evaluated. The expectations of the role of being a political leader in the community are in conflict with her role of being a sound businesswoman. She owns a large, local construction company and is interested in keeping the business growing.

Many factors should be evaluated in order to make a choice when a person experiences role conflict. Often there are rules or laws about a "conflict of interest." The rules help a person, who is caught in such a dilemma, to move in the right direction. In this case, the rules may require that Ms. Free withdraw from the decision-making process about the bids and contract awards.

She may decide to develop a Citizens Advisory Board of community volunteers to work with the task force that examines the bids for construction. She may have decided at the beginning of her political career to avoid submitting such bids during her political office.

Solving role conflicts often involves a long process that considers several choices. In the following paragraphs three methods of making choices will serve as examples. The three methods are (1) decision-making, (2) communication strategies, and (3) selective assertiveness. More information about these three methods appears in PART I of this book.

1. DECISION MAKING (From CHAPTER 2, CHANGE): The first method, DECISION MAKING, involves thinking about the issue, one's feelings, available choices, possible alternatives, and consequences that may occur. Decision making is demonstrated in the following situation.

A 47 year old woman is in role conflict with (1) her desire to be a good mother and (2) her desire to be a leader in her real estate company. Should she stay at home as a full time mother-homemaker or work full-time at the office?

After looking at the circumstances, her needs and feelings, available alternatives, and possible consequences, she may decide to compromise. She may choose to work part time until her children are in high school. At that time, she will begin to work full-time. The compromise involves gradually increasing the sharing of tasks with other members of the family at home. Ranking choices by priority, from the most important choice to the least important choice, and working through a decision-making model helped her to choose actions that resulted in her feeling fulfilled as a homemaker and career person. She feels happy because she feels as if she is accomplishing significant goals in life.

2. COMMUNICATION STRATEGIES (From CHAPTER 3, COMMUNICATION, and CHAPTER 4, BASIC COMMUNICATION SKILLS): The second method uses some COMMUNICATION STRATEGIES. The communication strategies demonstrated in the following example are:

1. "I" statements, using direct expressions that begin with "I,"
2. facts, the exact, objective information, or
3. opinions, personal feelings or attitudes, and
4. positive feedback, responding in a positive way to the efforts of other people.

Two neighbors are in role conflict with (1) the desire to be caring neighbors and (2) the desire to protect their property as homeowners. The issues involve their dogs who dig holes along the base of the fence that separates their property.

Discussing their concerns with "I" statements, clarifying opinion and fact, and keeping a positive frame of reference will strengthen their communication. Being aware of each other's trilevel communication will help them provide clear messages to each other. They will establish the actual facts, such as the locations of the holes, the number of holes, and the costs of repairs. They may disagree with each other's opinions about which dog is digging the holes or whose dog is the better protector of property. They may be able to reach a compromise, such as selling both dogs. Or they may determine a creative resolution such as planting holly along the fence. Holly thorns may help to discourage the dogs. They decided to keep the dogs and put in new plants together. As a result, they enhanced the landscaping and cemented a neighborly relationship.

3. SELECTIVE ASSERTIVENESS (From CHAPTER 5, SELECTIVE ASSERTIVENESS): The third

method, SELECTIVE ASSERTIVENESS, involves choosing the method of action that is open, appropriate, respectful, and the most desirable solution for the situation. Selective assertiveness is demonstrated in the following example.

An older couple, Mr. and Mrs. Gere, are in role conflict with (1) the desire to be supportive parents and (2) the desire to be loving partners. The issue involves a sum of money that they have saved during the last seven years. Should they use it to contribute to a down payment for the new home that their children are trying to buy? Or, should they spend the summer in Europe as they had planned?

After looking carefully at the choices and honestly thinking about each other's wants and wishes, Mr. and Mrs. Gere choose to spend the money on themselves. They decide to talk candidly to their adult-children.

Mr. and Mrs. Gere explain their need as older parents to be self-sufficient and independent. They are trying to plan carefully for their own needs in later life in order to avoid being a financial burden to others, especially the children. Part of their plans include sharing some of their unfulfilled, long-term dreams together while they are still interested in traveling.

They are respecting their own wishes. They are treating their children as capable adults. They are not being critical of or hurtful to their children. Mr. and Mrs. Gere are being open about how they want to spend their time and resources. They are coping effectively, loving each other, and caring for the other people in their lives.

In the three examples above, each individual tried to be a good person. Each one wanted to act in a caring, responsible way. With the effective use of communication skills, they were able to work through difficult situations and develop some good resolutions.

The Sick Role

As people age, their sensory systems undergo change. The sensory systems that help them to see, hear, taste, smell, and feel go through a transition. For some people, the transition is gradual, occurring slowly over a period of many years. For others, it is rapid. The transition may occur over a short period of time, such as the result of a car accident or during a health crisis.

As people adjust to slow, gradual changes, most of them modify their lifestyles easily. They may get a new prescription for eyeglasses to cope with their changes in vision. Changes in taste are accompanied by changes in style of cooking, perhaps using less cooking oil or more honey. With a few adjustments, their lifestyles continue to be basically the same.

Sudden changes in the sensory system seem harder to handle. Changing from one way of behaving to another way in a few minutes or hours may require a great deal of effort. For some, the sudden change may seem overwhelming. This is especially true when a physical or emotional trauma occurs. People struggle to cope. Sometimes it takes a great effort to survive. It may take an even greater effort to want to survive.

Struggling to cope.

For example, a sudden injury or illness that results in the loss of hearing may be so traumatic that the persons seem to become distant with others. They avoid conversations. They may stay away from friends.

Some individuals refuse to wear a hearing aid. The inability and unwillingness to cooperate may lead to a change in personality. A person who was active and sociable before may act withdrawn and angry when friends try to visit.

With support and caring from others, these people may be encouraged, one step at a time, to adapt to their hearing loss. With the help of others who are patient, they will find the proper hearing aid, learn how to listen better, and/or ask people to speak more clearly. With the encouragement of others, they may become willing to cope with the change and return to an active, fulfilling lifestyle.

Hearing and participating.

Some older persons experience physical change as terminal loss. They interpret the physical transition of aging as a loss of youth, time, energy, and opportunity. They begin to feel inadequate. They start to act unsure, dependent, and simple-minded. They have interpreted change as a permanent illness.

By assuming the "sick role," some older persons fulfill their expectations of old age as the state of helplessness. The sick role is an acceptable way for them to gain attention, self-esteem, and assistance.

They see the sick role as a temporary situation. It seems as if they expect to recover from being sick and, at the same time, recover from being old. After all, society expects a quick recovery, self-sufficiency, and a youthful vitality from its members.

In the sick role for a short while, a woman is willing to be the lady who needs help because of a skin condition. For a short while a man is willing to be the one who needs help because of a breathing problem. The recognition they receive for being sick helps them to feel special. They may gain a sense of status from the attention. After a long while, being sick becomes a more permanent role.

The "sick role" for many dictates a lifestyle of bondage. Older people who are sick for a long time are made to feel helpless, inadequate, and undesirable to care for and serve. This may be seen in long-term care facilities for the elderly in the United States.

The bondage of the sick role may restrict social interaction, physical activity, and self-determination. The level of alienation experienced by elderly residents in some group housing is partly a result of the limitations imposed upon them by staff members. Sometimes the limitations are safety precautions, such as obeying fire rules or health codes in the kitchen. Sometimes the limitations accommodate the needs of the staff, such as keeping patients in their own rooms or in the hallways for easier supervision. Instead of facilitating better care, however, the limitations increase the dependence and isolation of the elderly residents.

As older people experience change in physical ability, they become anxious about being less able to cope. After a while, worry mounts. Worry demands quite a bit of attention. It uses up a great deal of energy. Those who are busy with worry often show signs of being tired, preoccupied, and forgetful. They begin to fulfill their fears by becoming less able to cope with the concerns of daily life. Caring from other people helps the older person to deal with the stress of worry, to adjust, and to plan for the physical changes. The support of others preserves physical and emotional well being.

Helping.

Programs, such as exercise groups, growth groups, book exchanges, foster grandparents, friendly visitors, telephone reassurances, meals on wheels, volunteer services, and lifelong learning groups, encourage relationships. The programs provide social and psychological support. Spurred on by the interaction and caring from others, the person becomes eager to find new ways to adapt, cope, and maintain an independent, rewarding lifestyle.

SUMMARY

Satisfying relationships and meaningful roles result in fulfilled living. Relationships are essential to well being. A positive self-concept or self-image is the result of strong caring relationships throughout one's development. Roles in a person's life also contribute to the shaping of the self and a life of quality.

Many roles involve interactions with others. The interactions may involve the nuclear family, friends, or a changing surrogate family.

As a member of a group outside of the family, individuals sometimes behave in different ways. Some of the names given to these different ways or roles are: leader, follower, debater, questionner, information-giver, job-finisher, caretaker, noisemaker, starter, rejector, nonjoiner, silent one, custodian, and helpless.

A position or role of leadership carries a great deal of responsibility. As a leader, a person may be centered on the goal or job to be done. Working with a different style, a leader may be more concerned about caring for the needs of the group members than about meeting the goals of the group.

As people become more involved in group roles with each other, they reach out to participate in the concerns of society. Older persons should be involved in the issues of society so that their needs and interests are part of the policies and programs of the future.

Information About the Final Pages of Chapter 13

The next few pages of this chapter show a digression from the typical format of this book. Right after this SUMMARY is a discussion exercise, WHO I AM NOW. It is important for this exercise to be done after studying this chapter on the roles and relationships in people's lives.

Then after the exercise is a list of books. As in previous chapters, SUGGESTIONS FOR FURTHER READING carry additional information on the important topics of this chapter.

The next discussion exercise, WHO I AM NOW, provides an opportunity to think about the factors in life that contribute to the identity and development of the reader. Follow the directions on the next page. The directions will explain how the discussion exercise, WHO I AM, at the beginning of this chapter fits into the next exercise, WHO I AM NOW.

DISCUSSION EXERCISE

Who I Am Now

DIRECTIONS FOR THE LEARNER: List 15 words or phrases that identify who you are. Think about how you see yourself as a person. What parts of your personality or actions in your life give information about who you are?

Answer as if you were giving the information to yourself. Do not worry about your responses "making sense". Do not try to organize what you write. Just write down your ideas as they come to you. Think about what has meaning for you. Use symbols to represent any information you prefer to keep private.

1.

2.

3.

4.

5.

6.

7.

8.

9.

10.

11.

12.

13.

14.

15.

DIRECTIONS FOR THE LEADER: Generally, this exercise works well as an individual homework assignment that is discussed at a later meeting of the group. The purpose of the exercise is to become aware of all the parts, experiences, and relationships that make up the identity.

Participants should take a few minutes to compare the 15 responses above with the discussion exercise, WHO I AM, at the beginning of this chapter. Then, some time should be taken to reflect on and discuss the following questions.

How are the lists in the two WHO I AM exercises the same? What specific responses in the lists contribute to your being as unique as you are? What new information about yourself have you confirmed by working through these two lists? What kind of relationship do you prefer before other people become aware of some of these characteristics about you?

For most people, who have done this comparative exercise, it is much easier for them to find words or phrases that describe them after they have read the chapter. Then they understand the importance of self-awareness, relationships, and roles in the make up of their whole beings.

At the beginning of the chapter, people usually struggle to find words to capture their feelings about their identity. It is unusual for a reader to be able to write down 15 different identifying words or phrases the first time around unless they have studied or had experience in human relationship skills. When the reader is able to identify the self more fully in the second exercise, the reader begins to see others more fully.

Comparing the two exercises and discussing the results as a group take about 30 minutes.

Suggestions for Further Reading

FAMILY (EXTENDED FAMILY)

Okun, B. F., & Rappaport, L. J. (1980). *Working with Families.* North Scituate, MA: Duxbury Press.

Regnier, V. (1981). *Normal Elderly in the Community: Interpretations Leading to Products.* Paper presented at the National Research Conference on Technology and Aging, Racine, WI.

FAMILY (SURROGATE FAMILY)

Donelson, E. (1973). *Personality.* Pacific Palisades, CA: Goodyear Pub. Co.

Troll, L. E., Miller, S. J., & Atchley, R. C. (1979). *Families in Later Life.* Belmont, CA: Wadsworth.

MATURING ADULT

Neugarten, B. L. (1976). Adaptations and the life cycle. *The Counseling Psychologist,* 6(1), 16–20.

REFERENCE GROUPS

Hansen, J. C., Warner, R. W., & Smith, E. M. (1976). *Group Counseling: Theory and Process.* Chicago, IL: Rand McNally College Pub. Co.

Sussman, M. B. (1972). An analytical model for the sociological study of retirement. In F. M. Carp (Ed.), *Retirement.* New York: Behavioral Publications, 28–73.

RELATIONSHIPS

Donelson, E. (1973). *Personality.* Pacific Palisades, CA: Goodyear Pub. Co.

Hawkins, B. L. (November, 1983). Group counseling as a treatment modality for the elderly: A group snapshot. *The Journal for Specialists in Group Work,* 8(4), 186–193.

Okun, B. F., & Rappaport, L. J. (1980). *Working with Families.* North Scituate, MA: Duxbury Press.

Sussman, M. B. (1972). An analytical model for the sociological study of retirement. In F. M. Carp (Ed.), *Retirement.* New York: Behavioral Publications, 28–73.

ROLES

Atchley, R. C. (1980). *The Social Forces in Later Life.* Belmont, CA: Wadsworth.

Bolles, R. N. (1981). *The Three Boxes of Life.* Berkeley, CA: Ten Speed Press.

Donelson, E. (1973). *Personality.* Pacific Palisades, CA: Goodyear Pub. Co.

Dye, C. J., & Richards, C. C. (1980). Facilitating the transition to nursing homes. In S. S. Sargent (Ed.), *Nontraditional Therapy and Counseling with the Aging.* New York: Springer Pub., 100–115.

Hansen, J. C., Warner, R. W., & Smith, E. M. (1976). *Group Counseling: Theory and Process.* Chicago, IL: Rand McNally College Pub. Co.

Hausman, C. P. (1979). Short-term counseling groups for people with elderly parents. *The Gerontologist,* 19(1), 102–107.

Meyer, G. (1980). The New Directions workshop for senior citizens. In S. S. Sargent (Ed.), *Nontraditional Therapy and Counseling with the Aging.* New York: Springer Pub.

Ohlsen, M. M. (1977). *Group Counseling* (2nd ed.). New York: Holt, Rinehart and Winston.

Sobel, M. (September–October, 1981). Growing old in Britain. *Aging,* (321–322), 8–16.

Super, D. E. (1957). *The Psychology of Careers.* New York: Harper and Bros.

SELF

Bills, R. E. (1981). *Self-Concept and Schooling.* West Lafayette, IN: Kappa Delta Pi.

Carkhuff, R. R., & Berenson, B. G. (1977). *Beyond Counseling and Therapy* (2nd ed.). New York: Holt, Rinehart & Winston.

Donelson, E. (1973). *Personality.* Pacific Palisades, CA: Goodyear Pub. Co.

Okun, B. F., & Rappaport, L. J. (1980). *Working with Families.* North Scituate, MA: Duxbury Press.

SELF–CONCEPT

Bills, R. E. (1981). *Self-Concept and Schooling.* West Lafayette, IN: Kappa Delta Pi.

Marlowe, D., & Gergen, K. J. (1968). Personality and social interaction. In G. Lindzey & E. Aronson (Eds.), *Handbook of Social Psychology* (Rev. ed.). Reading, MA: Addison-Wesley, 590–665.

Reck, U. M. L. (Spring, 1982). Self-concept development in educational settings: An existential approach. *Educational Horizons,* 60(3), 128–131.

Super, D. E. (1957). *The Psychology of Careers.* New York: Harper and Bros.

SICK ROLE

Dudley, C., & Hillary, G. (1977). Freedom and alienation in homes for the aged. *The Gerontologist,* 17(2), 140–145.

Linn, L. (1977). Basic principles of management in psychosomatic medicine. In E. D. Wittkower & H. Harnes (Eds.), *Psychosomatic Medicine: Its Clinical Applications.* New York: Harper & Row.

Parsons, T. (1951). *The Social System.* Glencoe, IL: Free Press.

Sobel, M. (September–October, 1981). Growing old in Britain. *Aging,* (321–322), 8–16.

Special Committee on Aging. (July 26, 1982). *Long-Term Health Care for the Elderly.* Washington, D.C.: U.S. Government Printing Office.

14

Completing an Experience

It is commonly said that "all good things must come to an end." Good things may refer to parties, relationships, or even sessions of learning. Each year comes to an end on December 31st. The end of each year, however, marks the start of a new year. The beginning of a new year provides a fresh opportunity for new experiences. Each ending, in a way, represents the potential for a new beginning.

In a sense, ending does not mean stopping. Parts of the experiences and the relationships continue. They continue with the person who carries their memory. Also, the impact of learning is carried away with each participant. At the end point of the shared learning, they carry new ideas, new skills, and a new eagerness to share their learning with others. This provides a continuation of the meaningful, desirable parts of the shared adventure that has just been completed.

In this text, the readers have had adventures with basic and advanced communication and assertion skills. They experienced the adventure of learning something more about themselves and something new about each other. Now will come opportunities to reach out to new experiences with friends at home in the days ahead. The awareness and learning developed in the previous pages provide a foundation for a richer future experience in living.

Viewing oneself with a greater level of awareness, the reader may use communication strategies to enhance relationships. Making selective assertiveness a part of one's personal lifestyle, the individual may begin to live more fully.

THE GOOD–BYE

Saying good-bye is a way of ending an experience. It brings out into the open the separation between the person and the experience. Most of the time, it is difficult to end a pleasant situation. It is difficult to say farewell to the family car that has been worn out through usefulness. It is hard to say good-bye to a mountain retreat when vacation time is over.

Probably the most difficult situation to leave is a person or group of people with whom one has developed a relationship. It is very difficult to say good-bye to people.

Saying good-bye ends the experience in a way that is complete. Issues that have been worked on together can be summarized. The times that were really helpful can be identified. Special words of appreciation may be given to the people who will not be seen for a while or, perhaps, never will be seen again.

The purpose of saying good-bye is to end the experience. Issues that people have worked on together should be discussed in a light, though serious manner. This is a time to wrap things up; it is not a time to explore deep concerns. It is a time to put on the finishing touches, not the time to start exploring intense issues or involved problems. It is not a time to get involved with strong feelings about concerns other than the issue of leaving the immediate surroundings and people.

When people say good-bye, they should talk in terms of the positive learning, growth, and development that occurred. They should think about the process of ending. They should concentrate, here and now, on the situation in which they are currently involved. They should think about what it means to them. They should try to think about the parts of the experiences that are now part of them. What parts have been woven into the fabric of their lives? How does the experience fit now into the next steps that are taken in the continuing adventures of their lives?

Finishing precedes a new beginning. As time passes, the sadness that accompanies change or loss seems to decrease rather than completely disappear. In time, the memory occupies a small place in a person's vast mosaic of life experiences. The design of the mosaic is enriched continuously by the complex, exciting activities of life and of aging.

The following discussion exercises, A HANDSHAKE and SAYING GOOD-BYE, have been developed to help people conclude an experience. Bringing a matter to a point of closure is especially important when people have been together for a series of meetings. The exercises are ways that may help to put a finishing touch to issues or relationships that have developed while readers have progressed through the pages of this book.

The exercises may be used in sequence as they are described in the following pages. They may be combined together as one exercise with two steps, Part I and Part II. First, the activities of PART I: A HANDSHAKE, and then, PART II: SAYING GOOD-BYE. After the activities of both exercises, the discussion of the experiences from both parts may be combined as one discussion.

DISCUSSION EXERCISE

A Handshake

DIRECTIONS FOR THE LEARNER: Everyone shakes hands with as many people as possible in the group. Shake hands as if you were greeting each other for the first time. Do it the same way you would shake hands when meeting a group of people for the first time. Try to feel a sense of what each person is like when you shake each hand. Try to give a caring, but gentle handshake to people who may have tender spots in their hands or fingers.

Take some time to discuss each person's style of shaking hands. How did all the group members perceive each person as they shook hands? Remember to keep comments positive.

Now each class member may choose a partner who is among those whom the member knows least well. The partners stand up facing each other. They shake hands, and then close their eyes. With hands still clasped and eyes closed, they try to communicate a message through hand contact. No words are allowed.

Next, they open their eyes and tell each other in words what they felt from one another. Feedback is provided about the accuracy of the reported information. Then with eyes closed, hands clasped, the message is transmitted again. Once more, partners tell each other what messages they felt and give feedback to each other about the reported information.

To see how your handshake feels to other people, try to shake hands with yourself. Shake your left hand with your right hand. Can you feel in your own left hand to right hand contact what other people picked up when they shook your hand?

Then try to hug yourself. Put your arms around yourself. What do you feel like to yourself? How does it feel to put your arms around your own body?

DIRECTIONS FOR THE LEADER: This exercise depends upon interaction in a group. The purpose of the exercise is to increase the awareness of the self and others through socially acceptable touching.

The participants should take some time to talk about the experiences. Consider the following questions in your discussion.

How close did you come to communicating accurately the first time around? During any of the handshake experiences did you send or receive information that is hard to put into words?

How did you feel when you first closed your eyes? What kind of sensations did you experience when you hugged yourself? How does your body actually feel to you?

What do you experience when you meet others for the first time? Use your imagination and try to think about what it feels like to meet you (yourself) for the first time? When you shake hands with a person, what are some of your actions that you use to communicate about yourself? How do you communicate to yourself? Are the ways you communicate about yourself to others and to yourself the same or different? How are they the same or different?

This discussion exercise works well to help people become acquainted during a first meeting. However, it has been used in a more powerful way as part of the last meeting of groups of older people. As a result, the people linked the ending of some experiences with the beginning of other experiences in life. Also, the topic of permanent separation or the ending of life, the experience of death, has been discussed as another kind of beginning.

This exercise and discussion take about 20 minutes.

DISCUSSION EXERCISE

Saying Good-bye

DIRECTIONS FOR THE LEARNER: Form small groups. Each member takes a turn saying something positive to each of the other group members. The remarks may concern a special, personal characteristic of other group members. They may focus on specific actions of the other people that contributed to individual learning of the group member.

The format is informal, rather than formal. Pairs may form briefly within the group as positive remarks are shared. Then new pairs may form as new positive comments are shared.

After each small group shares, the group members remain seated with their group, but shift position slightly so that the total group may share messages of appreciation.

The members of the group should be encouraged to be open, assertive, and positive during the interaction. The comments by group members should be somewhat brief. Positive feedback should be included.

For example, one person may say, "Thank you, Lois, I enjoyed getting to know you in the group."
Another person may say, "Joel, I learned to listen better by observing how alert you are when you listen."

Responses which may be made to the previous comments:
Lois: "Thank you, I like hearing that."
Joel: "Thanks, I am glad I helped you."

DIRECTIONS FOR THE LEADER: This is a group exercise. The purpose of the exercise is to provide practice in finishing an experience or a relationship, in other words to say good-bye.

The function of the leader is to foster the unity of the total, larger group. In addition, the leader should try to support the sense of belonging that has developed in the smaller units during the previous small group activities.

The leader helps people to complete the experience of close emotional contact that has developed among group members. The leader facilitates the open expression of emotions, such as tears or respectful, appropriate touching.

Being open to sadness and other intimate emotions is a part of ending an involved relationship. Allowing feelings about ending a relationship to occur encourages a willingness for people to be more open to the experience of other emotions, such as excitement, happiness, and joy. Finishing a current experience is a step toward beginning the next, new experiences of life.

It takes about 60 to 90 minutes to complete this discussion exercise.

Bibliography

Aging America (2nd printing). (1984). Washington, DC: U.S. Senate Special Committee on Aging, & American Association of Retired Persons.

Alberti, R. E., & Emmons, M. L. (1974). *Your Perfect Right.* San Luis Obispo, CA: Impact.

Alberti, R. E., & Emmons, M. L. (1975). *Stand Up, Speak Out, Talk Back!* San Luis Obispo, CA: Impact.

Allen, E. E. (1982). Multiple attending in therapy groups. *The Personnel and Guidance Journal, 60*(5), 318–320.

Alpaugh, P., & Haney, M. (1979). *Counseling the Older Adult.* Los Angeles, CA: The Ethel Percy Andrus Gerontology Center.

The American Heritage Dictionary (2nd ed.). (1982). Boston, MA: Houghton Mifflin.

Ary, D., Jacobs, L. C., & Razavieh, A. (1979). *Introduction to Research in Education* (2nd ed.). New York: Holt, Rinehart & Winston.

Asch, S. (1952). Effects of group pressure upon the modification and distortion of judgments. In G. Swanson, T. M. Newcomb, & E. L. Hartley (Eds.), *Reading in Social Psychology.* New York: Holt, pp. 2–11.

Atchley, R. C. (1980). *The Social Forces in Later Life.* Belmont, CA: Wadsworth.

Axelrod, S., & Eisdorfer, C. (1961). Attitudes toward older people. *Journal of Gerontology, 16*, 75–80.

Bankoff, E. A. (1983). Aged parents and their widowed daughters: A support relationship. *Journal of Gerontology, 38*(2), 226–230.

Banziger, G., & Drevenstedt, J. (1982). Achievement attributions by young and old judges as a function of the perceived age of stimulus person. *Journal of Gerontology, 37*(4), 468–474.

Barkan, B. (September–October, 1981). The Live Oak regenerative community. *Aging,* (321–322), 2–7.

Belbin, R. M. (1972). Retirement strategy in an evolving society. In F. M. Carp (Ed.), *Retirement.* New York: Behavioral Publications, pp. 174–196.

Berne, E. (1966). *Principles of Group Treatment.* New York: Oxford University Press.

Biddle, W. E. (1969). Image therapy. *American Journal of Psychiatry, 126*, 408–412.

Billings, A. G., & Moos, R. H. (1981). The role of coping responses and social resources in attenuating the stress of life events. *Journal of Behavioral Medicine, 4*, 139–157.

Bills, R. E. (1981). *Self-concept and Schooling.* West Lafayette, IN: Kappa Delta Pi.

Birren, J. E. (1964). The psychology of aging in relation to development. In J. E. Birren (Ed.), *Relations of Development and Aging.* Springfield, IL: Charles C Thomas.

Birren, J. E., Schaie, K. W. (Eds.). (1977). *Handbook of the Psychology of Aging.* New York: Van Nostrand Reinhold.

Bolles, R. N. (1981). *The Three Boxes of Life.* Berkeley, CA: Ten Speed Press.

Brenton, M. (1970). *The American Male.* Greenwich, CT: Fawcett Pub.

Brickfield, C. F. (April–May, 1982). New federalism: Its promise and its dangers. *Modern Maturity, 25*(2), 4;5.

Butler, P. (1976). Assertive training: Teaching women not to discriminate against themselves. *Psychotherapy: Theory, Research and Practice, 13*(1), 56–60.

Butler, R. N. (1963a). Facade of chronological age: An interpretive summary. *American Journal of Psychiatry,* 119, 721–728.

Butler, R. N. (1963b). Life review: An interpretation of reminiscence in the aged. *Psychiatry: Journal for the Study of Interpersonal Processes,* 26(1), 65–76.

Butler, R. (1975). *Why Survive? Being Old in America.* New York: Harper & Row.

Butler, R. N., & Lewis, M. I. (1973). *Aging and Mental Health.* St. Louis, MO: The C. V. Mosby Co.

Canfield, J., & Wells, H. C. (1976). *100 Ways to Enhance Self-concept in the Classroom.* Englewood Cliffs, NJ: Prentice-Hall.

Carkhuff, R. R. (1973). *The Art of Helping.* Amherst, MA: Human Resource Development Press.

Carkuff, R. R., & Berenson, B. G. (1977). *Beyond Counseling and Therapy* (2nd ed.). New York: Holt, Rinehart & Winston.

Carlson, E. (May–June, 1982). Gaining on the fountain of youth. *Dynamic Years,* 17(3), 48–54.

Cavan, R. S. (1948). Family life and family substitutes in old age. *American Sociological Review,* 14, 71–83.

Childers, J. H. (1979). Building group leadership skills: Intervening after the critical incident. (Paper presented at the Southern Association of Counselor Education and Supervision, Daytona Beach, FL).

Christiansen, J. (January, 1984). Grace Hopper boosts computers far and wide. *The Institute,* 8(1), 16.

Coleman, J. C. (1976). *Abnormal Psychology and Modern Life* (5th ed.). Glenview, IL: Scott, Foresman and Co.

Corby, N. (1975). Assertion training with aged populations. *The Counseling Psychologist,* 5(4), 60–74.

Corsini, R. (1973). *Current Psychotherapies.* Itasca, IL: F. E. Peacock.

Cumming, E., & Henry, W. E. (1961). *Growing Old: The Process of Disengagement.* New York: Basic Books.

Dangott, L. R., & Kalish, R. A. (1979). *A Time to Enjoy.* Englewood Cliffs, NJ: Prentice-Hall.

Davidoff, H. (Ed.). (1942). *Quotations.* New York: Pocket Books.

Dilworth-Anderson, P. (September–October, 1981). A social structure that works: The case of Green nursing home. *Aging,* 39–41.

Donelson, E. (1973). *Personality.* Pacific Palisades, CA: Goodyear Publishing Co.

Donnelly, G. F. (1981). Freeing the nurse to practice. In E. J. Forbes & V. M. Fitzsimons, *The Older Adult.* St. Louis, MO: The C. V. Mosby Co., pp. 128–129.

Doty, L. (July, 1981). Planning and preparation for the new life. *Resources in Education.* ERIC/CAPS Clearinghouse, (ED 198408).

Doty, L., Tolbert, E. L., & DiLeo, J. (March, 1981). Using career development theory to help older persons. *Resources in Education,* ERIC/CAPS Clearinghouse. (ED 193573).

Dubos, R. (1965). *Man Adapting.* New Haven, CT: Yale University Press.

Dudley, C., & Hillary, G. (1977). Freedom and alienation in homes for the aged. *The Gerontologist,* 17(2), 140–145.

Dye, C. J., & Richards, C. C. (1980). Facilitating the transition to nursing homes. In S. S. Sargent (Ed.), *Nontraditional Therapy and Counseling with the Aging.* New York: Springer Publishing Co., pp. 100–115.

Egan, G. (1975). *The Skilled Helper.* Monterey, CA: Brooks/Cole.

Erikson, E. H. (1959). Identity and the life cycle. *Psychological Issues,* Monograph 1.

Erikson, E. H. (1963). *Childhood and Society* (2nd ed.). New York: W. W. Norton.

Erikson, E. H. (1964). *Insight and Responsibility.* New York: W. W. Norton.

Erikson, E. H. (1982). *The Life Cycle Completed.* New York: W. W. Norton.

Fallot, R. D. (1979–1980). The impact on mood of verbal reminiscing in later adulthood. *International Journal of Aging and Human Development,* 10(4), 385–400.

Fensterheim, H. (1971). *Help without Psychoanalysis.* New York: Stein & Day.

Fensterheim, H., & Baer, J. (1975). *Don't Say Yes When You Want to Say No.* New York: Dell.

Flanagan, J. C. (1978). A research approach to improving our quality of life. *American Psychologist,* 33, 138–147.

Flowers, J. V., & Booraem, C. D. (1975). Assertion training: The training of trainers. *The Counseling Psychologist,* 5(4), 29–36.

Flowers, J. V., Cooper, C. G., & Whiteley, J. M. (1975). Approaches to assertion training. *The Counseling Psychologist,* 5(4), 3–9.

Folkman, S., & Lazarus, R. S. (1980). An analysis of coping in a middle-aged community sample. *Journal of Health and Social Behavior,* 21, 219–239.

Forbes, E. J., & Fitzsimons, V. M. (1981). *The Older Adult.* St. Louis, MO: The C. V. Mosby Co.

Fromm, E. (1955). *The Sane Society.* New York: Rinehart & Co.

Fromm, E. (1956). *The Art of Loving.* New York: Harper.

Gainesville Sun. (July 18, 1982). Soon the country will be pagerized. 107(12), 18F.

Ganikos, M. (Ed.). (1979). *Counseling the Aged.* Washington, DC: American Personnel and Guidance Assoc.

Gazda, G. M., Asbury, F. R., Balzer, F. J., Childers, W. C., & Walters, R. P. (1977). *Human Relations Development* (2nd ed.). Boston, MA: Allyn & Bacon, Inc.

Gelatt, H. B. (1962). Decision-Making: A conceptual frame of reference for counseling. *Journal of Counseling Psychology,* 9(3), 240–245.

Gershon, S., & Raskin, A. (Eds.). (1975). *Aging* (Vol. 2). New York: Raven Press.

Glasser, W. (1975). *Reality Therapy.* New York: Harper & Row.

Goebel, B. L. (1982). Age preferences of older adults in relationships important to their life satisfaction. *Journal of Gerontology,* 37(4), 461–467.

Goldberg, H. (1976). *The Hazards of Being Male.* New York: Nash Pub.

Golembiewski, R. T., & Blumberg, A. (1970). *Sensitivity Training and the Laboratory Approach.* Itasca, IL: F. E. Peacock.

Guardo, C. J. (April, 1982). Student generations and value change. *The Personnel and Guidance Journal,* 60(8), 500–503.

Hamachek, D. E. (1971). *Encounters with the Self.* New York: Holt, Rinehart and Winston.

Hammer, M. (1967). The directed daydream technique. *Psychotherapy: Theory, Research and Practice,* 4, 173–181.

Hansen, J. C., Warner, R. W., & Smith, E. M. (1976). *Group Counseling: Theory and Process.* Chicago, IL: Rand McNally College Pub. Co.

Hausman, C. P. (1979). Short-term counseling groups for people with elderly parents. *The Gerontologist,* 19(1), 102–107.

Havighurst, R. J. (1963). Successful aging. In R. J. Williams, C. Tibbetts, & W. Donahue, (Eds.), *Process of Aging.* New York: Atherton Press, pp. 299–320.

Hawkins, B. L. (November, 1983). Group counseling as a treatment modality for the elderly: A group snapshot. *The Journal for Specialists in Group Work,* 8(4), 186–193.

Helms, F. C. (August, 1965). An inside look at retirement. In selected papers of Fifth Annual Conference of State Executives on Aging, Washington, D.C., May 2–5, 1965. U.S. Department of Health, Education, & Welfare, pp. 69–70. (OA No. 123).

Hess, B., & Markson, E. (1980). *Aging and Old Age.* New York: MacMillan.

Holmes, S. B. (August, 1965). An inside look at retirement. In selected papers of Fifth Annual Conference of State Executives on Aging, Washington, D.C., May 2–5, 1965. U.S. Department of Health, Education, & Welfare, pp. 65–68. (OA No. 123).

Horney, K. (1945). *Our Inner Conflicts: A Constructive Theory of Neurosis.* New York: W. W. Norton.

Huber, J. T., & Millman, H. L. (1972). *Goals and Behavior in Psychotherapy and Counseling.* Columbus, OH: Charles E. Merrill.

Hughes, P. W. (April–May, 1982). How AARP will protect older Americans' rights. *Modern Maturity,* 25(2), 5.

Iacobuzio, T. (1982). All alone by the high-tech phone. *Psychology Today,* 16(4), 46–47.

Ilfield, F. W. (June, 1980). Coping styles of Chicago adults: Description. *Journal of Human Stress,* 2–10.

Ivey, A. E., & Athier, J. (1978). *Microcounseling.* Springfield, IL: Charles C Thomas.

Jackson, J. J. (1980). *Minorities and Aging.* Belmont, CA: Wadsworth.

Jourard, S. M. (1964). *The Transparent Self.* New York: Van Nostrand Reinhold.

Jourard, S. M. (1967). *To Be or Not to Be . . .* Gainesville, FL: University of Florida Press.

Kaasa, O. J. (April–May, 1982). What two years have meant to me. *Modern Maturity,* 25(2), 4.

Kalish, R. A. (1975). *Late Adulthood: Perspectives on Human Development.* Belmont, CA: Wadsworth.

Kalish, R. A. (1977). Social values and the elderly. In R. A. Kalish (Ed.), *The Later Years: Social Applications of Gerontology.* Monterey, CA: Brooks/ Cole, pp. 64–68.

Kastenbaum, R. (Ed.). (1981). *Old Age on the New Scene.* New York: Springer Pub.

Kastenbaum, R., & Candy, S. E. (1981). The 4% fallacy: Many die where few have lived. In R. Kastenbaum (Ed.), *Old Age on the New Scene.* New York: Springer Pub., pp. 262–282.

Kosbab, F. P. (1974). Imagery techniques in psychiatry. *Archives of General Psychiatry,* 31, 283–290.

Krause, D. R. (September–October, 1981). Institutional living for the elderly in Denmark. A model for the United States. *Aging,* 29–38.

Krumboltz, J. D., & Thoreson, C. D. (1969). *Behavioral Counseling: Case and Techniques.* New York: Holt, Rinehart & Winston.

Larson, R. (1978). Thirty years of research on the subjective well being of older Americans. *Journal of Gerontology,* 33(1), 109–125.

Lawton, M. P. (1974). *Planning and Managing Housing for the Elderly.* New York: Interscience.

Levinson, D., Darrow, C. N., Klein, E. B., Levinson, M.H., & McKee, B. (1978). *The Seasons of a Man's Life.* New York: Alfred A. Knopf.

Linn, L. (1977). Basic principles of management in psychosomatic medicine. In E. D. Wittkower & H. Harnes (Eds.), *Psychosomatic Medicine: Its Clinical Applications.* New York: Harper & Row.

Little, V. C. (1980). Assessing the needs of the elderly: State of the art. *International Journal of Aging and Human Development,* 11(1), 65–76.

Loneliness shortens longevity. (July–August, 1982). *Dynamic Years,* 17(4), 60.

Lowenthal, M. F., & Haven, C. (1968). Interaction and adaptation: Intimacy as a critical variable. *American Sociologist Review,* 33(1), 20–30.

Marlowe, D., & Gergen, K. J. (1968). Personality and social interaction. In G. Lindzey & E. Aronson (Eds.), *Handbook of Social Psychology* (Rev. ed.). Reading, MA: Addison-Wesley, 590–665.

Maurer, J. F., & Rupp, R. R. (1979). *Hearing and Aging: Tactics for Intervention.* New York: Grune & Stratton.

McCrae, R. R. (1982). Age differences in the use of coping mechanisms. *Journal of Gerontology,* 37(4), 454–460.

Meyer, G. (1980). The New Directions workshop for senior citizens. In S. S. Sargent (Ed.), *Nontraditional Therapy and Counseling with the Aging.* New York: Springer Publishing.

Miller, F. (1972). *College Physics* (3rd ed.). New York: Harcourt Brace Jovanovich.

Mindel, C. H., & Wright, R. (1982). Satisfaction in multigenerational households. *Journal of Gerontology,* 37(4), 483–489.

Muson, H. (1982). Getting the phone's number. *Psychology Today,* 16(4), 42–49.

Neugarten, B. L. (1973). Developmental Perspectives. In V. M. Brantl & S. M. R. Brown (Eds.), *Readings in Gerontology.* St. Louis, MO: The C. V. Mosby Co., pp. 31–36.

Neugarten, B. L. (1976). Adaptations and the life cycle. *The Counseling Psychologist,* 6(1), 16–20.

Neugarten, B. L. (1977). Personality and aging. In J. E. Birren & K. W. Schaie (Eds.), *Handbook of the Psychology of Aging.* New York: Van Nostrand Reinhold.

Ohlsen, M. M. (1977). *Group Counseling* (2nd ed.). New York: Holt, Rinehart and Winston.

Okun, B. F., & Rappaport, L. J. (1980). *Working with Families.* North Scituate, MA: Duxbury Press.

Ordal, C. C. (September–October, 1981). To "grow side by side." *Aging,* 25–28.

Palmore, E. B. (1979). Predictors of successful aging. *The Gerontologist,* 19(5), 427–431.

Parsons, T. (1951). *The Social System.* Glencoe, IL: Free Press.

Passons, W. R. (1975). *Gestalt Approaches in Counseling.* New York: Holt, Rinehart and Winston.

Pelletier, K. R. (1977). *Mind as Healer, Mind as Slayer.* New York: Delta.

Peterson, G. W., & Burck, H. D. (1982). A competency approach to accountability in human service programs. *The Personnel and Guidance Journal,* 60(8), 491–495.

Phelps, S., & Austin, N. (1975). *The Assertive Woman.* San Luis Obispo, CA: Impact.

Press, F. (Fall, 1983). Commercializing new knowledge. *Educational Horizons,* 62(1), 3–4.

Rathus, S. A. (1975). Principles and practices of assertive training: An eclectic overview. *The Counseling Psychologist,* 5(4), 9–20.

Reck, U. M. L. (Spring, 1982). Self-concept development in educational settings: An existential approach. *Educational Horizons,* 60(3), 128–131.

Regnier, V. (August, 1981). Normal elderly in the community: Interpretations leading to products. Paper presented at the National Research Conference on Technology and Aging, Racine, WI.

Reich, W. (1949). *Character Analysis* (T. P. Wolfe, trans.). New York: Orgone Institute Press.

Reigel, K. F., & Reigel, R. (1960). A study on changes of attitudes and interests during later years of life. *Vita Humana,* 3, 177–206.

Riker, H. C. (1980). Older persons. In N. A. Vaac & J. C. Wittmer (Eds.), *Let Me Be Me.* Muncie, IN: Accelerated Development, Inc.

Romano, J. L. (April, 1982). Biofeedback training and therapeutic gains: Clinical impressions. *The Personnel and Guidance Journal,* 60(8), 473–475.

Rychlak, J. F. (1973). *Introduction to Personality and Psychotherapy.* Boston, MA: Houghton Mifflin.

Sarason, I. (1961). Intercorrelations among measures of hostility. *Journal of Clinical Psychology,* 17, 192–195.

Schein, E. H. (1969). *Process Consultation.* Reading, MA: Addison-Welsley.

Schlossberg, N. K., Troll, L. E., & Leibowitz, Z. (1978). *Perspectives on Counseling Adults: Issues and Goals.* Monterey, CA: Brooks/Cole.

Schultz, D. (1977). *Growth Psychology.* New York: Van Nostrand Reinhold.

Schulz, J. H. (1980). *The Economics of Aging.* Belmont, CA: Wadsworth.

Selye, H. (1976). *The Stress of Life* (Rev. ed.). New York: McGraw-Hill.

Silverstone, B. & Hyman, H. K. (1976). *You and Your Aging Parent.* New York: Pantheon Books.

Smith, M. J. (1975). *When I Say No, I Feel Guilty.* New York: Dial Press.

Sobel, M. (September–October, 1981). Growing old in Britain. *Aging,* (321–322), 8–16.

Sokoloff, L. (1975). Cerebral circulation and metabolism in the aged. In S. Gershon & A. Raskin (Eds.), *Aging* (Vol. 2). New York: Raven Press, pp. 49–56.

Special Committee on Aging. (July 26, 1982). *Long-Term Health Care for the Elderly.* Washington, DC: U.S. Government Printing Office. (99–345 0).

Spencer, M. E. (1979). *Truth about Aging.* Washington, DC: NRTA–AARP.

Standards for the Use of the Laboratory Method. (1969). Washington, DC: NTL Institute for Applied Behavioral Science.

Super, D. E. (1957). *The Psychology of Careers.* New York: Harper and Bros.

Sussman, M. B. (1972). An analytical model for the sociological study of retirement. In F. M. Carp (Ed.), *Retirement.* New York: Behavioral Publications, pp. 28–73.

Szafranski, L. M. (September–October, 1981). Using patient co-leaders in group sessions. *Aging,* (321–322), 21–24.

Tibbits, C. (1979). Can we invalidate negative stereotypes of aging? *The Gerontologist,* 19, 10–20.

Tobin, S., & Neugarten, B. (1961). Life satisfaction and social interaction in the aging. *Journal of Gerontology,* 16, 344–346.

Troll, L. E., Miller, S. J., & Atchley, R. C. (1979). *Families in Later Life.* Belmont, CA: Wadsworth.

Tuckman, J., & Lorge, I. (1958). Attitude toward aging of individuals with experience with the aged. *Journal of Genetic Psychology,* 92, 199–204.

U.S. Department of Health and Human Services. (December, 1983–January, 1984). SPICE and the schools work together. *Human Development News,* 1;12.

Weiner, M. B., Brok, A. J., & Snadowsky, A. M. (1978). *Working with the Aged.* Engelwood Cliffs, NJ: Prentice Hall.

Weitz, H. (1964). *Behavior Change through Guidance.* New York: John Wiley.

White, R. W. (1966). *Lives in Progress: A Study of the Natural Growth of Personality* (2nd ed.). New York: Holt, Rinehart & Winston.

White, R. W. (1972). *The Enterprise of Living.* New York: Holt, Rinehart & Winston.

Wilmott, P., & Young M. (1960). *The Family and Class in a London Suburb.* London: Routledge and Kegan Paul.

Wingard, J. A., Heath, R., & Himelstein, S. A. (1982). The effects of contextural variations on attitudes toward the elderly. *Journal of Gerontology,* 37(4), 475–482.

Wingate, A. (Fall, 1983). Communicating with business. *Educational Horizons,* 62(1), 15–17.

Wittmer, J., & Myrick, R. D. (1980). *Facilitative Teaching* (2nd ed.). Minneapolis, MN: Educational Media Corp.

Wolff, H. C. (1953). *Stress and Disease.* Springfield, IL: Charles C Thomas.

Wolpe, J. (1969). *The Practice of Behavior Therapy.* New York: Permagon Press.

Yalom, I. D. (1975). *The Theory and Practice of Group Psychotherapy.* New York: Basic Books.

Index